MY LAST
EIGHT
THOUSAND
DAYS

Valerie Boyd and John Griswold,
series editors

SERIES ADVISORY BOARD

Dan Gunn

Pam Houston

Phillip Lopate

Dinty W. Moore

Lia Purpura

Patricia Smith

Ned Stuckey-French

MY LAST

An American Male

EIGHT

in His Seventies

THOUSAND

Lee Gutkind

DAYS

THE UNIVERSITY OF GEORGIA PRESS | ATHENS

Published by the University of Georgia Press
Athens, Georgia 30602
www.ugapress.org
© 2020 by Lee Gutkind
All rights reserved
Designed by Kaelin Chappell Broaddus
Set in 11/15 Kinesis Std by Kaelin Chappell Broaddus
Printed and bound by Sheridan Books, Inc.

The paper in this book meets the guidelines for permanence
and durability of the Committee on Production Guidelines for
Book Longevity of the Council on Library Resources.

Most University of Georgia Press titles are
available from popular e-book vendors.

Printed in the United States of America
24 23 22 21 20 C 5 4 3 2 1

Library of Congress Control Number: 2020937962
ISBN: 9780820359601 (hardcover : alk. paper)
ISBN: 9780820358062 (ebook)

For Michele *and* Patricia,
my lifelines of love and support

Acknowledgments

I wish to thank the many smart and sensitive people who have read and generously responded to drafts of this book over the years. Your time and insight have been invaluable.

Walter Biggins
Andrew Blauner
Jess Brallier
Becky Cole
David Goehring
Anne Horowitz
Daniya Kamran-Morley
Emily Loose
Dinty W. Moore
Debra Monroe
Jill Patterson
Matthew Sharp
Mike Shatzkin

MY LAST
EIGHT
THOUSAND
DAYS

One

THE MORNING OF MY SEVENTIETH BIRTHDAY BEGAN LIKE ANY
other: my alarm blared at 5:30 a.m. Then: grope for the TV remote
to change from my *Law and Order* middle-of-the-night rerun station
to CNN for morning news; slip out from under covers, bare feet on
floor; stagger into bathroom; relieve myself; brush teeth; splash cold
water on my face, closing my eyes to avoid my reflection in the mir-
ror; then back to bedroom; pull on Levis and top from the night before; check iPhone for texts; descend the stairs, knees creaking; yell
goddamn, fuck, fuck, fuck because my joints are in morning rebellion;
open the front door; bend, wince, retrieve my *New York Times*; put on
coat—it is January—and head four blocks to Starbucks.

Everything the same, the identical routine I had followed for the
past I don't even remember how many years, except maybe for the
creaking knees, although I could not recall when they weren't creaking, or sometimes also clicking, annoyingly, like a light switch, *on/off,*
every step, *clickety-click*. I had no idea then, nor have I now, when
or why my knee would start or stop clicking, except that that might
be the only way to distinguish among my early mornings, the days

it clicked and the days it didn't. All else consistent. The morning I was sixty-eight, flowing into the morning I was sixty-nine. And then came the morning I was seventy. Just another year passing, nothing changing. One day later, one day older, but the same life I had been leading and would continue to lead until . . . until . . . until . . . whenever. Didn't matter. Seventy, I had repeated to myself, was only a marker. An unremarkable number.

This, of course, was a goddamn lie. A sham. A way of steadying myself and keeping calm. Or keeping going, even though things weren't going too well for me back then, to say the least. The stuff of my life—what had, in fact, kept me going—seemed to be gradually falling apart.

For one thing, my mother, Mollie, my most trusted confidante, had died—at a really bad time. Not that there could be a good time for my mother to die, but she had closed her eyes and said—or to be more precise, *moaned*—her last goodbyes to me and the world just five days before my seventieth birthday.

And to be honest, I was having trouble processing that it had actually happened, though I had expected it, and she, and even I on some level, had wished for it. For the past eight months, she had been wasting away before my eyes in an assisted living facility, no longer able to keep her thoughts and words straight, or her balance, or hear much of anything I tried to talk with her about. It had been painful to visit with her, to remember the vigorous woman she once was, the one who ran up and down the stairs, basement to second floor, lugging the bulging family laundry basket, intermittently gossiping on the phone with her gaggle of neighborhood friends, the one who worked 10 a.m. to 9 p.m. Saturdays at our family's shoe store, the one who protected me from my crazy, temperamental, unpredictable father, whom I invariably agitated and feared. It wasn't much of a life anymore for her, and her death should not have been a shock to me.

But I was stunned and unaccepting. I felt like one of those amputees you read about in stories about the severely wounded in war—soldiers in bed in hospitals recovering, who know they have lost legs or arms, but who continue to sense their missing limbs anyway. Phantom limbs, the doctors call it. My mom was a phantom presence to me—maybe dead, but not at all gone.

My mother wasn't the only missing limb of my being; there was an entire procession of people in my life and things that had kept me going that had been slipping away, one after another, during that shitty seventieth year. One of my two best old friends, Frank, had just died a few months before. My relationship with my girlfriend of nearly ten years had ended. And my son, my so very brilliant offspring, in whom I had thus far invested more than $250,000 at an exclusive private university for geniuses, where he was studying mathematics and philosophy and where, I had assumed, he would begin research that would change the world, had stopped taking classes with only a semester or two to graduate. I had been aware for a while that he was smoking a great deal of marijuana, but I was obviously in denial about the extent to which he was experimenting with other harmful substances. I guess that parents aren't necessarily the last to know about the bad things their children are doing to themselves, but it is easy, when you love someone so deeply and wholeheartedly, to hold on to the hope that, when you do find out, "he will grow out of it" or "he will wake up and see what he is doing to himself (and to his parents!)." Still, I had come to realize finally that my son was in deep trouble, not just with drugs but with the mental illness behind his attempts to medicate himself, and as hard as I tried, I hadn't the slightest idea what to do about it.

And then there was my second ex-wife, Patricia, with whom I had been communicating more frequently those days because of our troubles with our son. She's a hospice nurse, and she's got a great memory and a knack for telling stories, especially about the people she sees dying, which she often shares with me when we talk. I don't want her to tell me all this stuff—it creeps me out. But I am a writer, and when she starts a story, I want her to finish it, no matter how uncomfortable it makes me. You should hear her describe the "death rattle thing," as she sometimes calls it, when a person's lungs are bursting with fluid and they can no longer breathe, and you can hear this rattle even before you enter their room. Or maybe you shouldn't hear any of this. It would creep you out, too.

To make matters worse, I had been gaining weight. As always, I exercised like crazy, running six or eight miles a day, or as many miles as I needed to stay calm and focused. But gradually, despite my efforts, I had been developing a bit of a paunch—a soon-to-be-bulging belly if I didn't put a stop to it. After years of abeyance, I found myself frequently stopping in at the local convenience store after my runs, buying potato chips, cashew nuts, and other snacks, promising myself each time that this was a one-time treat—a rare "deviation" from my heretofore careful diet.

"Deviation" is what my former girlfriend, Michele, a nutritionist, called it when her clients went off the careful food intake regimen she prescribed for them. It wasn't cheating. "Cheating," she had frequently reminded me, "is much too negative and guilt-producing." Whether potato chips or French fries or chocolate biscotti, another of my deviations, it is okay to allow yourself this thing, this food fling, but only, of course, if you rarely repeat it. Inevitably I repeated it, until I was deviating regularly, cheating, I guess you could legitimately say, despite her admonitions on my deviations. Not just after running and not just snack stuff, but often leftovers late at night before I went to sleep, maybe because I was suddenly sleeping alone. A microwaved chicken drumstick or a greasy grilled cheese sandwich was soothing. Not nearly as satisfying or comforting, I should say, as a warm woman's body beside me, but it filled up that awesome hole of aloneness. As a former fatty, a teenager who had tipped the scales at 220 pounds, who had worked diligently to keep his weight in control since, over all those years, the deviations were embarrassing and downright intolerable.

So, too, was the sudden termination of the book I had been writing for nearly five years, the one I thought would vitalize my heretofore unremarkable literary career. Throughout my adult life, my up-and-down relationships, my books had always sustained me, kept me grounded. My books, my writing, meant everything to me—absolutely everything. I came to fatherhood later in life than most dads, and despite the difficulties with my son, being a parent has been my greatest challenge and adventure. But I had always replied, before the birth of my son, to those who asked if I ever wanted children, that my books, from conception to full-blown living entities, alive on the page, were my progeny. My footprint on the world.

But now my magnum opus, the book I had always hoped to write, had been fading away in front of my eyes, and there was absolutely nothing I could do about that, either—except eat, drink, worry, curse, and maybe cry.

On top of all this, did I mention? I was suddenly seventy years old. And as hard as I tried, I could not pretend that this was not a milestone, a landmark. I could not pass it off as if nothing had occurred. You don't have to tell me that seventy is just a number. I dig that. I've heard it before. I've said it to myself. It's not how old you are but how old you feel. And I felt fine in many of the most important ways for someone my age. Damn good, in fact. I was healthy, for one thing, no diseases or afflictions except for clicking knees, and safe and secure at that moment financially—and I still am now. No one was or is threatening to fire or retire me, or in any way impede my life or work.

And yet, as I think back, the inevitability of aging and what it might mean to me, personally, and to how I am perceived by others—

the in-word these days is "ageism"—nagged at me long before seventy, like an annoying and relentless itch in the middle of my back I could not reach to scratch. Each passing year had brought to the surface questions that made me uneasy and on edge. What would happen if I could not write anymore? Or continue to exercise like a madman? Or walk up Walnut Street, the main drag in my Shadyside neighborhood in Pittsburgh, to Starbucks ten times a day? Or think with clarity? Or speak articulately? Or remember where I was yesterday, or what book I read last week?

Aging for most of us is a silent process, of which we are often unaware—until a transition, an awakening, occurs. When you are a kid, you want to be older, sixteen, eighteen, twenty-one, so that you can drive, vote, and then legally drink. Later, it is okay to be a little older so that people will stop telling you that you are too young to understand life, marriage, politics, or too inexperienced to qualify for a job. Getting older to a certain point is okay, good in fact, until suddenly you cross the line and you're too old—or even if you're not quite too old yet, you're very aware that age and over-the-hill-ness, as noted and judged by society, the world at large, is catching up with you. And you have to do something about it, fast, before you begin to circle the too-old, doomed-for-the-rest-of-your-life drainpipe.

So one night thirty years ago, when I turned forty, I acted. Patricia—we were then married—took me to dinner to celebrate my birthday. We went to Klein's Restaurant, a long-established steak and seafood place in downtown Pittsburgh. The moment we walked into Klein's, I realized it was all wrong. The room suddenly buzzed and whirled in my head. As the hostess led us to our table, I noted that most of the diners at the other tables were old—I mean very old, as old as I am now. And the carpet was worn thin. There were parts of the carpet so translucent you could see the floor underneath. The carpet symbolized what I would one day become—a buried skeleton—or so I visualized then. You could look right through me and see the ants gnawing at my rapidly disappearing corpse. The whole thing had made me dizzy, out of synch, out of whack.

We sat down at our table. The waiter put a basket of dinner rolls in front of us. I picked up a roll. I bit into it. Dry and stale. I looked around again. The old fuckers, the frayed carpet, the stale bread—it overwhelmed me, and I felt like I was somehow sucked into this entire disintegrating milieu, ambushed actually, and I could not stand the thought of becoming an old fucker myself, like these old fucker people. And so I bolted. I dropped my roll, jumped up, and fled Klein's, leaving Patricia behind to make apologies and excuses and chase after me. I felt bad doing this to my wife, but I couldn't help myself. I was not being rational.

I don't remember driving home, rushing into my apartment, shedding suit and tie. Details of my cowardly retreat remain buried to this day. The next thing I remember is lying in bed, blankets to my chin, eating from a box of soda crackers, sucking on the salt, drinking a Diet Pepsi, and watching *M*A*S*H* on TV. I am so old now that the episode of *M*A*S*H* that I watched was not a rerun. And that, like I say, was when I was forty.

Now I am thirty more.

The Klein's debacle was the last time for a very long time that I was a birthday boy. From that day forward, I told all my friends and family not to send cards or call me up with celebratory greetings. I would rather suffer in silence, pretending that nothing different or significant was taking place, until the dreaded day was over, and I could sigh with relief and make believe it hadn't happened, that I was the same guy I had been the day before yesterday, just two days older.

Two

THE PREEMPTIVE DENIAL OF MY GRADUAL AND OBSESSIVELY feared irrelevancy, starting at forty, worked for a while, but as the years and the non-birthdays passed, reality came creeping up on me, and I began wondering how much time I had left and what I could do to delay or deter the inevitable. Not my inevitable seventieth birthday—I was stuck with that—but my inevitable disintegration, my inability to be productive and make an impact, turn heads, connect with readers, achieve significance, whatever that might mean, before my eventual demise.

So I conducted some basic research. That's what writers and reporters do, the way we begin any book or article, to discover stuff that will introduce us to the world we are going to observe and write about. Devote a few hours to surfing the internet and you can find out plenty. But it is one thing to research other people and another to research subjects related to yourself. You will learn stuff you don't want to know or remember.

I discovered, for instance, figuring from seventy onward, when I was going to die, more or less—or, as TV commentators say when they poll political contests, "plus or minus and within the margin of error." The Institute for Health Metrics and Evaluation at the University of Washington noted that men born in Pittsburgh were expected to live to 75.1 years, compared to 76.2 nationally. So I calculated that I had 5.1 years to live—approximately 1,825 days from that measuring point, my seventieth birthday.

How to avoid aging—or, at the very least, showing your age? Again, more research, sometimes helpful and other times nonsensical. Eat a cup of Greek yogurt every day to calcium-load, thereby safeguarding against osteoporosis. I did that for a while. When you leave the house, sunscreen to decrease wrinkling and shriveling. And that. I contemplated getting a pet because pets boost your mood and lower blood pressure and cholesterol levels. And if the pet is a cat, according to the Minnesota Stroke Institute, you decrease your chance of dying from heart disease. What happens, I wondered, if your pet is an alligator or a frog? Some of the research was totally off base for me. Like a study from Cardiff University that suggested that marriage increases one's lifespan by 15 percent. I had tried the marriage route twice. Which was worse, I wondered, marriage or divorce? The longer the marriages and then the divorces dragged on, the more I felt I would be better off dead.

My friends and family resented my birthday moratorium. Susan from New Jersey told me straight out, quite angrily, that I was being unfair. Birthdays, she scolded, bring friends together at significant moments in their lives, especially when they live far apart and don't see each other regularly. I always visited Susan and her husband, Iggy, in mid-June to celebrate Susan's birthday. Iggy had been a father figure to me in high school and afterward in Pittsburgh. Even when they moved to New Jersey, he and Susan remained my oldest and most cherished friends. We celebrated Iggy's birthday, too, every September. Iggy's real name was Bob; Iggy in Yiddish was slang for oversized protruding ears.

Every year after the moratorium, as my birthday neared, friends and family began distancing themselves, afraid they would somehow slip and violate my moratorium and thereby not honor my request. A couple of days before the dreaded day, their phone calls, e-mails, and general regular contacts would fade away. So not having a birthday turned out to be rather isolating. My birthday was the elephant in the room, and the elephant and I were in the room all by ourselves.

But why would I worry? No one would ever know how old I was—unless they googled me. And even then, I had lied about my age in every interview I had ever given since I turned forty. They could never be certain how old I was. That's kind of hilarious, I know. Silly. But sometimes making fun and doing or saying dumb things are the best ways to avoid the pain of reality.

Like when you are having a conversation with a friend and you can't remember his wife's first name, even though you have known them both for thirty-five years, have had dinner at their house, went to their kids' bar and bat mitzvahs. Or when you can't bring up a word—a common, ordinary, easy word you've used a thousand times, like "frantic" or "elevator." And you say to yourself or the person you're talking to, "I am having an early Alzheimer's moment." What else can you do but wisecrack and laugh, masking embarrassment, avoiding shame? It is serious business. But you laugh anyway. It is a way of getting by.

When I was writing a book about liver transplantation at the world's largest transplant center—in the mid-1980s and into the 1990s, when more people were dying on the operating table or after the procedure than living—there was this one woman I will call Lizzie who was yellow with jaundice all over, skeletal and brittle as bark, but she never cried or complained, was always polite and respectful to the nurses and cooperative with the physicians. She had waited a very long time for an available liver, one that was her size and blood type, which was always the rub. You needed a good fit for a liver. Lizzie was literally on the edge of death when her turn finally came, the matching brain-dead person, and the surgeons jumped into their Learjet and rocketed out to Halifax, if I remember correctly, where the brain-dead donor was. I went with them. In the Halifax operating room, they opened up the donor and prepared to remove the liver—a procedure called a hepatectomy—only to discover that the liver was diseased. It looked terrible, dry, brownish, awful and ugly, and one of the surgeons said, matter-of-factly, "That's not liver—it's burnt bacon."

It was a weird comment, since the organ didn't look anything like bacon, burnt or raw. He just blurted it out of exasperation. Later, in the jet coming home, all of us, who admired Lizzie and maybe even loved her a little bit, knew that without this liver Lizzie was going to die, perhaps that day. But that "burnt bacon" observation just kind of struck a chord. And as we jetted back to Pittsburgh, to the luckless and soon to be lifeless Lizzie, one of the surgeons repeated the words, "Burnt bacon. Burnt bacon." He was speaking ruefully and regretfully, but then he started laughing, and then a nurse began laughing, and before you knew it, we were all sitting there in the dark, twenty thousand feet above the earth, laughing and laughing. We laughed and laughed and laughed, until we were so spent and exhausted and broken, we no longer had the energy to do what we all wanted to do, which was cry.

You'd think, considering my experiences and observations in a liver transplant unit, I would have come to grips with my feelings about aging. Or, more to the point, mortality, because when you come right down to it, when you're dead, you're dead. I don't believe in heaven or hell, or any notion of paradise that might follow.

What concerned me the morning of my seventieth birthday, the first day of my seventy-first year, were the remaining years leading up to my demise, how I might stretch them out and, at the same time, accept that there was a time limit to them. I hadn't been able to do that. I was not ready. Are we—can we be—ready? I had plans and goals and exploding energy and ambition, not just to hang in for as long as possible, but to generate new ideas and follow them to fruition, and to write one really great book people would actually buy and read, then act on my messages, praise my insight and creative expression.

More than that, I wanted to figure out who I was, who I had become, how my seventy years had been invested, why I did what I did—and why I did not do, perhaps, in retrospect, what I should have done. I wanted to answer questions that had been intriguing and troubling me. Like why was I, or why did I feel, so isolated and alone when, maybe, surely, there were people in my hometown and elsewhere who might want to interact with me? Why did I feel so vulnerable, considering that I was in good health and, professionally, if not at the top of my game, then at the very least consistently productive? In the process of this exploration, perhaps I would be able to cope with and accommodate myself to what was going to happen to me—what was already happening to me. Old age . . . and, more frightening, irrelevance.

I don't think this transition and quest for self-understanding were confronting only me. I am not so damn special. Many of my contemporaries, I suspect, are attempting to come to terms with their own life experiences, to face the foibles and inevitable indignities of their twilight years with more equanimity. In fact, I could have asked them, initiated conversations, about how aging sucks for them, but then I would have had to admit that I was aging too. And that people perceived me differently now, in a way that might shatter my ego, that might weaken my spirit and resolve. So I did not want to talk about it. It was embarrassing, made me feel so damn *exposed*.

All these questions converged as I became seventy. I felt like a deer caught in the headlights of an oncoming car—frozen. Should I run? Should I duck? Should I close my eyes and wait to see what happened? That's what my mother used to say when faced with difficult decisions: "I don't know what's going to be. Let's wait to see what happens." I wasn't sure I had time and patience to wait to see what happened. What if nothing happened? What if I could not keep working? And worse, what if I did continue to work, and nobody paid attention? I didn't want to feel that the next big events of my life would be my infirmity, followed by disability and then my death. And what if, when I died, nobody noticed—or cared?

As I headed for Starbucks that morning, proceeding and pretending as if my seventieth birthday was exactly like all other days, the word "loss" prefaced every thought and every step. My son. My mother. My book. My best friend. My death rattle thing, the foreshadowing echoes of which I imagined as I walked up the street. And, even more important, the self-confidence and inner strength, the public persona, I had worked so hard over the years to establish, nurture, and sustain.

Three

AS USUAL, THAT MORNING, I WAS THE FIRST STARBUCKS SHADY-side customer. Six a.m. on the dot, when the lights went on and the doors unlocked. Since it had opened thirty-one years ago, I'd almost always been the first customer any morning I was in town. The baristas know what I want, a takeout venti dark roast, and usually have it ready or start pouring when I walk in the door. But that day, as I stood at the counter waiting, Tony the barista was taking longer than usual to fill my venti cup. And as I looked more carefully, I noticed he was leaning backwards, then suddenly he was falling, ever so slowly, hovering at first, momentarily balanced in midair, stiff and rigid, then gaining momentum, propelling downward, like a lumberjack's felled tree. He landed, squirmed, and twisted on the ground.

How long did I stand there, frozen, processing what had happened? Maybe fifteen seconds. But it seemed much longer. I wanted to help him, but I couldn't force myself to move. I knew, as I stood there, what had probably happened, but my boots were glued to the ground.

A couple of weeks earlier, I had arrived at Starbucks in time to see the ambulance pull away. It was Tony then, too. He had had a seizure. So this was a repeat incident, I assumed. And yet I was hesitating, unable to act decisively.

Once in Oklahoma, while motorcycling the country for a book I was writing, my cycling partner, Burt, took a razor blade to his wrist. Burt's moods had seesawed erratically throughout the trip. He had left his wife, three children, and a struggling business in a generic strip mall to join me for a few weeks on my nomadic cross-country odyssey. Motorcycling America was a dream come true for both of us, but his guilt over abandoning his family, if only for a short time, surfaced off and on in erratic waves, periodically overwhelming him.

The cut on his wrist wasn't too deep, but there was a gash and some pulsing blood. I knocked the blade from his grip and pounced on it, so that he couldn't get at it. Burt calmed down. Then I wrapped a towel around his bleeding wrist, borrowed a car from the owner of the motel where we had stopped for the night, and rushed him to the nearby hospital ER, by which time he had regained control of himself and begun weeping, regretting what he had tried to do. But I had reacted instinctively, correctly, back then—the nurses praised me.

Yet decades later, here I was, hesitating to dash behind the counter and help Tony. All kinds of scenarios ran through my head. Would I be accused of looting the cash register—or trying to—digging my gnarly old fingers into the drawer? Was Tony really in distress? Or would he suddenly jump up like nothing had happened and gaze at me like I was delusional and addled, an old fool, a lame and overly panicked gray ghost, for trying to help? And besides, what does one do for a person having a seizure? I hadn't the slightest idea. Lift his head? Turn him around? Shake him? Slap him silly and tell him to wake up? What if I do the wrong thing, I thought, and kill the sonofabitch?

Then I suddenly remembered my cousin Shimmy. I don't spend a lot of time thinking about Shimmy, and I didn't know him that well, just from family gatherings when I was a boy, but his stupid tragic story, often retold with shame and sympathy on those rare occasions, mostly funerals, when our cousins got together, periodically haunted me.

"Shimmy" is a Yiddish nickname for Sam—usually conferred on those Sams with a bit of personality and panache, which is exactly how to describe Shimmy. A character, to say the least—and, you might say, a trouper. He kept himself going well past his prime. Or, to put it another way, imagined and gambled on an extended prime.

Shimmy liked to sing and dance—and people all over loved and appreciated watching him. He was the life of any party. Sometimes he wore black-and-white saddle shoes with taps on them—he could dance like Fred Astaire—and he played the piano with verve, lots of ragtime. Long time ago, he sold his business and retired—I can't remember what he did for a living, but he made a lot of money—and moved with his wife to Miami, where he could dance, sing, and play the piano all the time.

Until that day, when he was on his way home, driving from the Jewish Community Center where he had been entertaining some people his own age, and confused the sidewalk with the street, which, when you are eighty-eight and still have the ragtime in your head, and you are tapping your saddle shoes to the beat, maybe on the accelerator, is probably easy to do. Shimmy mowed down and killed two people who were standing on the sidewalk waiting for a bus, which is what Shimmy should have been doing. Waiting for a bus, instead of shimmying in his car. He never played the piano or tapped those saddle shoes again, and he died soon thereafter, from grief and old age.

Although I hardly even knew him, Shimmy's story pops up in my mind from time to time, primarily because I don't want to do what I have come to call "pulling a Shimmy," by which I mean fucking up—getting too old, so old that you lose control and suddenly can't do what you know you should, must, do. Right then, standing motionless in Starbucks as I stared at Tony, frozen like a fool, gawking, for those maybe fifteen seemingly endless seconds, I realized, I feared, that I might be on the verge of pulling a Shimmy.

It required a massive effort to unglue myself, but finally I came to my senses and dashed around the counter. I laid Tony flat on the floor, put a towel under his head, and called 911 for help. It was easy, nothing to it, the right thing to do, instinctively, and yet I had hesitated. I felt so dumb, unraveling the way I did.

That incident with Tony scared the bejeezus out of me. My hesitation, my inability to instantly act, was not good—not me. I had never been a procrastinator. Ask the people who know me, work with me. I get on everyone's last nerves because I am such a take-charge fellow. "Actions speak louder than words" is my mantra. I annoy people constantly by asking them, did they do their research, did they make a back-up plan, did they take advantage of obvious opportunities, did they follow through, did they act with authority and decisiveness? Now look at me: I can't even act decisively and follow through to save a life.

"This will never happen again," I vowed, as the paramedics arrived to tend to Tony. "No more backsliding or bungling for Mr. Lee!" But when you get old—too old—perhaps you lose your judgment. You don't see or comprehend everything as instantaneously and unambiguously as you once did. At least, I don't think you do. But how can I be sure? It's hard to know what you really know at seventy. You think you know a lot, age leads to wisdom and a rich bank of knowledge, but sometimes you behave like there's a goddamn screw loose. You want to tighten it, but then you can't remember where you put the screwdriver. Or what a screwdriver is.

Four

ON MY WAY HOME FROM STARBUCKS THAT DAY, I TOOK A DEEP breath. "Okay, it's over, and you've handled it, right? No more hesitation. This isn't who you are. Never again." And that helped—until I realized that what I had just said, I'd said out loud. I was talking to myself, as if I were two people, which is okay, I guess, lots of people talk to themselves, but not in public, for God's sake!

This seems to happen more frequently as I get older. For instance, I might leave Starbucks after having a casual conversation with someone in the coffee line. I say goodbye, exit out the door, then continue the conversation, aloud, as I walk up the street. The sound of my voice, carrying both sides of the conversation, eventually startles me, and I say, also out loud, "Oh shit. You better stop this." And I do—until I begin to think of something else that's on my mind, and my resolve to shut up fades, and the dialogue in my head gradually flows out of my mouth and into the street. And again, I have to shut myself up—"Stop talking!" I command—and again, for God's sake, out loud.

Sometimes I express, in public, out loud, and for no particular reason and to no related reference . . . nonsense. Total nonsense, which sticks in my head for days on end, like the lyrics of a song you hear on the radio or as Muzak on an elevator, which you cannot, as hard as you try, shake. That day after Tony was whisked away in another ambulance, as I was walking home, I said to no one, except maybe to the sidewalk or the storefronts on the street, "What do you think of Mr. Skink?"

Why did I say that? Who is Mr. Skink? But this Mr. Skink business became a noise in my head I couldn't shake. All day long, during my feverish runs, and at home, drinking glass after glass of wine before dinner, and more after dinner, alone, at night, I repeatedly asked myself the question of the moment: "What do you think of Mr. Skink?" I stopped asking myself the question after a few days, but the Mr. Skink mystery, why he popped into my head, has forever eluded me. And he does come back to confuse and taunt me from time to time. Maybe I know Mr. Skink. And maybe I am slipping. Maybe just a little. Maybe, perhaps, Mr. Skink is me?

But I don't want you or anyone else to think I was or am some sort of neurotic because, honestly, it's simply not true, or not completely true, anyway. But I have come to understand that there are two different and often conflicting Lees.

First, there's the Lee who presents himself to the public. I am one confident cat—or, at least, that's my persona or façade. What people see of me professionally. I teach at a large public university, travel and conduct workshops primarily for graduate students, postdocs, and faculty folks, most of whom are usually way past thirty and have achieved a great deal in life. I have no problem lecturing to hundreds of people, during which time I am animated, articulate, and quite spontaneous. I've been on national TV various times, including *Good Morning, America* and *The Daily Show with Jon Stewart*. I do well, also, one-on-one. I know how to listen, to charm, to flirt and joke even in difficult circumstances, all generally in a timely and responsive manner.

But then there's the other Lee. The behind-closed-doors me, another persona entirely. Not that I get crazy when I am alone, screaming and yelling and throwing things. Or punch out my TV when Wolf Blitzer or Oprah Winfrey get on my nerves. But when I am home and alone, especially when I am preparing to go out and play the public me, the pressure mounts, and I become anxious and more than a bit OCD. I guess I am pretty damn insecure, and the insecurity is or was getting worse and more troublesome. As I got older, I became increasingly afraid of looking foolish, making mistakes, showing my age. Like I had with Tony. I worked hard, ceaselessly and obsessively, to prove to the world that I was a superman—a guy who's got it all together quite naturally. As if it was in my blood.

Since I am not a superman, this ease of seeming so together in public requires a lot of preparation and resolve in private. But it's often the little things that get in the way of my careful preparation and drive me crazy and make me feel so lame and out of synch.

Soon after I got home after watching medics pack Tony into the ambulance, I had an important morning meeting to attend. I was making a presentation to a large foundation interested in funding the literary magazine I founded and edit. This magazine represented a lifetime professional effort for me; I had conceived the idea of a literary magazine, the first devoted to true stories—a genre called creative nonfiction—and I had devoted many years, while teaching and writing my books, to keeping it running and growing and, most important, independent, not reliant on any institution or individual that could zap it and take it away. This happens with literary magazines/journals, mostly supported by universities or wealthy individuals. The powers that be decide at the drop of a hat that you are no longer worthy of support, or that you have been around too long (like me!) and that you have become a financial drain or a pain in the ass, and you are unceremoniously dumped. Cancelled. Left to swing in the wind.

And I wasn't going to allow that to happen, so I had worked all the previous night to get prepared. That's what I do. I prepare my ass off in secret so that it looks spontaneous, this natural, ready-for-anything me. But just as I was about to leave my house and get on the road—early, so as not to be late for the meeting—things went wrong, and my mania to make certain I had put myself and all the loose ends together got the best of me.

For one thing, I couldn't seem to zip up my jacket. I mean, I was at the door, heading for my car in the garage behind my house, when the zipper stuck to the fabric of my jacket and I began fighting to get it loose. You know how that goes. The more you tug, the more it sticks and resists. I was making some progress, but then I dropped my car keys. Seemed like I was dropping everything I touched. Coins and keys, pens and pencils. How did my fingertips become so smooth, as if there was none of that gluey stick-to-it grip left in my fingers anymore? The week before, I had dropped my credit card while paying for items at the grocery, so I bent down to scoop it up. Then I dropped it again. And when I bent down a second time, the damn plastic seemed laminated to the ground. It wouldn't budge. So I wedged my fingernail under the corner of the credit card, or tried to, but my fingernails were too short. I tried three times before I snagged it. And then I dropped it again.

Eventually I gave up on the zipper, pulled the jacket over my head like a sweater in order to examine closely the stuck zipper, to see and then gently but stubbornly tug the material loose from it. But first the sweater-jacket caught on my eyeglasses, which I had been too lazy to remove, and my glasses clattered to the floor, necessitating another bend. I felt like a fool, so lame—one thing after another. Thank God I was alone! But you can't do anything about this stuff, except to yell and swear out loud. *Fuck-fuck-fuck!* Not helpful.

When these annoyances happen, they don't end. You get off your game, lose your confidence. At least, I do. Even when I had my keys in my hand, my jacket zipped up neatly, and I was ready to go out the door, I felt unsure. Did I have everything I would need for my meeting? Notebook? Yes. Laptop? Yes. File folder? No. Well, maybe I wouldn't need it—but maybe I would. It had some relevant papers, and I didn't want to rely on my memory if I was asked any questions; I needed the folder, just in case.

So I went back to the second floor of my house, where my office is located, and on the way to the office I adjusted the thermostat. I wasn't going to be home for half a day; no need to have the heat running full blast. But then I realized I would probably need to pee sometime during the middle of the meeting, and the last thing I wanted was for my potential funders to believe my kidneys were failing. Even though I had visited the bathroom right before I began wrestling with my stuck zipper, I detoured into the bathroom once more.

I relieved myself for the second time in about fifteen minutes— better safe than sorry—then retraced my steps downstairs and headed for the door. And stopped. Something was not right. Then I remembered: the file folder I had gone up to my office to retrieve. I went back upstairs for the folder, but then I realized I hadn't shaved that morning—which was okay. I don't need to shave every day, but I wanted to remember to shave later, or the next day, so after I retrieved the folder, I took my razor from the bathroom and placed it on top of the stairs to remind me to shave when I returned. I have learned that this reminder device works: whenever I think of something I need to do, I place an item somewhere in the house that will jog my memory, and I keep it there until I fulfill whatever task I needed to do. On the TV table in the living room, beside the front door, I will place empty packages of English muffins or Sweet'n Low—whatever—to remember to buy. Or letters to mail. Checks to deposit. My mania not to forget is relentless; I don't want anyone to realize I'm slipping. No one except me: I will not slip in public. I need to remain viable, no matter how hard I must work to do so.

This doesn't happen every day. But when little things go wrong, angst and anxiety take over, and I feel quite out of control. It takes a while to settle down and regroup, and I always do manage to get things together and get myself back into gear—moving from my private persona to the way I am when I am playing the part of public me.

By then, I was running late for my meeting and had to hurry. I left the house and locked the door. I put my keys in my left pocket by habit, so I would remember where they were. I have a pocket ritual. Left pocket for keys. Right pocket for money and a Listerine Cool Mint PocketPak—thin wafers of gel mouthwash, because I am afraid of having old man's breath. I've heard people say, "He looks like death warmed over—and he smells like it, too," and I know and have smelled what they mean on old geezers, like they are sour and musty, so I continually coat my tongue with these wafers before I meet up with someone. You can never be too careful at my age; you must be relentless in playing the game to be convincing.

I headed off, late but finally in meeting-the-public mode, ready for anything, thinking and going over in my mind what I needed to talk about and, at the same time, considering how to get where I was going. Sometimes, these days, I can't remember even the most familiar streets. I must concentrate carefully or I will end up somewhere else, or get the entire endeavor confused—the wrong meeting time on the right day, or the right meeting time on the wrong day. This has happened.

But in the end, the meeting with the foundation went well. I was in first-class super-Lee shape, amusing, insightful, thoughtful, persuasive ("What a guy, considering his age!"). And I got some funding. So, you see: I am okay in public, more than okay. It's when I'm in private and alone, unwatched, overthinking everything, that I sometimes lose my moxie.

And Tony, it turned out, was okay too. He returned to work the following day, and when I walked into Starbucks that next morning, he was all over me, hugging and thanking and complimenting me about my fast action, quick thinking, on his behalf. I listened and played along, but he did not know what I knew: that it was all I could do to muster the strength and the will to help him. I had barely escaped pulling a Shimmy.

And that is what happened the day I turned seventy.

Five

NOT LONG BEFORE MY SEVENTIETH, AN OLD FRIEND, DICKIE Diamondstone, invited me to get together with a bunch of guys I graduated from high school with. They were meeting at one of those chain restaurants, Panera Bread, in a suburban shopping mall called the Miracle Mile, just outside Pittsburgh. Right away, I did not want to go. Too many years had gone by, and I had made it a point to disconnect from my past and become in every way possible a different person.

But Dickie was the lone figure from my elementary and high school days who had kept in touch, mostly through e-mail, and even though I did not want to go back in time and confront those memories again, I appreciated his efforts to connect. And I appreciated that he had kept his name from when he was a kid—Dickie! Not Dick or Rick or Richard or Ricardo. But Dickie Diamondstone! I liked saying it—the alliteration made me smile—and sometimes I would chant it real fast after receiving one of his "Here's what our old friends are doing these days" e-mail blasts: *Dickie Diamondstone, Dickie Diamondstone, Dickie Diamondstone!*

When Dickie said the mini reunion was taking place in the middle of the morning at a suburban shopping mall, a gigantic red flag began waving in my mind. I hate the suburbs and shopping malls, and hanging out in the middle of the morning, when everyone should be working, was anathema—and at a Panera, for God's sake, a dreary, drab, soggy-soup cafeteria chain. How dreadful! And getting there would be such a pain. So infrequently do I head into the suburbs, even though I have lived in Pittsburgh off and on throughout my life, that I use my GPS, although I sometimes find it more annoying than useful. Watching the road, while struggling to glimpse the GPS screen out of the corner of my eye, listening to that artificial-voice asshole inside the dashboard telling me what to do, requires too much coordination. Sometimes I can't understand what he-she-it is telling me.

But I considered the invitation for a while, going back and forth in my mind, the pros and cons of this reunion, and then agreed. Maybe it would be nice, helpful, to reconnect with a few folks from the old neighborhood. Might offer a different perspective. I had hated where I grew up.

Greenfield, where Dickie and I lived as kids, was strictly a blue-collar, Catholic bastion, a dreary, worn-down peninsula of provincialism. The men worked in the mills—J&L Steel, U.S. Steel, Mesta Machine—multibillion-dollar Trojan horses, gone and forgotten now in what some citizens call the revitalized Pittsburgh, although many of their children, my high school classmates, also ended up in the mills for a while before confronting unemployment. This situation caused great resentment, especially toward Jews.

It was an unwritten rule in elementary school, a tacit understanding among the non-Jews in Greenfield, that you beat up on the Jewish boys because they'd be back in the neighborhood ten or twenty years later as doctors, accountants, real estate hucksters, and attorneys, beating up on you by squeezing your pocketbook dry. I was a favorite target, with two strikes against me: Jewish and fat. The kids in my grade school, Roosevelt, called me Slim and sang a parody of the then-popular song by Tennessee Ernie Ford about coal miners when I walked into class or onto the playground: "Sixteen tons and whadda you got? Lee and his mother sitting on a cot."

I had always assumed that once I left Roosevelt, escaping the gang of Greenfield Catholics led by Billy Sopira, the older boy next door who made me his official punching bag "because the Jews killed Christ," and started high school in the predominantly Jewish Squirrel Hill, my life would be better and I would have friends who liked me. But I immediately discovered my miscalculation. Because I lived in Greenfield, the kids in Squirrel Hill—the group to which I thought I belonged because I was Jewish—ignored me. Squirrel Hill was and is basically the cultural and intellectual district of the city, where the university professors, doctors, lawyers, and CPAs lived. I was Jewish, but my family didn't pass the white collar "professionalism" test.

But Dickie, too, was Jewish in a neighborhood of Greenfield goyim, non-Jews, and he had grandparents from the old country—Russia, I think—just like me. He was fat, too, even fatter than I was. And yet neither his disconnection from Squirrel Hill nor his weight ever seemed to affect him. He was a good athlete. He could run and hit, and, unlike me, he could catch a fly ball and hurl it from the outfield to second base or home plate like a missile. More to the point, no one ever seemed to ridicule him, calling him Slim or Jelly Belly or Fat Fuck. Or "Jew boy." I didn't know him all that well, but I had observed and admired how comfortable and confident he seemed to be—fat and fit at the same time. I too was fit and fat back then, but no one seemed to take note of that, including me. Of course, I didn't inspire much confidence in my contemporaries because I couldn't, or wouldn't, catch a fly ball.

The boys would all get together at the dusty, rutted playground field adjacent to Roosevelt after dismissal, rain or shine, for a pickup softball or baseball game. Tommy Spooner, the best athlete, and muscular, rock-jawed Stuart Caplan took over: born leaders. Always the last to arrive, they'd swagger onto the field and take command.

Tommy and Stuart picked their teams, taking turns, one kid after another. Tommy might choose Johnny Davin, a short, quick, wiry guy, for shortstop, and Stuart would nab Billy Keener, tall, lithe, muscular, the reliable left fielder, or Sonny Cofsky, a steady, deadeye pitcher. On and on, the group would dwindle down as the teams took shape, and those of us left would yell, "Pick me! Pick me!" until it was just the dregs. Like Marc Lindenbaum, a gangly pimple-faced kid who would die of leukemia in junior high school. Then, finally, Mr. Last-to-Get-Picked-Every-Single-Time. Me.

I stood out in right field, every time I had the chance to play, and prayed to God that no one would hit the ball in my direction. Everybody on my team also prayed to God that the ball wouldn't come to me, because they expected me to blow it. That was why I was in right field, because that's where the fewest balls were hit, so when I did get picked, right field was where the captain invariably banished me. Where I could do the least harm.

Ironically, I was good at the plate. In fact, I could hit like crazy, and I could catch a ball coming at me when I practiced. But during a game, when it counted, I suddenly turned inept. It wasn't as if I had difficulty paying attention. I watched every pitch, every swing, and I could always see the ball when it was coming in my direction. Off the bat, into the air, way up high, evaporating momentarily into the sun, and then dropping back into view, descending toward me, and I'd angle, shuffle around, position myself, get under it, watch like a hawk as it plummeted down, that elusive white speck growing larger and larger and riveted into my eye. I was focused, anchored, waiting exactly in the right place—or so I thought.

Because then, in that split second when ball and glove met, or were supposed to meet, that white sphere, which I had squarely homed in on, suddenly disappeared! Gone. Bouncing behind me, in front of me, or to the side. More than once it hit me on the head or banked off my chest, and then I frantically scrambled around to find it, humiliation increasing with pain as I chased it down and hurled it to an exasperated infielder in hopes that I could still make amends by getting the runner tagged out. Hardly ever happened.

Six

THE FIRST TIME I HUNG OUT WITH DICKIE, HE INTRODUCED me to pizza. We were on the ball field after a game. It was one of those rare events when I had been allowed to play. I got a couple of hits—and, fortunately, no fly balls came my way for me to muff. Dickie came up to me as we all headed home and, out of the blue, said, "Let's walk to Beto's."

"What's Beto's?" I asked him.

"Where you can get pizza."

This was in the mid-1950s. Maybe pizza was a big deal in Chicago or New York, but in Pittsburgh the P-word when it came to food was *pierogi*—dumplings filled with sweets or meats. I had never heard of pizza, I told him.

"It's the greatest," he explained. "Tomato sauce with spices and pepperoni and hot melted mozzarella cheese on a pie crust. Pizza pie!" he added.

I didn't know what pepperoni was either, but I figured I would find out. Besides, I had plenty of time on my hands, no one to talk to or hang with, so Dickie and pizza pie and pepperoni seemed fine.

Turned out that Beto's was far away, at least an hour's walk, even though Dickie set a rapid pace; he evidently walked to Beto's quite often. And so we had a long time to get acquainted and talk, mostly about our fathers and our inability to deal with their disciplinary demands.

Dickie's father's first name was Julius, but when Dickie was a kid, because he didn't get along with his dad and wanted to say critical things about him right in front of him, he said his father's name backwards—*Suiluj* (pronounced "Swilage"). And for a while, I also, inspired by Dickie, was introducing myself, mostly to girls, backwards: "Good evening, I am Eel Dniktug." At the time, I felt backwards—like I was going nowhere. These days, I would like my life to go backwards. I don't want to go anywhere forward at this late date.

Suiluj was a CPA and had his own accounting firm downtown. He was a stickler for academic achievement. Dickie wasn't much of a scholar, didn't care about school, was often truant, and was regularly punished for bad grades and low test scores by having his privileges suspended—his "freedom," he said, like being able to leave the house after school, hang out with friends, play ball at the field, or walk to Beto's for pizza.

I didn't know exactly what to say to Dickie about my father because, frankly, I was embarrassed, humiliated, puzzled about our situation at home—and helpless to do anything about it. My father was also a strict disciplinarian, like Suiluj. But my dad, unlike Suiluj, was filled with an anger that flared up and exploded often without warning or reason. Like the Zippo lighter he used to fire up his cigars, any little thing I might say or do that pissed him off—a subtle flick of the thumb, so to speak—would ignite his temper and he would suddenly lose all control. When that happened, he would unbuckle his belt, which he called "the strap," pull it out of his trouser belt loops, order me to bend over, swirl it around like it was a bullwhip, and begin to flail away. If I didn't bend over, or bend over fast enough, that strap would make its mark anywhere, creating red blotches on my arms or my face.

Greenfield, as I said, was a transitional neighborhood mostly made up of lower middle-class blue-collar people who worked in the steel mills not far from our homes, and it would be no surprise to learn that these men strapped their kids—it could be expected, maybe—but this kind of uncivilized behavior from a Jewish family, the Chosen People, was unheard of. Who would believe it? Why would God condone such hostility? Jews did not rain down a strap on their children, right? Rather, they nurtured and protected them and prepared them to negotiate and achieve in a hostile Jew-hating world.

Spilling the beans about my family would have made me more of an outcast than I already was, so I kept silent. Explosive anger was the family secret. The trauma of what happened at home seems now to be finally fading, but I still find it uncomfortable to write about those days, my father's rages, and I can't quite escape remembering or dreaming about the way in which I was trapped at home, that little fat boy rolling into a ball of self-protection, the swish of the strap, the crack as it slapped into me, and the knife of pain that was, in retrospect, more humiliating than hurtful.

So, I listened to Dickie and his troubles with Suiluj, but I never fessed up to what happened behind closed doors at my house. And I told him about the garage door because it represented my father's craziness and intransigence, and my sheer inability to do anything about anything that really went on at home.

Every morning, before heading off to work, my father recited this order religiously: "Don't forget to close the garage door. And make sure it is open for me when I get home."

"Why is the garage door so important?" I asked him repeatedly.

He was in a hurry in the morning to take care of business, so he didn't have time to get out of his car and close the garage door, was his answer. And he was tired when he came home from work at night, so the garage door should be open and waiting for him. This was when automatic garage door openers and closers were rare, if available at all. I don't remember. And my father would probably not have purchased one of those gizmos anyway, just so he could harass me about doing my garage door duty. I had two brothers, twins, Michael and Richard, seven years younger, much too young at the time for garage door duty. And besides, they were good kids, did what they were told. Kept to themselves and stayed out of his way. I was the troublesome child.

It is not that I decided not to fulfill garage door duty. I just couldn't or wouldn't focus on it, like catching a fly ball. I had my mantra every morning as I brushed my teeth, ate my breakfast, headed to school: *Don't forget the garage door, don't forget the garage door, don't forget the garage door.* I invariably forgot. Which I realized even then was a symbol of rebellion. Which led to all sorts of punishments. I was banished sometimes to the basement to sit alone in the dark and ponder my indiscretions or sent to my room for the night without supper. Or both. And there was always the looming threat of the strap if I argued or refused.

By the time Dickie and I got to Beto's, trash talking our dads, I realized that I had missed supper and would probably be sent to my room for being late when I returned home—so pizza pie, with spicy tomato sauce and delightfully tongue-titillating pepperoni, would be perfect.

Which it was.

SOON AFTER OUR WALK TO BETO'S, DICKIE FIGURED A SECRET way to pay back his dad for all the punishments he had endured. It was ingenious.

Suiluj was obsessed with that musical riff or couplet, "Shave and a haircut, two bits." We all know how it goes. Seven notes, beginning with five notes, *bum bum-bum-bum-bum*, followed by the ascending "two bits"—*bum-bum*. Suiluj was always tapping it out, in the car on the steering wheel, or at home in response to TV commercials. That's how he knocked on doors when visiting friends and neighbors. Or woke Dickie up in the morning. *Bum bum-bum-bum-bum . . . bum bum.* Suiluj, Dickie said, couldn't stop himself from finishing the riff, if someone didn't finish it or didn't do it fast enough.

So, Dickie let me into his house in the middle of the night. His mother and father were sleeping in their bedroom down the hall. Dickie walked over to the piano and ever so softly and gently played out, in G major, *Bum bum-bum-bum-bum*—"Shave and a haircut"—and then rushed back behind the sofa.

We waited maybe just a few minutes until, finally, we heard his parents' bed creak. Then the bedroom door opened, and steps thudded down the hall.

Suiluj's figure, dark in the shadows—he was a short, rotund man—appeared in the middle of the room. We held our breaths, hoping he wouldn't discover us. Then he plunked out: *bum bum*. And went back to bed.

Seven

DICKIE AND I HAD, FOR A WHILE, CONTINUED OUR FRIEND-
ship after high school. In our early twenties, we hung out regularly
with a bunch of other guys who, like us, were trying to find themselves
and figure out what they were going to do for the rest of their lives.
They all had crazy names, like Boo-Boo, Tooth, Mad Dog, Villain, Fast
Eddie, Animal. I was known as The Cleat, because of the big cleated
motorcycle boots I had adopted as a trademark to go along with my
fascination with motorcycles and Jack Kerouac, who had written a
book I had, at that point, read maybe a dozen times, *On the Road*.

We did a lot of crazy things befitting our crazy names, mostly mis-
chievous stuff like drag racing and crashing parties. We got into a few
skirmishes in bars because we were drinking or smoking too much
grass—"weed" in today's terminology. It was fun, harmless, but like
I said, we were all in transitional periods—that limbo time in your
life when you are searching for direction and trying in one way or
another to ease yourself from extended adolescence into responsible adulthood. If those were the guys I would be meeting at Miracle
Mile, I would have been more enthusiastic. But Dickie's e-mail said

this was to be a different group—none of whom, I surmised, I had seen since high school, or known very well, which is why I hesitated for so long before agreeing to join them. This would not be a reunion with old friends. More like a reunion with old semi-acquaintances. So I approached the day with more than a little apprehension.

I arrived late, purposely, at the Miracle Mile Panera to meet Dickie Diamondstone—for two reasons: first, I figured I wouldn't have to stay as long as everyone else, and second, I admit, I wanted to make an entrance. I know that is somewhat egocentric, but I wanted these people from my past to notice me, to see how different I was from how they might remember the fat kid who couldn't catch a fly ball, and who graduated with them in the bottom fifth of our high school class. The kid who walked away from Greenfield, the bullying Catholics. And, perhaps more important, from the wealthy, smug Jewish kids in the adjoining "ritzy" Squirrel Hill, the group I had wanted so much to connect with, and create a larger life. A memorable, significant, big-deal writer, professor, different me.

But there wasn't anyone around when I walked into the Miracle Mile Panera. The place was quite empty—not even a hostess on duty at 10:30 in the morning on a workday Tuesday. I wandered around, thinking perhaps I had the wrong day. There were two men at a table in a front corner, a salesman and his customer, going over an order form, and a half dozen or so old men together in the back, clustered around a table near the men's room.

I headed that way—I can always use a men's room—hoping I had missed Dickie and his pals. But as I got closer, these old guys at the table came into clearer view. They were mostly way overweight, bulging and balding and gray-whiskered, craggy and unkempt, and dressed in clothes that had gone out of style with Billy Joel. Or worse: baggy sweatpants, sandals with black socks. Typical pitiful old men whiling away the morning hours talking about the world a half century ago when they thought they were vital and active.

A feeling of sickness and dread came over me as I passed their table—or rather I desperately wanted to pass their table, but I had to stop and sit and talk, because I suddenly realized who these old men were: Dickie and his gang of geezers. My contemporaries! I was mortified. And I was even more mortified by the possibility that I looked more like them than I wanted to admit.

They were all retired. The discussion centered around grandchildren and great-grandchildren and the people with whom we had grown up who were now dead. One of the guys was excited because he was going to California—his first trip across the country. Another said that he went to Panera every morning because the coffee was only a dollar a cup and refills were free. I vaguely remembered them all—but there was nothing we could share. Different lives. We were more than out of synch. We were in the outer limits of separation. I could have been in Uzbekistan. I would have preferred to be in Uzbekistan.

I felt empty and nervous. I didn't belong, which is how I had always felt about myself when I was a kid. Even then, clearly, nearing seventy, I was still missing that something that could make me feel like part of the group, any group—although it was absolutely okay and, in fact, somewhat of a relief that I did not feel a part of this group.

The thing is, though, they all seemed to be pleased with the lives they were leading and the fact that they were sharing their waning years together at that moment. I did not want to be like any of them. And yet I was amazed by the aura of contentment that flowed like some sort of mild intoxicant around the table that late morning. Why was I feeling so jealous of something I did not want?

I was happy to see Dickie. He was the same good guy he was when I met him, and he was undeniably at ease, sitting there with those old folks, reminiscing about and reconnecting with the people with whom he grew up, and in that way solidifying and justifying his long life. He was still heavy, way overweight, just like the old days when we walked to Beto's, yet he seemed at peace with himself. I guess some people just have the gift of being comfortable with who they are and how they look, while others, like me, may never be comfortable with themselves, no matter how many personas they create and try out.

And if someone, anyone, noticed that I was no longer fat that day as we sat around the table and sipped dollar-a-cup coffee, they didn't mention it. Perhaps my fatness had never affected the way in which they thought about me—if they thought about me at all. I was so uncomfortable with myself back then that I worked tirelessly not to stand out, not to be noticed.

What was Dickie doing now in retirement? He was riding his bike, playing golf. And shooting his guns. Dickie had become a champion marksman while serving in the army. He owned some great firearms. I don't remember the models, exactly. Shooting is not my thing. But I do remember his favorite weapon: a Kimber Ultra Carry II, which, along with his other revolvers, he shared generously. Over the years, he had taken my son and me, once or twice, to the range. He was a great teacher, incredibly kind and careful. He had a license to carry, we found out, which was kind of cool and mysterious, in a way. He was not an FBI agent or a mobster, as my son had once speculated. I think he was just one of these people who wanted to exercise his Second Amendment rights, and clearly enjoyed shooting, especially that Kimber Carry. That was okay.

But what else was he doing? This is what got me! Driving around the country, visiting people he went to high school with, reconnecting and laughing about the old days and having great fun. He had remained in regular and intimate touch with Boo-Boo, Tooth, all of the old gang. They were meeting, frequent reunions, in Florida, California, antique car shows, the Rock and Roll Museum in Cleveland, on and on. And he was still calling me Cleat. I thought that all of that was amazing and downright wonderful. I did not for an instant want to be like Dickie, doing those things with the old gang, visiting one another (who would I visit, anyway, except maybe for Iggy and Susan and, of course, Dickie?) but I was jealous as hell of how he—they all—had achieved such satisfaction in life. Out of nothing. These visits, excursions, reunions, was that nothing? Or was it something I just didn't get?

One thing I realized after coming home and thinking about my interaction with Dickie and his friends is that I wasn't particularly open to those people at Panera. I didn't really participate in the dialogue. I sat and listened to their back-and-forth conversation, smiling and nodding, but not engaging. Writer and crack interviewer though I was, I hadn't really taken the time or made the effort to dig behind what they looked like, or go beyond the few bits of information they offered as conversational gambits, to find out who they really were, what they had done in their lives, who they had cared for, how they, too, had confronted the Greenfield–Squirrel Hill roadblocks and produced families with successful children and beautiful grandchildren, and how and why they had seemed to find such evident satisfaction. I wasn't interested, maybe. Or, I wondered if, really, down deep, my aloofness meant that, selfishly, I just wanted them to be interested in me.

Who was I to feel so superior to these folks just because they had chosen a different path to follow in their lives? I thought about it later. What bothered me is how they focused on their age, couldn't stop talking about it. This made no sense to me. Probably because I worked so hard to look forward in time and worried so much about what I would do in the future, whatever future I had left. I was constantly annoyed and resentful when people my age called attention to their age, which reminded me about my own age, my feelings of vulnerability, my approaching seventy.

As a matter of principle, and self-protection, I never discussed my age—nor anyone else's age, if I could help it. I did everything in my power to dodge these "How old are you" or "Do you realize how long ago that was?" discussions that seem to come about more frequently as time passes.

"Can you believe it? I was a kid when Kennedy was shot," people will say. "Time flies."

Yes, I do believe it—I know it and feel it. At that moment, when Walter Cronkite announced on national TV that JFK was dead, I was with my father—now dead. With us was his best friend Bob Sherman, now dead. We were in a restaurant called Joe's Tavern, now closed, owned by Joe DeCicci, now dead.

I was nineteen years old and I had the whole world ahead of me. Which is precisely why I avoid eye contact, and I nod to the person talking to me on these "remember when" occasions, waiting for the opportunity to transition to another subject. I understand that people who so incessantly talk about the past with that sense of wonder and dismay are verbalizing their amazement and apprehension to someone they consider to be an obviously like-minded person, a codger in the same boat. They are looking for reinforcement and understanding, but I can tell you, at least at that time, that they are not, or were not, going to get it from me.

Like the guy I encountered at the edge of the ice field at the summit of Alaska's Exit Glacier the day I climbed to the peak with my son more than a dozen years ago.

After we had eaten our lunch, I was lying on the ground, my eyes closed, soaking up the sun, and enjoying the triumphant feeling of accomplishment after three hours of slipping and sliding through ice and snow, when I heard a gravely, elated voice: "What's an old man like you doing all the way up here?"

I opened my eyes. He was a man with gray hair and a beard similar to mine, a face creased with wrinkles and a tanned, generous nose, and he was grinning like he thought he was funny. "We're the two oldest people on top of this glacier by twenty-five years," he said. "You don't belong up here," he continued. "Neither do I, know what I mean?"

Of course I knew what he meant. I just didn't want to admit it.

"We're too damn old," he said. "We're not supposed to be able to do what we just did—climb this goddamned mountain!"

I didn't answer. I had felt like a teenager on top of this mountain: it had been a struggle and a triumph getting to the top, and the experience was rejuvenating—or I had felt that way until this man invaded my space and spoiled my fantasy.

"You know," he said, as he walked away, "I'm about your age, and I fought my way up here just like you. I know what it's like—how you feel. So, I can talk to you that way, can't I?"

"No," I said, turning around once more to face him, "you can't."

Later, thinking more about it, I realized that I was being downright mean to this man, who was just trying to be friendly. I regretted it. I still do now, years later. Sometimes I wish that I possessed a "do-over option" that I could activate periodically. All I had to do was blink or sniff or wrinkle my nose in a special way and time would stop and go backwards, so that whatever mistake I made, I would get to take back and try all over again. If only—just once. Or even maybe if there was a wearable item I could purchase or invent, like a Fitbit. Anytime you were about to say or do something stupid, a hidden warning sensor would be activated and there'd be a buzzer or a subtle flashing light that would go off and on, *wait-think-don't be-dumb*, until you paid attention. But then, even with that, I wondered if I wouldn't do or say the same thing again, even double down, because I could be so damn stubborn, no matter how wrong I knew it was.

Like the lines I once read from a novel by Samuel Beckett, *Watt*: "And if I could begin it all over again, knowing what I know now, the result would be the same. And if I could begin again a third time, knowing what I would know then, the result would be the same. And if I could begin it all over again a hundred times, knowing each time a little more than the time before, the result would always be the same, and the hundredth life as the first, and the hundred lives as one."

Like I said, this happened a long while back, but that guy on the glacier top came back to me once in a while because I realized he was so right and I was so wrong—or anyway half wrong. That old guy was still climbing mountains, like me, and what we were doing, despite our age, was in fact cool, all things considered. I just wished he hadn't said what he said out loud. I wished he had just smiled at me, winked or something, a secret signal between two aging but vigorous men. I would have smiled back, maybe nodded in affirmation. But laying it out in front of me in that way with my son listening was annoying and even to a certain extent threatening. I wondered what my son was thinking and whether he thought about and judged or reevaluated his old geezer dad.

I find it so much easier to accept being old if I don't think about or talk about being old. I am, rather, just me, doing my thing. I have no idea if this is true, but I am guessing that people with handicaps, say blindness, don't want to be reminded all the time that they are functioning like everyone else, more or less, as best they can, although they cannot see, and praised for it. They just do what they need to do; it's who they are, not what they are, that matters. Maybe they get points for extra effort.

I realize that most people who have called attention to my age in those ways, like the mountaintop guy, were just being kind. But it is not so kind in my way of thinking, or in the way I thought back then. Like clerks in stores or waitpersons in restaurants, people I don't know, who ask me if I am retired, or why I am not retired when I tell them I am not. Or who say stuff like "How can I help you, *young man?*" It is meant as a compliment about my appearance, maybe my vigorousness, *young man*, but to me it is a zinger. They are reminding me that I am old. Like I didn't know that, for God's sake.

This guy on the glacier was really my kind of guy. He was still climbing mountains, while Dickie and his friends were coasting. Maybe they didn't think they were coasting—and maybe coasting is not a fair way to describe the essence of their lives. Or maybe they did think they were coasting but didn't feel that coasting was such a bad thing. Why should they? Dickie, from Dickie's point of view, I am certain, did not think that there was anything but good, productive, fun stuff going on in his life. Besides, is there a law against coasting, enjoying your remaining years, you know, like they say, retiring, "doing your own thing," and "smelling the roses"? Or the "funny" bumper stickers you see on cars, which I don't think are funny at all.

"I'm retired, go around me."

"Adventure with dementia."

"I'm so old I fart dust."

Maybe I was being stupid, defensive, because I was so damn uncertain and insecure about what was going to happen in my life next.

I remember a woman I was talking to at a party who was embroiled in a contentious situation at work with her boss. She was rambling on about her soon-to-be-ex-boss (she was quitting) and maybe she was drinking too many martinis, but she said something that resonated with me, and I couldn't help myself, I laughed out loud about what she said because it was sort of silly, to say the least. But then later I thought that what she said might be true, if not profound—at least for me. I could, unfortunately and embarrassingly, relate.

Railing against her employer, his intransigence and refusal to listen to her, she stated in frustration, "You can't change an asshole."

Did that comment, I thought, looking back on the many miscues in my life, including my treatment of that man on that Alaskan glacier top, also pertain to me?

Was I an asshole for resisting reality, for not accepting who or what

I was? Was I just denying the obvious? I went round and round about this for a long time, another one of my mantras: *I feel so young . . . I am so old. I feel so young . . . I am so old.*

How to come to terms with, reconcile, these annoying, nagging, conflicting realities?

Eight

MY DAD DIDN'T HAVE SUCH A GREAT LIFE GROWING UP, AND I honestly feel bad for him now, looking back. One day in 1927, right before the Great Depression, when he was only thirteen, his mother, Lena, my namesake, had signed a permission slip to allow him to enter Hebrew Polytechnic High School. Evidently my dad hoped to become an architect or engineer. His father, Isadore, who owned a dry goods and tailoring shop in Brooklyn, hadn't been too keen on that idea, but Lena, ill and buried under blankets, bed-bound for months with liver cancer, persisted until he agreed. I am not sure my father remembered the name of this school correctly, for I have been unable, in a cursory search of the internet, to find evidence that Hebrew Polytechnic High School existed back then, although it may well have been renamed over the years. But I think it hardly matters, since my dad's time there was cut short. For when he came home from school that first day, he learned that Lena was dead.

Some months after Lena's death, my father came home from school and a second situation, maybe even worse than the first, confronted him. Isadore was absent. A cousin who was minding the store directed my father to the home of another relative. A wedding had just taken place, and my father arrived in the middle of a celebratory dinner. He was ushered into the room and seated across from a woman he had never seen before. This was Isadore's new wife—my father's new mother, stepmother, Molly.

I can't imagine how bad he felt meeting his new mother in that obviously insensitive way. And why his father did that to him—such unnecessary ambush!—is anyone's guess. My father shared that and other bits of his personal history in a letter he wrote to me when I was in my forties. He wrote it in ballpoint pen on blue-lined paper, like a grade school tablet. My mother had warned me that the letter was coming—he had been working on it for a long time, she said, his attempt to explain himself and his own growing-up hardships to me. But the moment I received it in the mail and recognized his scrawled, slanted handwriting on the envelope, I tossed it in a drawer and refused to open it until many years later.

I had spent a half dozen years with a therapist at that point trying to deal with the trauma of my father's violent outbursts, the threatening strap, and the imprisonment in my room or often in the basement when I misbehaved, and for a long time afterward I had no interest in learning his side of the story. There couldn't be a story he could tell me, no matter how gruesome, no matter what the circumstances, to justify or explain his behavior and the impact it had on me. After all, what happened to him was not my fault. So I never had the chance or, for a long time, the interest, or perhaps the courage, to ask him to fill in the details. Even today I don't know if I want to know any more than I know now. Enough, as people tend to say, is sometimes enough.

But I do know his life changed significantly the day that Lena died and then even more significantly when his new mother, Molly, suddenly came on the scene. Molly, a seamstress who had just recently arrived from the old country, Russia, was totally devoted to Isadore, and had absolutely no interest in becoming a parent or doing anything but cooking and cleaning for her new husband. My father's siblings, two older sisters, Hattie and Ethel, had already graduated from high school and had jobs somewhere in the city, but still lived at home. They shared the extra bedroom in the house. My father slept on a cot in the hallway. In that letter, he told me that from the moment of Molly's arrival, the people in the family and in the neighborhood referred to him as "the orphan." When he graduated from high school—the neighborhood high school; his father had made him quit Hebrew Polytechnic to help out in the shop—he immediately left home and went out on his own, working part-time jobs.

My dad clerked in a fruit store, then was a Western Union boy delivering telegrams, then worked in a machine shop as a draftsman. But this was at the height of the Depression, and the company soon went bankrupt. He went into business on his own. He sold college football souvenirs, which he designed and made himself, with the appropriate school colors. Then he began reconditioning used automobile spark plugs, which he purchased for a penny apiece. My father sanded and repainted them, set the gaps, had special boxes made that said Jack's Spark Plugs, Guaranteed Reconditioned, then resold them back to the garages for retail sale. He learned to drive as a night watchman in a taxi parking garage, one of his spark plug customers, by zipping around in the garage with the taxis in the dead of night, when he was all alone.

He also traveled a bit; I know he hitchhiked to the Chicago World's Fair in 1933 and then he went to Washington, DC, to look for work. He walked all the way to the nation's capital because, although he was sticking out his thumb, no one would give him a ride. When he finally got there, he roamed the streets—no jobs, no friends, no one to talk to. So he went to Pittsburgh, where Isadore had relocated with Molly. But my father remained independent, sleeping in rented rooms, sometimes even sharing beds with the many other men and women lost and destitute during the Depression. He never went back home, and for a long time he was rarely in touch with his family.

Eventually, as times got better and the FDR New Deal recovery took hold, he got a job selling shoes, and soon discovered what became his life's work. He worked as a salesman in shoe stores all around the Western Pennsylvania–West Virginia corridor, in a 150-mile radius of Pittsburgh. He met my mother in 1942, courted her zealously, wrote her love letters every week, about how much he missed her, wanted her in his life forever, to build a family, to share in every way the good and the bad times, and commuted from wherever he was working back to Pittsburgh to spend Sunday afternoons with her. A coincidence, for sure, that might have given him pause: from Molly, the dreaded stepmother, to Mollie with an -ie, the love of his life. They were engaged in three months and married soon after.

I often wondered, as did my mother, what had happened to this romantic and love-struck young man, to cause him to become so angry, set in his ways—and bitter. Was it me, I thought, such a rebellious boy, also in certain ways angry and difficult, who reminded him of his own life as an "orphan"? I never felt like an orphan, despite my dad's treatment, because, of course, I had a mother to comfort and protect me. Surely if Lena had been around for him, his life, and maybe mine, would have been different.

My father devoted every ounce of energy and ingenuity to becoming and remaining totally independent. He often warned me about the dangers and pitfalls of counting on others. You cover yourself at any cost or sacrifice. Plan ahead. Know your options. Never rely on anyone for anything you can do for yourself, except perhaps opening and closing your goddamn garage door—ask your firstborn son to do this. He was, he said, a man in control of his destiny. That's exactly what I have attempted to achieve in my life, I realize now, not just with my little literary journal and my books but beginning long ago with shaking myself loose from the man who was trying in his own way to teach me independence—my dad. I should say he succeeded, but the sacrifice and the loss we both suffered was hardly worth the effort on his part, and maybe mine as well.

He was drafted in late 1943 and eventually went to France, where he served as a quartermaster, moving supplies by rail to the front line. My mother had a photo of him with his double-peaked khaki army hat set jauntily on the side of his head, and he was smiling, looking quite happy, a rare event from my point of view. For so many years, when I thought of him, I always pictured him snarling: pressed-in lips, puffed-up face, eyes squeezed into slits, what my mother called his "mad-on sour puss." He was also always yelling at me—or at my mother for trying to protect me from him. That's what I remember when I think of him. "Yelling" doesn't do justice to his anger fits; his "mad-on sour puss" face got all red, and he bellowed like a boar, or what I thought a boar might sound like had I ever heard one. If only he had stayed in the army after the war, I often thought, then we would only have had to put up with him when he came home on leave.

In the late 1950s he opened his own store, a children's shoe store primarily, specializing in orthopedic footwear. He called it Tryson's (pronounced "TRI-sons") for his three sons. He used Tryson's instead of Tri-sons because it looked better with a Y. Most people thought Tryson was his last name; they didn't get the three sons significance. I think, maybe, my father didn't get it either.

Until he took charge of his own life, working for himself, my father didn't have much control over what happened to him, and maybe exerting control over me became a challenge and an obsession to him. Maybe he was trying to teach me life lessons, like learning how to do the right thing by honoring your father, following orders even if the orders made no sense. And maybe he was also testing me, my love, my loyalty, and most of all, like I say, my obedience. His garage door mania was a mental glitch, and he might have realized that, but the moment he instigated it, he was irrevocably stuck with it. Backing down, changing your mind after making such a big deal out of the garage door, or after insisting on the last word in an argument, no matter how many times we went back and forth, would have been humiliating to him. The harder you fight for something, especially when it is not something of substance, the more perspective you lose about the essence and meaning of what you are fighting for. This same thing happened to me on my fortieth birthday when I declared the moratorium on celebratory well-wishing. Sometimes you just get something in your head, and it gets blown way out of proportion, an obsession that becomes an unstoppable runaway train.

Today, I like to think of my father as a pioneer of consumer branding—first with his Jack's Spark Plugs, then later in his little shoe store in the Pittsburgh suburbs, where he began selling shoes he bought from small, unknown companies, mostly in eastern Pennsylvania, Amish country, settled two centuries back by German leather craftsmen—shoes high in quality but considerably less expensive than well-known brands like Poll Parrot and Stride Rite. Back in the corner of the stockroom was a tiny workbench with razor blades and pliers where a worker would rip out the original heel pad emblazoned with the unrecognizable brand name, trace the pad on a sheaf of leather with a ballpoint pen, then cut out and glue in the replacement pad with my father's brand, Tryson's—gold and blue, a nice combination of colors. My father's leather heel pad was of higher quality than the composition material it replaced, justifying an increase in the retail price by a dollar or two. This was branding, long before Apple and Starbucks and McDonald's became household names.

It has taken me a while to recognize the brilliance of my father's vision, probably because the worker he dragooned into ripping out the original labels and gluing in the Tryson's ones was his firstborn son, me. Eight hours every Saturday, and also a couple of days every week after school. My head still aches with the memory of the fumes from the petroleum-based rubber cement. Usually, back in that lonely cubbyhole where I worked, I was permitted to play the radio, as long as I didn't play it too loud, thereby distracting his customers.

My father loved that shoe store—it was his ultimate accomplishment, the symbol of his independence, the proud response to his rejection and abandonment as a kid. Just as I loved and was devoted to my own literary magazine and, even more, the books I had written over the years. I made my mark with the words I wrote, edited, and published. My father made his intimate connection with the world through shoes and feet—certainly not through me and my two younger brothers.

I cannot remember my father ever kissing or touching anyone with tenderness, but at Tryson's he caressed his customers' feet, which made him a natural "shoe dog," a nomenclature for the cadre of shoe merchants he networked with. People sometimes laugh when I tell them my dad was a "shoe dog," but he was fond of the phrase and the profession. "It's my lifeline," he said. And it was, he admitted, how Jack Gutkind defined himself.

But he never defined himself as a dad. Or maybe he came to believe that dads were supposed to shape their sons' characters, to help or force them to understand that life can be, as a friend once told me, a "shit sandwich." You learn to eat it, digest it—and never show how repugnant it is. So my dad was likely responding to his past and his relationship with his own father when teaching his eldest son about the brutal and unfair facts of life. He always told me when I complained or rebelled, "What I am doing is for your own good." Maybe he believed that.

I am beginning to see, as I look back, that I have done many things to emulate my dad over the years, first and foremost to escape the life I was leading at home, emulating his disconnection with his family by fleeing him—being, in a sense, close to him, and who he wanted me to be, precisely by being far away. I had no idea what I was looking for, but after high school I knew that anywhere had to be better than where I was then. I had fantasized constantly about running away, wresting control from my father, being on my own. This is what I wanted more than anything—independence, the confidence and ability to do whatever I wanted to do, whenever and wherever.

The funny thing is, as I turned seventy, I felt in some ways just like I did when I was so young, out of high school, needing a new direction. Not to be my own man—I was that, whatever that meant—but to become a different man. I could not enlist in the military at seventy years of age, a starting-over thought that I periodically fantasized about, although that might have been interesting and certainly change-making. It would make a great book—a seventy-year-old guy in boot camp, along with all of those feisty, full-of-themselves post-adolescents, flexing their muscles and parading around in their spiffy uniforms. But I could show them a thing or two in boot camp, I mused. "You think you're tough? In shape? Well, watch me!"

I can't tell you how often these imaginary me-against-wise-guy-kids scenarios run through my head, especially since the humiliating Tony incident. Some young person, or let's say someone a lot younger than me, suddenly makes fun, wisecracking about how damn old I am. Why he or she would do this, I don't know. But in this scenario, I hold my temper and my comments for a while, and then I say, softly but with steel-edged grit: "Why don't we take a run? Let's go five miles, or even ten miles, or let's just run until the first one drops. And then you will see how damn old I am!"

That's never happened, and probably never will, but I imagine the possibility quite frequently. And what if it does, one day, actually happen? What if the wise-guy kid takes up my challenge, and we meet the following day at the running track in the park, like a duel, with water bottles and running shoes instead of boots and musket single-shot pistols. And then, what if this kid runs circles around me and I am the guy who drops? What would that prove?

I actually, foolishly, once reached out to the Defense Department to see if such a scenario, a seventy-year-old boot camp recruit, was a possibility. A publicity idea they might consider. The officer I talked with in the press office politely explained that that was unlikely, that they couldn't be responsible for what happened to me, even if I was only there for a week. That there were, for one thing, age limitations. And that, frankly, no matter how healthy and youthful I was, I'd be pretty damn outclassed in too many ways to explain, not just physically, but psychologically. I would have to take a lot of abuse. And it would distract from the training of the real recruits. I don't think I would have really gone through with it had they, indeed, actually considered my proposal. I was not thinking too clearly then. I was trying to prove something—my own self-worth—by doing something that was way out of proportion to my problem.

But that's exactly what I did when I turned eighteen—a decision that was absolutely not out of proportion to my problem, back then: I signed up! Enlisted.

Nine

I WAS STANDING IN AN ABANDONED AIRCRAFT HANGAR, IN A line of fifty-five men. We had been boys when we'd come together at the start of boot camp training at the U.S. Coast Guard station on the tip of Cape May, New Jersey. Raw recruits from all over the United States, we had suffered through constant hazing, marching in snow and rain until our feet were numb and bleeding and our fingers frozen blue, and we were still there, most of us. All we had to do to receive our assignments and start our new lives as enlisted men, Seamen, was to pass what Chief Petty Officer O'Reilly was calling "the rope test."

The rope test was the culminating experience of boot camp training—proof that we had truly achieved a measure of fitness and readiness that would allow us to perform our duties as military personnel in a professional and respectable manner. This wasn't just another test, by the way: the rope test was a necessity. We were the Guard, the service designated to protect the coast from enemy infiltration. There were other ways of boarding an invading or otherwise suspicious ship, but when a rope on the side of a ship was the only option, a Coast Guardsman had to be able to climb it.

We were nervous as we stood in a line along the wall of the hangar waiting for the signal, excited and optimistic. The ropes cascaded down from the sloped ceiling of the hangar, knotted here and there and swaying in the drafty building, teasing and tantalizing us. Passing the rope test meant we would receive two weeks' leave to go home and show off our uniforms and svelte new bodies to family and friends before proceeding to new postings. Some of us would be sent to schools for further training, while most would be serving on buoy tenders or patrol boats along the Atlantic Coast. Exciting stuff for young men in the 1960s, boys from the backwoods of Alabama, New Mexico, Indiana, or industrial ghettos like Pittsburgh.

I was especially anxious to make a triumphant journey back to Pittsburgh, for I had progressed both intellectually and physically more than almost anyone else in the company—or so I thought. First, having just squeaked out of high school in the bare bottom fifth of my graduating class, I was one of the youngest men in the company; a few of the men were college graduates. Before I enlisted in the Coast Guard—the only service that would take me; I'd tried the Marines, the air force, and the navy, and they'd laughed and pointed at my stomach—one recruiter scanned my flabby upper body, shook his head, and referred to my fatty, jiggling "yo-yo arms."

But in the Guard, having been forced to march around the compound endlessly, do thousands of push-ups and sit-ups, and run and dive maniacally through the U.S. Marine–style obstacle course, I had lost seventy pounds. Six meals a day was not an option, like at home. Snacks were disallowed. In the Guard, I'd learned to work harder and eat less, obey orders, perform menial tasks, nonstop. I was as ready as I had ever been to achieve something that a few months before had been inconceivable. The rope test: climbing fifty feet straight up to glory and advancement.

Chief Petty Officer O'Reilly raised his whistle, counted to three, hesitated momentarily, and blew. We all raced like mad to the ropes, jumped up as high as possible, grabbed a knot, and started to climb. The screams and yells and groans echoed all around me in the large high-ceilinged room as I began to put one hand over another and pull myself skyward. For a moment, I felt invigorated, consumed by the challenge, almost as if I were flying up the rope along with everyone else.

But when Chief Petty Officer O'Reilly blew his whistle a second time, most everyone in the company was hanging at the top of their ropes, waving their fists and cheering triumphantly. Only one lowly sailor, one dejected young man, flapped and flailed about halfway up to the top of the rope, holding on precariously, breathing heavily, stunned and confused, like a dying fish. Then, as everyone watched, that sailor lost his grip and plunged to the ground.

That sailor was me.

Lying on my back, I could see my new friends, soon to become full-fledged Seamen, "Coasties," looking down from the tops of their ropes, and I felt humiliated. I hadn't failed to get to the top of the rope by just a few feet or a couple of seconds; I hadn't come close. I had plummeted from the most confident and exhilarated period of my life to one of the lowest. In an instant. A heartbeat.

I had entered that hangar thinking I had made some sort of a unique transformation, from the whipping boy of my neighborhood and one of the fattest kids in school to a normal human being. And I had demonstrated that I could survive, fit in with many different men, from all walks of life and of various ages. I'd believed I was not an outcast, which is how I had once perceived myself; I was an accepted part of something, a new person, a legitimately slim person, burgeoning with invigorating confidence.

Until I failed the rope test. What the fuck had happened?

Ten

AFTER BOOT CAMP GRADUATION CEREMONIES, I SAID GOODBYE
to my fellow recruits, who'd been assigned to units across the country. I, however, Chief O'Reilly informed me, would be anchored to
the boot camp base until I passed the rope test. At first I didn't think
this was true. I mean, they weren't going to keep me there forever.
Or were they? But I got the message, loud and clear, that I better get
my act together.

During the day, I worked with a maintenance crew—men who
were incarcerated in the brig for minor offenses—inside a large abandoned furnace, chiseling away at the burnt-in soot and debris, without seeing natural light between breakfast and lunch, and lunch and
supper. At that time, masks were unheard of—or, at the very least,
not for us ne'er-do-wells. I breathed in the coal dust in the morning
and coughed it out, staining black fresh white Kleenexes, at night.
Being surrounded by those filthy windowless walls made me feel
trapped and impotent, just as I had felt in high school and in my parents' Greenfield house, imprisoned by circumstances and my inability to find a way out, chart another direction. And then that fucking

rope test had tainted my dream, and I regressed back into that state of helpless limbo—inside a goddamn furnace. What they would be doing with this furnace after we chiseled it out was a question no one could answer. Or maybe there was no answer.

At the same time, I realized that the rope test symbolized a potential direction, a way forward to the future—something that had been lacking at home, where there was no line of escape whatsoever, no goal or mission worth working for or achieving. All I had to live for at home was waking up to another disappointing and deflating day and eating my way through it. So now there was the rope test, a challenge and a way out, which, as it turned out, would in many ways define the next fifty or so years of my life.

Two things happened during that furnace period in the Guard. First, I had a lot of free time at night since I was forbidden to leave the base and was banned, as a lowly recruit, not yet an official Seaman, from the enlisted men's club, where I would have been able to drink beer, eat burgers, hang out. So I went to the library and started reading. It was a meagre dusty place, one midsized room, with rows of old books and a few featured publications in a rack in front of the librarian's desk. There was, of course, no librarian, and I will never know who, periodically, put those books out on the rack to read. But as it happened, I was usually the only person using the library, so it became a private hideaway. First I read books that were on the rack, popular back then, mostly because of movies or TV shows: Leon Uris's *Exodus*, Neville Chute's *On the Beach*, and Budd Schulberg's *What Makes Sammy Run*. But when I finished those and explored the shelves along the walls, I found books that were surprisingly inspiring and cathartic: Philip Roth's *Goodbye, Columbus*, J. D. Salinger's *Catcher in the Rye*, James Baldwin's *Giovanni's Room*, and John Knowles's *A Separate Peace*.

Here were protagonists with whom I could relate, young men, boys, whose stories mirrored my mood and the sense of isolation I felt back then. I carried their struggles and insecurities with me, reading again and again the passages that most affected me, as I went through my repetitious furnace days, wondering all the while if they would save themselves, and how understanding and learning from their struggles might inspire and guide—and save—me.

Here was Philip Roth's protagonist in *Goodbye, Columbus*, frustrated by his inability to be accepted in a world that, ironically, he knew in his heart he did not want to be a part of, just as I wanted to be accepted in my neighborhood although I did not want to live there and did not actually admire the people who rejected me. I came to an important and frustrating realization: those people weren't any better than I, yet they perceived me as so inferior that they didn't know or wouldn't care that I repudiated them.

I picked through various collections of short stories by Ernest Hemingway. "Big Two-Hearted River" captured and fortified my search for solitude; I found in the library that peace and privacy that Hemingway had savored, healing on the Upper Peninsula in Michigan. I, too, was healing (and shrinking, getting skinny) behind those closed library doors.

And "Indian Camp," in which a country doctor, Hemingway's dad in real life I assumed, performs a caesarean section with a jack-knife on a pregnant Indian woman in an isolated camp, and the boy, Hemingway, Nick in the story, grudgingly and fearfully assists. At the end of the story—what an ending—the woman's husband is discovered dead, having slit his throat because of the pain and fear he experienced for his wife and his newborn child and, obviously, himself. I don't know, don't remember, if I thought about being a writer then. I only knew that living inside these stories, being swallowed and captured by every detail and image and the collective power of the reading experience, when you wholeheartedly give yourself to it, was magnificent and overwhelming and downright ecstatic.

And Jack Kerouac blew me away in a different way but also provided sheer ecstasy in the voice and the explosive energy. His obsession, the passion, the electricity of his *On the Road* odyssey, with those weirdo maniacs Ginsberg and Moriarty, narrated by the Kerouac character, Sal Paradise, excited me like nothing else I had ever read, for it helped me to recognize my options and potential. As Moriarty, Sal's crazy, nomadic, sleazy antihero, says, you choose your own road in life. "What's your road, man?" he says. "Holyboy road, madman road, rainbow road, guppy road, any road. It's an anywhere road for anybody, anyhow."

That's what I wanted to do, exactly, I thought: take a road to a new world, a different destiny. I vowed I would give that anywhere, anyhow holyboy road a try—in a couple of different ways.

As soon as I passed the rope test, that is.

Which led me to another realization: I was no longer thinking about food, when and what I might eat, and how gorging myself would soothe and tranquilize me and ease my anxiety. And it dawned on me that my situation had nothing to do with who or what I had been at home. I was a different person now. I really was! Groping and poking and exploring with my fingers, I could feel my body! The bone and tissue—the real me—and not that awful congealing marmalade that had encased me. Jelly in the belly made me jelly in the head. I had to focus, and I had to commit. I had to wring my old fatty self, my past self-image, out, and push the real me, the new me, from my body to my brain.

This furnace was a temporary entrapment that could be eradicated by direct action. There was a way out, a recognizable path, and I embraced it with a rare sense of clarity.

I began to get up early in the morning, before reveille, and pad barefoot into the men's room to practice pull-ups on the toilet stall doors. At lunch, instead of eating or smoking, I would take long walks around the compound and periodically drop to the ground to do sit-ups and push-ups. I knew I looked silly to people on the base who might catch a glimpse of what I was doing, but I didn't care. I drank quarts of water. I practiced visualization: I focused my mind on the dangling, daunting rope and how I would conquer it. Not that I knew, actually, what visualization was at the time; I was simply frustrated and angry at myself, and I could not figure out anything else I could do except force myself to be disciplined in order to get the hell out of those furnaces and the boot camp jail I was stuck in.

My effort worked: under my secret regimen, perhaps no more than two weeks passed before I showed up at the gym one evening during a training session and bounded up the rope, from floor to ceiling, almost effortlessly. I touched the top with one sure hand and then skittered down again without using my feet. When I got to the bottom the first time, I showboated by going up again—and back down—impressing Chief O'Reilly and the few other recruits who were trying to get to the top. It was a triumphant, magical moment, not just because I succeeded, but more because of the ease with which I pulled it off.

I've used the term "magical moment" here because I like the message it conveys: there are certain seemingly spontaneous events in life that make an impact and change you, and "magic" conveys the unique aura of that experience. But when you come down to it, there's no real magic in any breakthrough moment. The spontaneity and the magic are results of a variety of forces coming together that allow an instant action to occur. Like climbing the rope. It didn't just happen. There was no "instantly" about it. There was a long preamble of effort, in mind and body. The entire process was spiritual and awesomely intense: visualizing, focusing, squeezing out each image and idea, step by step, and making the steps work or finding new ways to problem-solve, then locking in the goal, the reward, the fulfillment of the mission, inside your head, viselike.

This is how I think about and experience the act of writing today. Every day, every hour is a rope test, confronting the page, untangling your thoughts and ideas, pounding them out, forcing them to make sense, not just to yourself, but to how you think others will perceive them, and every day and every hour when you feel that you have achieved something worthwhile, something all yours, something that sings on a page, is a magical moment.

And that's how I perceived my coming-home experience after passing the rope test and earning my two weeks of leave, anticipating the glory of my return.

I pictured the headlines in my parents' favorite local paper, the *Jewish Chronicle*: "Former Fatty Now a New Man" or "Lee Gutkind Back in Pittsburgh: Triumphant—and Thin!" Wherever I would go, people would see the svelte new me and stand up—and applaud. It was a miracle that I alone made happen.

In my letters and weekend phone calls from Cape May, I had not told anyone from home how I had been changing. I said I was getting stronger and losing a little weight, but I avoided specific details: how many lost pounds or how hard I worked to make it happen. I wanted the new Lee to be a surprise. And when I jumped off the bus at the Greyhound station, just a few days after passing the rope test, I approached my anxious, flustered mother, her eyes darting to the left and right and beyond me. I stopped a few feet in front of her, spread my arms to embrace her, and . . . she walked right by me! "You don't recognize your own son?" I asked.

She turned and looked, as if she had never seen me before, and then began to cry. "Oh my God, what have they done to my child?"

That was a magical moment.

Eleven

MY PSYCHIATRIST, TO WHOM I AM REFERRING FOR THE MO-
ment as Dr. Mason, once asked me: "Who do you feel like when your
temper is out of control?"

"Who do I feel like? What kind of question is that? I feel like me,"
I replied, annoyed. I added defensively, "You think that when I lose
my temper, I turn into some sort of crazed lunatic? Like I'm Jack the
Ripper?"

"That's an interesting example," Dr. Mason said. "Your father's
name—Jack."

Dr. Mason had this infuriating way of stretching every coincidence to make a point and to prove that he was clever, insightful, and
brilliant. But I also realized he might be right. Of all the madmen in
the world, including Adolf Hitler and John Wayne Gacy, I chose to
spout the one who shared my father's name. Could that be me? Do
I become Jack? Am I, like Jack, sometimes over the edge and out of
control? I thought for a minute, remembering that Sunday, that really awful day in the 1970s when my first wife disappeared and my life
fell apart for a while.

She had been asking me for weeks to put the lawn furniture in our backyard away, into the basement, for the winter, and I had never gotten around to it. But each time she asked, I got annoyed, until this time I stomped out into the backyard and let those chairs and chaises fly, one by one, down the basement steps. I dragged them inside and then, for good measure, I kicked the basement door shut—hard! It was a quite a performance.

I regretted that kick and my entire rage the moment it happened. It wasn't the first time I had erupted into a temperamental outburst, and I realized how my behavior then, and in other instances, must have frightened my wife and precipitated her unpredictable defensive reactions, almost as if she were testing me. At moments when I least expected it, when I passed her on the staircase or when we ate dinner, she would suddenly, without warning, put up her hands and shield her face, jump back and start to whine: "Don't hit me. Please don't hit me!"

The chair incident had happened the morning I was waiting for my pal Larry to pick me up; we were going camping for the weekend, and my wife was especially nervous and out of synch. In fact, she told me, "I feel like killing myself." This wasn't the first or even the tenth time she had expressed such desperation, but I did suspect she was more serious than usual. The tremor in her voice or some fear reflected in her eyes—like a shining—gave me pause.

So when Larry honked the horn announcing his arrival, I said to my wife that I could just tell him something had come up and I couldn't go. I didn't mind staying home with her. She shouldn't be alone in this state of mind.

"No, everything is all right," she said.

"But you're very nervous; I don't want you to hurt yourself," I said.

"I won't," she whispered.

"I never touched you," I said. "I've never hit you, never would. Never even threatened. Why do you fear me like that?"

"I know you've not hit me, but you wanted to," she added softly.

She was right, I realized, maybe. Maybe I did want to, but I never would.

I was unable to say more at that moment. What was wrong with me?

After Larry and I set up camp, I hiked to the nearest pay phone, about a mile away on the highway, to check in with my wife. When no one answered, I continued to hike back and forth from our campsite to the road every couple of hours in an effort to reach her. I became so worried that I woke in the middle of the second night and hiked to the highway phone through the dark, careening against trees and tripping over roots and logs. It began raining. I slipped in the mud and tumbled down a hill, smashing into the side of a tree. I heard the crack of bone, a sickening sound, felt excruciating pain, but staggered to my feet and kept going, riddled with fear and guilt. I didn't realize until days later that I had cracked three ribs. But I had visions of empty bottles scattered about and my wife lying in bed, having ingested dozens of lethal pills.

That night, it began raining harder. The phone was in the open, anchored to a pole—no booth or shelter available—and the rain poured down with increasing intensity. I telephoned my brother Richard and persuaded him to drive to my house, knock on the door, and, if no one answered, to use the keys I had given him for emergencies and let himself in. Forty minutes later, he reported from my kitchen that my wife was not home. Her car was missing. The police—he had called them—had no information about bodies matching her description, and it was much too soon to designate her a missing person.

After hearing Richard's news and learning little from her friends, whom I had also telephoned, I spent the rest of the night slouched against the telephone pole in the rain, literally moaning in pain and shivering from fear of what might have happened back at home. By morning I had caught a terrible cold. Every time I coughed or sneezed, I thought I would die because of the excruciating pain from my ribs. I realized, admitted to myself again and again, that I deserved such punishment. I had been such a selfish fool for leaving her in that state, no matter how much she had assured me. Coming home the following morning, I found the house empty of many of my wife's possessions, but the answering machine contained a message with her familiar voice informing me that she was fine but that she had left me. Hurtful, jarring, but under the circumstances not a surprise, which didn't make me feel any better.

Weeks later, I would learn that she had planned her departure in advance. Days before my camping trip, she had rented an apartment—perhaps to share, I do not know—with a man whom she had met months before at a Greek food festival. I think that they were together for six or seven years before she found another partner, an engineer, who I can't remember ever meeting. As far as I know—I have only seen her a couple of times since that day so many years ago when I climbed into Larry's car and drove away—she and the engineer are still together. I don't know if they ever got married.

I don't miss my first wife, and I rarely think about her, but I do find it kind of amazing and perplexing that we humans can be so intimate with one another for so many years, sometimes many decades, and then, in the blink of an eye, disconnect forever, as if all the time and experiences, the problems shared and confronted, the vacations, the promises and pledges, the comfortable daily routines, the intimacies, the ups and downs of our lives, had never happened.

Why is it that, looking back, I can so vividly remember many of the minutest details of my early life at home, and yet those years, more than ten, as I calculate, from the time we met until the time she disappeared on that awful, excruciating, rain-soaked night—ten years with the first woman I loved, or thought I loved—are mostly a blur? I've lost one-seventh of my entire life! Now, that's pretty damn weird.

Twelve

I ONCE TOLD DR. MASON, WHOM I STARTED SEEING RIGHT AF-
ter my divorce, about being the "watcher boy" for the colored trash
men at Tryson's.

I had never associated with black men before. In my grandparents' and parents' world, black people were (in Yiddish) *schvartzees*,
who cleaned your house or shined your shoes. *Schvartz* was "black" in
Yiddish; *schvartzees* were people whom you paid a pittance to do dirty
work. Similar to another word we used, *goy*—"gentile" in Yiddish—
which meant "not like us," not as good as the Chosen People.

At my father's shoe store, the "colored men" came to carry the
trash out of the basement and haul it in their truck to the dump. Directed by my father, I stationed myself in the basement, pretending
to take inventory or sweep the floor or do some other menial task,
while I guarded the merchandise on the shelves, so the men would
not steal anything.

I hated doing this; it was so insulting to the trash men, and there
was no evidence, no reason to assume that they had any intention of
stealing. They seemed nice, rather exotic to a sheltered person like me,

singing and joking in a run-on word-scrambled language I could not fully comprehend, breaking out in blasts of laughter that I couldn't help but realize were directed toward me, a fat clueless kid pretending not to be a policeman. The color of their skin fascinated me. They weren't black—nobody was black; they were all different shades of brown, like the shoe polish in the rack adjacent to the cash register on the floor above. You could buy "rosy brown," "russet brown," "sandy brown," "beige," "beaver," not to mention "taupe" and "smoky topaz," and as I watched, I tried to match the trash men up with the available colors, wondering how I could apply the corresponding wax and brush them up and make their wrinkled, work-soiled faces smooth and shiny.

At the end, maybe twenty minutes at most, their job done, the trash gone, and the floor swept, the trash men's garbled language suddenly and miraculously gelled, ringing with unsettling clarity as they shouted at me, "Goodbye, watcher-boy. See you in two weeks"—and slammed the door behind them.

That got to me. Why did my father make me do this? It was his prejudice, for one thing: Jews were better than goyim, and Jews and goyim were better than *schvartzees*. But more than that, my father was exerting his power and dominance over me. Not only could he bully me, push me around—he could also force me to do something that humiliated me, something I would never do by choice, something I knew in my heart was wrong. It was as wrong as the wrong his father did to him so many years before, by springing a stepmother on an unsuspecting Jack one day after school without warning and perhaps without caring about the damage he might be doing.

I told Dr. Mason I could understand being persecuted and bullied, being pushed around, ordered about. My father was bigger than me, and the ferocity of his temper intimidated me. And he was my father, and therefore deserved a certain adherence to his wishes and rules.

But the fact that he was trying to manipulate my emotions, to create a prejudice or wariness that didn't exist, infuriated me. I didn't care about black people one way or another. This had nothing to do with black people. What I cared about was my father making me do something I didn't want to do, something that made me sick inside, something that was totally not me. If my father wanted to guard the trash men, well, that was his business. My business, what I needed to learn, was to follow my own moral code.

"Did you have a moral code at the time?" Dr. Mason asked.

I didn't answer. It occurred to me that I hadn't the slightest idea what a moral code was when I was a kid. I am not even sure, if I were asked, if I could clearly articulate my moral code now. I would have to think about it. Write it down. Study the words and contemplate what they meant. Moral code is not something you just spew out from memory like the first three presidents of the United States you learned in grade school or the Pledge of Allegiance to the Flag. This was heavy stuff. But I knew, as a kid, that what my father had ordered me to do may have been right for him, his moral code, but not mine.

"You were helpless," Dr. Mason said. "The important thing to realize is that you're not helpless now. You may not be able to control everything that happens to you, but you can learn to understand and moderate your responses, to influence or even change whatever confronts you."

He paused, waiting for me to respond, but I didn't really have anything I wanted to say, or could say. Anger welled up inside of me, anger at my dad, at his genes or legacy, at myself for being such an easy receptacle of rage, at my inability to deal with the humiliation and helplessness I felt at my wife's sudden departure, or policing the trash men, or opening and closing the garage door, and at my awareness of being manipulated by Dr. Mason himself. The way he stared and nodded at me all the time and asked me question after question I did not want to answer, or did not know how to answer, was infuriating. I wanted to scream and lash out, bang my fist against the end table beside me, or grab and throw something, anything, as I had hurled the lawn chairs years before.

But then, I didn't do anything. I just sat there. And as I sat, still as stone, I realized, something different was happening. I could feel some gradual sense of awareness processing inside me. A shaky, but soothing, hesitation.

I was learning, I realized, as Dr. Mason had frequently counseled me, to back away from a situation even though it was a rupturing experience, to picture it playing out in my mind, as if I were watching a cinematic reenactment, before I responded. Not to instinctively react. To hesitate. To study the interaction, as if I were disconnected, as if it were happening to someone else. Watching as the camera of my memory pulled back, from close-up to far shot to dissolve.

I was in the basement, and I had no choice but to be in that basement. I could not disobey my dad or he would lock me away in that very basement. The trash men also had no choice but to be in the basement if they wanted to make a living, to support their families, to work a job, maybe the only job they could get. My father was wrong, but he was also doing what he thought he needed to do. And maybe he even thought he was doing what a father needed to do by forcing his son to do a tasteless job, to fulfill a responsibility, to obey his elders.

Today I am not exactly certain I was thinking clearly in Dr. Mason's office, or that what I was thinking was right—but I was learning about processing, the idea of stopping to think before acting and reacting. Had I stopped to think and consider the act of kicking the chairs and frightening my ex-wife, I might not have done it. I might have put the chairs away in the basement, quietly and carefully, and maybe even apologized. I might have gone into therapy with my wife, as she had long requested, and maybe, just maybe, she would not have become my ex-wife.

I could not explode every time I felt the urge. In fact, that's what I learned more than anything else from my years of talking to Dr. Mason: to look for and sense the rising urge to anger, to feel the urge coming, and not to hate it or fear it, but rather savor the urge, to embrace it and focus rather than act on it. I could take advantage of the feeling, translate it into a warning, a preparatory stimulus to seize control of the situation. Because the urge to explode comes right before the explosion, the urge can be your best friend. If you look for the urge, if you feel its heat as it begins to ignite, then you can embrace it, because it is signaling to you that something awful is going to happen unless, of course, you control it, contemplate the ramifications and hold it steady inside of you as it plays out, so you can process before you make a mistake and act.

Thirteen

I'M NOT SURE IF DR. MASON WAS A GREAT PSYCHIATRIST OR IF
I was finally ready to confront my problems, but the transformation
in me was gradual and painful and therapeutic. It took, in the end,
eight years.

One of our sessions, later in our tenure together, was especially
revelatory. I was attempting to relate an incident that had occurred
when I was in junior high school, seventh grade, thirteen years old,
an event so hurtful I had been unable to remember it all at once, in
one moment. Whenever I started thinking about it—and I found myself reliving snatches regularly—I shut it down before it became too
threatening to endure. But that day it all came back.

I had been sitting at my desk in homeroom when suddenly a
group of the boys—the wealthy Jewish boys in my class—paraded into
the room. They came en masse, as if they were making a statement to
which we all must pay attention. And they were grinning as they entered, shoulders back, so that we could all see their blue-and-white
crew-neck sweatshirts emblazoned with a coat of arms and four bold

initials, WWMG, with the words corresponding to the letters: *Work, Wisdom, Morality, Goodness.*

To that point, I had hoped I could eventually become a part of this in-group, these Squirrel Hillers. I had tried to hang out with them before and after school, during lunch in the cafeteria, had led them to believe that I lived in Squirrel Hill by dropping Jewish family names I thought they might recognize, folks my parents knew or had, at the least, mentioned. They were not unfriendly or impolite; they simply weren't interested in me. Maybe because I was fat. Maybe because I wore dungarees and they all wore khaki pants with buckles in the back, all the rage back then. Or maybe because of the way I carried myself. Or didn't carry myself. Discounting my clothes and girth, there was something about those boys, the way they walked and talked, I could not emulate; they seemed so comfortable with who or what they were. So confident and at ease with themselves. So damn sure.

With their dramatic entrance into the room that day, I experienced an awful, sinking, empty feeling, a sense of abandonment, though I realized even then that they were not, in fact, abandoning me because they had never accepted me. All the effort I had invested in trying to connect with them had been fruitless. I had harbored a sliver of hope and trust that somehow, some way, I had made some inroads, enough so that I could at the least have been on the fringes of their world. But right then I realized I was clearly ever the outsider, an island of aloneness. I felt myself shrinking in that room—not my body so much as my sense of self, what meagre personal esteem I had tried to maintain, shriveling like a prune.

Later that day, walking home, contemplating my surprise and deep disappointment, I decided that I would have to soldier on in school and in life pretty much on my own, never completely trusting anyone—which was foolish, I knew, since I had never really trusted those boys in the first place—but I vowed to protect myself by never truly relying on anyone, to be wary of everyone who would ever come into my life. Including, as it turned out, Dr. Mason.

I remember when I walked into Mason's office for the first time, I had a feeling that I had seen him before, that I knew him, and I said so. He admitted that I looked familiar as well. He was balding, slender, and impeccably dressed in Brooks Brothers–like attire— button-down shirt, striped tie, and a blue blazer he carefully, each visit, arranged on a wooden hanger on a clothes tree in the corner of his office. Then he lowered his unwrinkled self into his leather chair, placed a black notebook on his lap. Pen in hand, he looked me square in the eye and encouraged me, with a slight nod, to begin speaking. He was giving me permission to vent—and that was all I needed.

We didn't dwell on if/how we had previously encountered one another after that first meeting. I was deeply hurt by my wife, who had left me for that guy from the Greek food festival. I was feeling abandoned, and afraid of being alone, and I needed to talk with someone—fast. I didn't want to take the time to figure out our possible connections. Maybe that was a mistake. But I was lost. So we started talking—or I started talking, and he started nodding and making these encouraging hhmmmming and uhhumming noises that shrinks tend to do.

Reliving this WWMG flashback in Dr. Mason's office, I realized something else—that I recognized and remembered one of those WWMG boys. He had been heavyset then, with a full head of hair and no eyeglasses, and, in fact, he'd had a different name. Still, there was no question that one of the WWMG boys who had trooped into that room and marked me forever as an outcast was the man I then knew as Dr. Mason. But his real last name, for God's sake, in junior high school, was Schwartz!

I sat there for a while in his office and silently relived that memory, replaying it in my mind, beginning to end, a continuous rewind of that moment, the boys walking into class, one at a time, grinning, chests puffed out, displaying the WWMG insignia on their sweat-shirts, settling into their seats, all of us watching and maybe, like me, wondering. I blinked and focused and then refocused, as I relived that incident, swallowing and breathing deeply until I could feel composed enough to speak.

"You were there," I finally said to Dr. Mason/Schwartz.

After a while, he admitted the possibility.

"You motherfucker," I told him. "You ruined my life."

I was being overly dramatic—and we both knew it—but there were serious questions that needed answering. Had the realization that we shared a history come to him at that moment, the same time it came to me? Or had he remembered me from the very beginning and led me on to collect his fees and/or to embarrass me? Was he going back to tell his old WWMG cronies how he was shrinking someone they had collectively devastated?

"Why did you change your name?" I demanded.

"I had my reasons," he said.

"What reasons?"

"I don't want to get into it."

After that I was silent and confused and angry. I wanted to bolt, to leave him in the dust of his cozy office oasis and just chalk this experience up to another disappointment and rejection—of which there had been so many since I was a kid from Greenfield fighting for recognition in Squirrel Hill that I couldn't count them. Then I realized that after devoting years to talking with this man and baring my feelings, it didn't make sense to scuttle a connection I had put so much time and effort into. Such an action would be destructive to me, and it might even hurt Dr. Mason.

I mean, after all, just because Mason was a shrink, it didn't mean he was any more well-adjusted than I was. If he had changed his name, well then, maybe he too had been hurt by something that happened to him long ago. Maybe he was ashamed of his parents. Maybe the Schwartz family had lived in Greenfield. Maybe his dad was a mobster. I remembered reading in the papers years before about the Pittsburgh Jewish Mafia, which was led by a crazy gun-toting criminal named Nutsy Schwartz. Maybe Mason was Nutsy's son? Or maybe he was just goddamn insecure, like me.

Besides, I had no idea whether this guy, Dr. Mason (I continued to call him by his chosen name; I never said the S-word to him again; he was and always would be Dr. Mason to me, even though he wasn't—not biologically speaking), or any of his WWMG friends, had meant to exclude me, only me. That would mean that they even thought of me as someone to exclude, and I am pretty certain that they didn't care one way or another if I even existed. If I was not one of them, then clearly I was just one of the "others," the kids who didn't matter.

So I sat there for a while and processed my resentment, realizing that I was doing exactly what he had been teaching me to do when I encountered my own irrepressible anger—sitting it out, considering all of its edges and angles, the reasons behind my fiery feelings, and weighing the extent to which others were responsible. And not reacting. Just contemplating. Thinking about how I might react and, if so, when. This was such a good thing to learn. I was not responsible for being rejected that day in homeroom, I repeated to myself again and again. How could I have been? The rejecters had their own issues. One of them couldn't even face up to owning his God-given last name!

Years after Dr. Mason and I parted, I went for the first and last time to a high school reunion. Dr. Mason was there, as were a few other alums of WWMG. And that's when I learned the best secret of all. I mentioned WWMG to one of the guys I was reminiscing with, who said, "That was a real scam."

"You guys didn't believe in Work, Wisdom, Morality, Goodness?" I asked.

"We took that name, WWMG, so we could be an authorized high

school organization," he told me, "but the initials really stood for something else that we all desired."

I didn't understand and shook my head, gestured for him to continue. "What did those letters mean, then?" I asked.

He rolled his eyes, raised his eyebrows, shrugged, and smiled: "We Want More Girls."

I was stunned by this revelation, and the irony of it. I laughed, and I laughed at the thought of my obsessive stupidity and naïveté. All through those years I had suffered from the scars of my imagined rejection because I did not have a sweatshirt with the WWMG initials, and suddenly I discovered that the whole thing had little to do with me, with who was the most hardworking, wise, moral, and good. It had to do with girls? Adolescent, gangly, screeching, mostly flat-chested girls? How ridiculous can we be? How stupid, self-critical, shallow, and self-obsessed I had been back then. And maybe also, alas, still was, at seventy.

Fourteen

MY MOTHER'S PHONE CALL CAME ONE EARLY MORNING IN the spring of 1973, a half dozen years after my return from the Coast Guard. She was with my father, she said, watching Tryson's Shoe Store burn to the ground.

According to newspaper reports I read later, the fire originated in Tryson's basement, the same basement where I had been imprisoned to do trash men watch duty. At the time, I couldn't help thinking there was more than a little justice to that. Although I don't think I was gloating, I did feel a tiny twinge of satisfaction, I admit. I imagined the Buster Brown scuff-toe oxfords, the Poll Parrot patent leather T-straps that were so popular for little girls during Easter Communion, and my father's specialty imprint labels, all of that rubber and leather boiling and burning. And the trash men were burning, bleeding brown in the intense heat, and they were pointing at me—the watcher boy—and laughing. I was burning too, the blubbery fat of my Haystack Calhoun (back then, a popular 600-pound professional wrestler on TV) body melting away, pouring down my trousers in yellow gel and onto the cement floor, making me skinny, then skeletal. And then, gradually, that little boy who was once imprisoned in the basement was gone. I felt no pain, only a great flood of relief, thinking that the memory could no longer live inside me, because the scene of the crime and the actors were now ashes and dust.

The fire had spread to Al Sesto's Barber Shop on one side of Tryson's and the Brookline News Stand on the other side. There was a basement restaurant, Zitelli's—an Italian place where my dad and mother often ate dinner—adjacent to the shoe store basement and under the newsstand. Evidently, the fire was so intense that it ignited the cooking oil stored in Zitelli's kitchen. Six firemen were hospitalized due to injuries and smoke inhalation; the fire burned for two hours, out of control.

When I arrived on the scene that morning, maybe an hour after my mother's call, a small crowd was lingering, watching the black filthy smoke wafting above the buildings. The stench of burning leather and rubber filled the air.

I detected the stench as I turned the corner and drove down Brookline Boulevard. It filled my lungs and nauseated me; I wanted to heave. I saw my mother as I parked. She was a bright butterball of a woman then, short, round, with a pretty face and the frosted gray bouffant hairdo with a bluish tint that middle-aged women, mostly Jewish, seemed to favor then. She was standing alone, behind the crowd of watchers. Her eyes brightened when I came up to stand beside her. I hadn't seen her for a while; I had been distancing myself from family, trying to settle into my first attempt at a marriage, which was, I realize now, already unraveling, and establish some clarity—a comfortable space—about my relationship with my dad.

I saw my dad in the front of the crowd, talking to a fireman. This guy was, I found out later, the chief of the local station that had been fighting the flames, and he was wearing one of those big, awkward fireman helmets with the long brim. A man in a suit stood on my dad's other side. Both were considerably taller than my dad—his head reached their shoulders—and they were all squeezed together, talking rather intensely. My father was fat and bald; a customer once referred to him as "portly," a fine and polite description. Watching him talking to these two men, I remembered how, when I was a kid, he seemed so massive and threatening, staring down at me, pushing, shoving, yelling. He seemed so inconsequential now, pressed in like a pimple by these men who were probably not even six feet tall but were nonetheless giants in comparison. I wanted to feel sorry for him—I knew that I should—but that store had been more important to him than his sons. *Shoes before sons. Feet before fatherhood. Now he is getting exactly what he deserves.*

In retrospect, I know that may not have been true. He was a troubled and flawed man who always thought he was doing right even though he was wrong as rotten piss most of the time. Even then I felt the urge, the necessity, to be what my mother would call a mensch, in Yiddish a person with integrity and honor, despite past bitterness, and go up to him, as an eldest son should, and comfort—embrace?— him. I could push my way in between the fire chief and the man in the suit and give my dad some space and support to debate, or discuss, whatever was going on. But I couldn't do it—or I didn't. I stood there and watched the swirling fumes with all the other curious bystanders, silent and feeling like a stone inside.

After standing around behind the crowd with my mother, I asked her who the guy in the suit was, talking so intensely with my dad. She identified him as Bob Haynor, their "insurance man."

"Well," I said, "at least we're insured." I remember using the word "we." Suddenly I thought, it was not just his store—it was ours. Even though I didn't want it, Tryson's was part of my past, an integral anchor of my roots, part of who I had become as an adult.

"No, we're not," she said.

"What do you mean?" I said. "Of course we're insured. Every business has insurance."

My mother acknowledged that my dad had always had insurance and paid the premiums on time. But recently, he'd had a cash flow problem. Business was down, and to pay the insurance premium, he would have had to take out a loan. So instead he'd let the policy lapse, figuring he would reinstate in the fall, just a couple of months away, after the back-to-school season when parents would purchase gym shoes and new oxfords and patent leather pumps for their children.

"Are you kidding me?" I asked. "Any business person knows . . ." I couldn't even finish my thought.

"He's over sixty years old," my mother said, and then she added, "I guess he wasn't thinking straight."

I couldn't get over it. "How stupid, how foolish," I told her. "What an asshole," I added. I don't remember now whether I thought that or said it out loud, probably the latter, but the intent was clear. My father had pulled a Shimmy—big time!

But I will never forget how my mother looked at me then, as if I had said something terrible and disloyal, even though, in the past, we had both talked dirty about my dad. Well, maybe not dirty. But we were both critical, and even downright mean and resentful sometimes.

I knew that my mother felt somewhat responsible for the rocky childhood I had endured. That's why she spent so much more time with me than with my brothers. It wasn't because I was her eldest son; I was, clearly, the neediest. Once, when I was newly married, we were sitting in my backyard one afternoon and reading, and she looked up from her magazine and commented spontaneously: "I'm sorry I never let you have a dog when you were a boy." I had a dog at the time, a friendly golden retriever called Spats because of two white patches on his back legs. My mother liked to talk with him and pet him. "I thought that dogs were dirty," she continued. "That they would make a mess in the house."

I hadn't remembered wanting a dog when I was a kid, but I felt good that she was saying that to me. Just as an acknowledgement of my childhood trauma.

Another time she said, not long after my dad died, also spontaneously and apropos of nothing, "I should have left him."

"Dad?" I asked.

"I didn't know where to go. The times, the circumstances," she added, "were different for women back then. I didn't know what to do. So, I stayed."

But that day, standing in front of Tryson's Shoe Store, 920 Brookline Boulevard, Pittsburgh, Pennsylvania, 15226, after I had called my dad "stupid" and "foolish," it was as if I had crossed a line. At a time of crisis, families were supposed to unite and support one another, no matter the resentments and wounds of the past, even if one of them had pulled a Shimmy. This is what *menschen* are supposed to do. I wasn't buying into that—not just yet. But my mother knew where her loyalties belonged, just as she knew that the rest of her life, despite his temper, was integrally tied to my dad. She looked at me for a quick moment, just a cursory glance, as this reality clicked in. Then she walked away, pushing through the crowd to stand beside my dad and watch the love of his life, his symbol of independence and achievement, burn to the ground.

Fifteen

IT WAS WHEN MY FATHER LOST HIS STORE THAT MY PARENTS began to come together as a couple. My dad would have to get a job. And he did, soon thereafter, working regular hours as a shoe dog for somebody else and taking home a paycheck, balancing budgets, like his employees once did. He was no longer Mr. Independent. He seemed, in fact, somewhat humbled by the experience of losing Tryson's because of his miscalculation. He became less temperamental, and a supportive companion for my mother. She relied on him greatly, especially after she experienced a traumatic surgical event in her seventies: a surgeon, doing a minor procedure, mistakenly nicked her intestine, which never properly healed and continually drained a pus-like substance, causing her to fear doctors—and much of everything else in the outside world—for the rest of her life. The draining, she had been told, could only be repaired by yet another surgery, a prospect she totally rejected. She became deeply neurotic, and my father, caring for her, taking over most of the shopping and household chores, made up for some of the damage he'd precipitated with his furies as a husband.

That moment on Brookline Boulevard, the simmering flames and the wafting, stinking curls of smoke, and my intransience when my dad was in need, came back to me years later, in the hospital, on the day he died. My mother, my brother Richard, my second wife, Patricia, and I were there, and we hadn't expected my father to die. He had rallied somewhat the day before and seemed stronger when we left him the previous evening. But by the morning, it was clear he was failing, fading away, from old age mostly, although he had not been well for the previous few months. He was eighty-eight, same age as Shimmy when he died.

"What to do? Give up?" I asked the nurse assigned to him.

She suggested we take him off the respirator and see if he would breathe on his own. She said that if we talked to him, he might very well rally—hear our voices, gain strength, come back, at least for a little while. I found this helpful. Here was something I could do—as opposed to sitting and doing nothing.

I admit that I wasn't totally sure I wanted my father to live, or if I even cared one way or another, but I wasn't going to wait for him to determine his own fate. If I could bring him back to life, then he would owe me big, I figured—and I owed him some support and understanding after he had lost Tryson's to the fire and I had totally ignored him.

I started to talk to him, quietly, whispering in his ear, encouraging him to respond. I don't remember what I said—random thoughts and ideas. Nothing mean-spirited or provocative, just stuff that came to mind. I don't remember if I mentioned Tryson's—but that day of the fire and my stony refusal to comfort him was in my mind.

I had tried to avoid him throughout most of my life. I had feared him and tried never to look him in the eye. The closest we ever came to connecting physically was when we shook hands, making up after our many arguments and the resulting punishments. The calm lasted only a short while until the next confrontation, when we were at each other's throats again. And he also, years before, had sent me that letter on blue-lined paper, describing his life as an "orphan," which I had only recently read. Now my hands touched his arms and shoulders—they were cold and clammy. My lips brushed his ear as I whispered to him. He didn't know it—or maybe, in fact, he did. But we were closer then than at any time during his life or mine.

I was happy to have had that intimate moment with my dad. Not that it made up for my distance and ambivalence on the day of the fire on Brookline Boulevard. I did not in any way regret my behavior at the fire, because I knew how I'd felt about him, my anger and disappointment at what he was—or was not—as a father. But as the years passed, I had grudgingly begun to admire him. I knew how much he loved that store, a symbol of his independence and his single-handed accomplishments. It wasn't a big-deal operation; it was just a family business. But he had built it from selling souvenirs to spark plugs to something that was all his own. His brand. His little empire.

In some ways, this was not too different from me, with my own little literary magazine. It was something I had started from scratch, all on my own, and it had blossomed to the point that by the time I reached seventy it was one of the largest independent literary publications in the world. In that way, I was like my dad. And, I feared, as Dr. Mason had helped me come to grips with, in many other ways.

But then my dad had not followed his own advice, had not covered himself or carefully thought through his actions. He must have felt awful about that, humiliated, haunted. And yet he never said a word about it, at least not in front of me. Now that I am more than the age he was when he lost Tryson's, I sure wish I had said something to my dad that somehow acknowledged his effort to adjust after he lost his beloved island of independence. Why is it that we often can't say or do the right thing, can't even realize what the right thing to say or do is, until it's too late to make amends, to balance the ledgers of life?

My dad did his best, under very difficult circumstances, to make his way through life and accomplish something special. And when he lost it, he had very few options to make a living. Being an aging shoe dog was not particularly lucrative, but he carried on and became a better person in the process. He could have faded away in shock and depression and guilt, like our cousin Shimmy.

I was impressed by his resiliency. I had assumed that he would become even more bitter and angry, lost and confused without his Brookline Boulevard Tryson's store. But something had happened inside of him, God knows what, and he evolved from the Jack he was to the better Jack he had become. As far as I know, there was no Dr. Mason in his life to nod and uhmmmmmm him and drag him, kicking and screaming, through the traumas of his life to his senses. And he certainly did not and would not have devoted eight years, or even eight weeks, to the process. He salvaged what he could from the meagre assets and inventory remaining at Tryson's and moved on.

I can't compare my dad's losses to mine at seventy, friends-lover-book-son, because we were different men in different times and circumstances. I was, in fact, in a much better position to survive and push on than he was. I did not have to start all over. But quite clearly his attitude and spirit far exceeded mine at the moment. I was stuck, confused, a little bit afraid. I am sure he felt the same way when he lost his store. And yet he quickly and gracefully turned the corner and found a direction, passed his most challenging rope test, while I, at seventy, fumbled and fretted, grappling for answers and direction.

Sixteen

THE YEAR TRYSON'S BURNED TO THE GROUND, I HAD JUST started teaching at the University of Pittsburgh. Which was incredible. No one who had known me in Greenfield or Squirrel Hill would ever have imagined I would end up on the faculty in the English department of a major university, least of all myself. But people can help you along the way, if you give them a chance. Casual conversations can lead to big ideas. Like this chat I had with Laird, a pipe-smoking guy I met during boot camp.

He had been a student at Princeton but had dropped out in his junior year and decided to join the military to learn more about life and growing up. We were sitting outside the barracks one day, smoking and talking about our fellow recruits, how little they seemed to be aware of current events, and I remember commenting about how "these guys never read." And Laird looked at me and said, in mild rebuttal, "But after all, Gutkind, you are a college man." I was astounded and flattered, and I explained to Laird that I was only eighteen, going on nineteen, and had, in fact, graduated in the bottom fifth of my high school class. But his observation planted a seed.

Maybe college was a possibility. I mean, I had nothing else in mind, except for the fact that I wanted to do something, anything, different, to continue the change I had initiated in the military.

After active duty, I wandered into the Cathedral of Learning at the University of Pittsburgh, the massive forty-story monument to education, the tallest classroom building in the United States, and registered for my first college course: Freshman English. It was in what they called night school then, or "general studies"—kind of a second-tier or second-class way of entering college where the academic requirements were far less stringent. For night school at Pitt, my classmates would often joke, there were only two requirements: paying the money and showing up. That was an exaggeration, but I guess you can compare night school then with the average community college today. Still, considering my Greenfield background—I had always been a second-class citizen—this night school suited me.

The following evening, notebook and pencil in hand, I went to class. Our teacher was a potbellied, pockmarked man in his late twenties with a long nose and greasy black hair. Robert Meyers, a teaching assistant working on his PhD, outlined his plan for the course and then told us to write an essay about a person or an experience that had caused a change in us. He would then critique our essays and return them the following week.

As I wrote this essay, about the push-ups and sit-ups, the obstacle course and the rigid discipline demanded in the military, I felt exhilarated. I had written book reports in high school, as well as a few essays for science and history classes, but this was exciting: telling stories about my life. All awareness of time escaped me. When I looked up, I was the last person remaining in the classroom. Reluctantly I ripped the pages from my blue-lined notebook, just like the paper my dad had used for his letter, and handed the stack in. It took me a couple of moments to pack up. Out of the corner of my eye, I could tell that Mr. Meyers was reading what I had written. As I opened the door to depart, he said: "This is pretty good." He was pointing at my essay. "What do you do?" he asked. "I mean, in life. Or what do you want to do?" I told him that this was why I decided to start college: to figure out what I wanted to do with my life. I was clueless.

"Well," he motioned at my essay, pausing to nod and purse his lips, "this is well written. You ought to think about being a writer."

Not that I jumped into the profession overnight, but his words resonated, even though I realized that he might have been half joking, just a flip comment to be friendly and encouraging to a student. But a writer could do anything he wanted, be totally independent, choose any adventure, write about it and make money, at least make a living. Or so I imagined then. I took two classes from Mr. Meyers, and many more classes from other good professors as well: political science, philosophy, history, all of which intrigued me. But I couldn't let go of the idea of writing. Sal Paradise—Kerouac—was a writer. Hemingway, Heller, Baldwin, Mailer. I worshipped their work. I bought a typewriter and began pecking away early every morning for many hours, a schedule that I have followed to this very day.

So, I became what they call these days a nontraditional student, working my way through the University of Pittsburgh part-time at night, while also working as a truck driver delivering beer, and then as an on-the-road shoe salesman with suitcases of samples. I traveled four states and called on general stores and army-navy stores, selling an array of boots for the J. W. Carter Shoe Company of Nashville, Tennessee: Wellingtons, engineer boots, steel-toed work boots, soft pliable kidskin boots with buttons for old men with bad feet and arthritic hands. And all the while, I woke early every morning, as if still in boot camp, to squeeze out words and ideas and dreams at my typewriter, like any respectable writer would do—stories nobody but me would probably ever read. Eventually, while still in school, I took a job as a gofer in an advertising agency—not because I wanted to be an ad man, but because it was another option, a different challenge, another rope test. I hustled my ass off, worked on weekends, and turned some heads. Soon I became an account executive with a challenging new client and assignment: the U.S. Department of the Interior, promoting the one-hundredth anniversary of the discovery of helium.

The cornerstone event of the centennial was the unveiling of a monument in Amarillo, Texas, where helium was first discovered. The Helium Centennial Time Columns consisted of three stainless-steel time capsules, narrow cylinders that came together like a tripod, supporting a fourth cylinder shooting straight up six stories into the sky—a dramatic, erect shaft, like a majestic silver penis glittering in the relentless Texas sun.

The day before the inaugural event, four helicopters lifted the corners of a gigantic black tarpaulin, hovered above the site, and dropped the tarp to conceal the entire monument from view. The corners of the tarpaulin were securely anchored as a safeguard against the relentless Texas Panhandle wind. Dozens of large helium-filled weather balloons were also attached to the tarp. Senators, congressmen, and government bigwigs came from all across the country. The airport was mobbed. Every visitor was personally welcomed by the Amarillo Greeting Club: two rows of twelve cowboys in red gabardine pants, white shirts, blue bandanas, white gloves, and hats, lined up like toy soldiers in front of the exit doors, waiting to shake each visitor's hand and thank him or her for coming to Amarillo:

"Welcome to Amarillo. Thanks for coming to Amarillo."

"Welcome to Amarillo. Thanks for coming to Amarillo."

"Welcome to Amarillo. Thanks for coming to Amarillo," each visitor heard twenty-four times. Much of this event was not organized by me, I should say; these Amarillo "helium-ites" were pretty damn way out. Whatever they did had to be "big." Overboard. You know, Texas-style. Like the "Texas toast" you got in diners, twice as thick and a couple of inches wider and longer than regular sliced white bread. But I was responsible for promoting this extravaganza, the man—the flak—in charge.

The ceremony featured high school bands playing the national anthem, the state anthem, and "The Yellow Rose of Texas." The three television networks sent cameras. At precisely noon, burly cowboys, stationed at the corners of the monument where the tarpaulin had been anchored, swung their axes, severing the ropes. With music playing and cameras rolling, the balloons began to rise, at first slowly but then ever faster, climbing higher into the sky until the tarp was lifted and the Helium Centennial Time Columns were dramatically revealed. The crowd hooted and hollered, then settled in for beer and barbecue, baked beans and, of course, Texas toast.

The monument was in the middle of the biggest slum in Amarillo. Down the road from the festivities were houses without plumbing and children playing in mud puddles in the middle of unpaved streets—a reality I subconsciously protested in a news release I wrote, which should have started with the following sentence: "People from throughout the country will have the opportunity to achieve immortality by nominating items to be included in the Helium Centennial Time Columns." Only after the release was sent to hundreds of newspapers and radio and TV stations nationwide did I realize I had omitted the first *t* from the word "immortality"—an honest mistake I have never regretted.

Seventeen

THE JOKE I TOLD AT THE TIME ABOUT WHAT I WAS DOING WITH helium was that my job was "a gas"—which led to a letter I wrote to the producer of *The Tonight Show Starring Johnny Carson*, persuading him to do a show with Johnny sucking in helium and talking like Donald Duck. Which was hilarious. Even now, when I mention my helium adventures to old-time *Tonight Show* aficionados, they remember this episode. I was on a roll, I thought then. I was having fun. I was making my way, although I had no idea what way I was making.

There was no plan here, except that the job was getting me out of Pittsburgh, providing new roads to follow, new people with compelling ideas to meet. Options and opportunities. Selling shoes on the road and promoting helium were hardly fitting for someone dreaming of emulating Sal Paradise or Dean Moriarty. My road was no holy road, but I was learning about the possibilities in a life. Which was, to me, exactly in the spirit of who Dean and Sal were and what they were doing. So I guess I had a plan, after all; I just didn't know where it would eventually take me or how I would get there.

Then I started riding motorcycles, shaping a rebellious image, a different me. Or different from what my family expected, and different and distinct from those kids in high school I grew up with. I wore leather—pants and jackets. And big heavy boots with large metal cleats on the toes and heels. At Pitt, where I began teaching after I graduated and published my book about riding across the country on a motorcycle, *Bike Fever*, those boots represented my new persona, The Cleat.

For my classes, I always timed my arrival to be about a minute late so that my students could hear me coming and be ready when I cleated through the door. They liked having a brash motorcycle thug as their teacher, especially in contrast to the pony-tailed, seedy, effete English professors with their Birkenstocks and battered leather briefcases—more the norm back then. During class, when I sensed they were losing interest, I jumped up on a chair or desk, stomping and pontificating, my cleats banging deafeningly. I threw chalk at those who seemed sleep-eyed. I kept them awake and alive. Professors didn't have to worry about being politically correct in the 1970s. In fact, the opposite was true.

They too, the students, wanted something different, and I could happily oblige them by playing the rebel-writer role to the hilt. But it really wasn't an act. Or if it was, I was fooling myself. Perhaps a decade and a half had passed since I had finished high school, an overweight outcast from the wrong side of the neighborhood without any identity or sense of self whatsoever. Now I was a professor and a writer. And I had, finally, if not a mission, a spiritual direction. The writing life.

The writing life was like a catalogue for me. I'd leaf through the pages of my imagination, seeking experiences, reaching for connections I could make, people I could meet, new things I could learn. I loved what Yogi Berra, the eccentric Hall of Fame New York Yankee catcher, once said: "When you come to a fork in the road, take it," and "If you don't know where you are going, you might wind up someplace else." That philosophy appealed to me, even though it didn't make a lot of sense. Unless, of course, you thought about it for a long time.

In the beginning I wrote articles and books in the style that Gay Talese called "the art of hanging out," throwing myself into all sorts of situations—clowning for Ringling Brothers, wrangling at a rodeo (I could ride a horse pretty well in my twenties), and traveling across country in a transcontinental truck. And then recreating my experiences in a story—a narrative that could be dramatic, suspenseful, and informative. These days, people call the genre, my genre, creative nonfiction. "Creative," meaning that the writer may use the tools of fiction, dialogue and description of character and place, for example, and write the story in the first person if appropriate rather than in the more journalistically accepted third person. And "nonfiction," meaning that the story is factually accurate and true from the writer's perspective and point of view. In the 1960s and 1970s, Talese, Tom Wolfe, Joan Didion, Norman Mailer, and many others labeled this form the New Journalism. Which, no matter what you call it, boils down to the combination of substance and style—the facts or information and the storytelling. Memoir, personal history, like this book, was and is included under the creative nonfiction umbrella.

The genre was rarely recognized in English departments and creative writing programs back then. In the academic world, journalists, reporters, were thought to be more like technicians, adhering to formulaic structures, more like word engineers than "literary" folks. Real writers were novelists, poets, and playwrights. And the "creative nonfiction" term was considered bogus at best.

"Nonfiction is a non sequitur! How can you describe what you do as something you don't do?" That was a constant complaint from my colleagues as time went on. But the more contentious and perhaps threatening word was "creative." "Why can't my work be considered creative, too?" they whined. Why, for God's sake, were their essays on Milton or postmodernism considered "criticism" while my prose about traveling the country on a motorcycle or hanging out with major league baseball umpires was artistic and literary and creative?

Over the years I persisted, though, at Pitt and throughout the country, lecturing and campaigning, and establishing my literary journal, until creative nonfiction became gradually recognized as an "art form," as legitimate as poetry and fiction, at many dozens of universities and eventually throughout the world.

Still, there were always detractors. At one point, a genuine magical moment as it turned out, the cultural critic James Wolcott, writing in a four-page takedown of the genre in *Vanity Fair*, dubbed me the worst offender, the "Godfather behind creative nonfiction." Wolcott believed, like some of my colleagues, that creative nonfiction was way too personal and often unnecessarily intimate and embarrassing; he called it "civic journalism for the soul." He also criticized English departments and creative writing programs, saying that he had learned more about writing by selling want ads for the *Village Voice* early in his career than anything he might have been taught in the academy. But the prestige and the reach of *Vanity Fair*, with more than a million readers, brought creative nonfiction—and me—into the limelight and, ironically, gave it legitimacy. Oscar Wilde said it best in the first chapter of *The Picture of Dorian Gray*: "There is only one thing in the world worse than being talked about, and that is not being talked about."

MY FIRST REAL WRITING GIG—I MEAN MY FIRST WRITING THAT counted, because it was widely published—came when, in the powder-blue VW convertible I had borrowed from my wife, I drove to Wyoming to follow Hemingway's path across that state.

I had read in the recent biography by Carlos Baker that Heming-way wrote parts of *Death in the Afternoon* and *A Farewell to Arms* in a cabin on an isolated ranch in the upper Tetons. Even in that very thorough biography, Baker had not written much about Heming-way's Wyoming. Hemingway had written a short story, "The Wine of Wyoming," which wasn't one of his best, but this trip, I thought, would open another door to his life and perhaps a door for me. I tracked down the only remaining child of the family that had built and operated the ranch, now a woman in her eighties, a short, plump, silver-haired widow. She was at first resistant, gruff but po-lite. Too many years had passed, and she wasn't healthy enough or even in the mood for such a journey. But I begged and pleaded with her to take me up to the ranch and show me where Hemingway had lived and worked. I had traveled so far, wanted this so much. Finally she agreed.

The going was slow. We bounced and banged in the surpris-ingly frisky powder-blue Bug, with the top down, dodging rocks, fallen trees, and nasty ravines. It was an hour and a half up the Red Grade Road to the site of the ranch. It was intact, considering it had been abandoned and reportedly uninhabited for three decades. The woman—her maiden name was Spear—led me through the property, a modest complex with a main house, a bunkhouse, a mildewed barn, rotting corrals, and a couple of guest cabins. She tired quickly and de-cided to return to the Beetle, but she pointed at one of the two guest cabins. "That's where he lived," she said. "That's where he wrote."

Amazingly, the cabin was well preserved. I could walk up the steps into the room and, with the light shining through the bare logs, see a table sitting by the window and facing a bank of lodgepole trees. I felt at that moment a sudden chill and a rush of emotion—a burning, exhilarating clarity. There I was, where the great man had written—maybe even at that very table, surveying the lodgepoles! And this was not some tourist place, like his homes in the Florida Keys, or even the famous Finca Vigía in Cuba; it was, rather, a secret spot that few had visited. I owned it, so to speak, at that moment. This was my experience. And I would write about it—which I did, for a newspaper syndicate. The piece was published in various forms across the United States. Since that time, I gather, the ranch has come back into operation as a dude ranch and later an educational facility. The last I heard, Hemingway's cabin still stands. It was a remarkable event for me which solidified the notion that I could simultaneously experience and write about new things, subjects, ideas, barely touched. I could live it and write it, an idea I pursued during the following few years.

I profiled and worked with a one-armed blacksmith and a cooper who practiced his craft in the old way with a schnitzelbank; I sparred with professional wrestling's heavyweight champion, Bruno Sammartino; I hunted rattlesnakes, chewed tobacco, ate nauseating bear meat with a mountain man named McCool, who had killed the bear. Once, in the hills of eastern Kentucky, writing for *Sports Illustrated*, I joined a group called Judo and Karate for Christ: members chopped, kicked, flipped, and hurled their fellow disciples in the name of the Lord Jesus. The leader of the group, an evangelistic preacher named Mike Crain, sliced a watermelon, which I had placed on my bare chest and stomach, with one massive chop of a gigantic, menacing Samurai sword. Pat Boone was in the audience at the time, serenading us.

But my motorcycle book, which I wrote a few years after my Hemingway odyssey, fulfilled my Kerouac dream of traveling around the country on my big black BMW, my Beemer. It was exciting and daring. And it was far from a leisurely Sunday outing—this was dangerous stuff. People were angry and at odds in the early 1970s; longhaired hippie "losers" like me were taunted and threatened, especially in the Deep South. In Alabama my riding partner, Burt, and I were once dusted off the road and knocked down by a hippie-hating redneck in a tractor trailer. Bartenders and motel clerks glared at us. Frequently, we were denied service. What happened at the end of *Easy Rider*—a cult movie that I also cherished and watched repeatedly—where Dennis Hopper and Peter Fonda are murdered by a redneck with a shotgun in a pickup, was a haunting scenario. Would we make the movie come true? It didn't matter. We felt legendary; we were having the time of our lives. This motorcycle odyssey demonstrated to me that I could fulfill my adventure dreams. I couldn't wait until I could dream again—and jump right into another milieu, another temporary life.

I wrote my second book, *The Best Seat in Baseball—But You Have to Stand*, about a crew of National League baseball umpires. These guys were eccentric, kind of like Yogi, but in a different way—so absolutely certain that, as the policemen of the game, they could never do wrong. They could not see past their own egos. That book made a lot of noise—nasty noise—because the crew I followed included Art Williams, the first black umpire in the National League. I observed nearly every game this crew officiated, and as the 1974 season progressed, I wrote about the way in which racism pervaded what was then still considered America's national pastime. Not just among the umpires but among the players, the management, maybe even the fans.

I had no idea that Williams's struggle was going to be the primary focus of my narrative. It was the main story that emerged, as I observed over the year, and I ran with it. I should say that the crew he was with that season was unique and, in a bizarre way, well meaning—although, if so, pretty damn dumb. Doug Harvey, the crew chief, was eventually inducted into the Baseball Hall of Fame, one of only ten umpires to be so honored. Harry Wendelstedt went on, after retiring, to establish a successful umpire school; his son, Hunter, eventually became a major league umpire, following in his dad's footsteps. And Nick Colosi during the off-season was the maitre d' at the chic Copacabana nightclub in New York.

Learning at the beginning of the season that they would be working with Williams, in only his second year in the majors, the three decided to "jokingly" direct as many insulting and prejudicial comments at him as possible, in the privacy of the locker room or while traveling, and, to make it seem acceptable and "fun," they would be self-deprecating at the same time. This in order, so they said, to strengthen Williams's resistance to the racial slurs with which he would undoubtedly be—and was—confronted. I captured in my book, word for word, many of these interactions, demeaning and insulting, no matter the intention, and this generated a great deal of controversy in the baseball world and in the media, not only because of the focus on racism but because I had, so some said, by revealing what happened behind the scenes throughout the season, tarnished the image of the game. I had, in fact, ambushed the umpires, who had no idea that I would be reporting what I observed. Maybe some people perceived the book that way, but it seemed to me that the appalling saga of Williams's isolation as a black man in a white man's world symbolized a bigger issue and a higher truth, a story that demanded to be told.

When he was fired two years later, Williams lodged a complaint with the Equal Employment Opportunity Commission over the racism he confronted while with this crew. But it was never fully examined and resolved. Tragically, he died of cancer, destitute, in 1979, unheralded in baseball lore for breaking the color line in a way that was not too different from what Jackie Robinson had done a quarter century before.

Williams's story put me on a different track. I loved immersing myself in other people's lives and writing true stories about what I learned. This was what I did best and what I liked most about my work, finding and writing stories that had not yet been told. And my book about a bunch of ignorant white guys, these umpires, thinking or maintaining that they were doing the right thing, while appallingly stupid and wrong, made an impact.

But then I wanted to dig deeper, go beyond motorcycles and mountain men and even baseball, delving into ideas and challenges—and stories, of course—that mattered in a larger world. Which is when I entered the organ transplant arena. Books about parents caring for sick children in a children's hospital and about the tragedy of child mental illness followed. Writers, I kept telling my students, bring clarity to difficult decisions and complicated predicaments, and fresh and illuminating points of view. Can we change the world? Probably not. But we can motivate and inspire our readers and, in the process, inspire and motivate ourselves to keep on writing and trying to make change. I believed that then. I believe it now.

Eighteen

"IMMERSION RESEARCH" IS A TECHNIQUE I HAVE EMPLOYED throughout my writing career: pick a subject and become intimately involved in that subject, be a fly on the wall, and then write about it from the inside out—no matter how long it might take. I usually remain with the people I shadow for months or years, until something happens that precipitates a change in their lives, for better or worse. Change is a key measure of failure or success, and a point at which evaluation and reflection can be helpful and appropriate. For an immersionist, it can also represent the end of the timeline for a story or a project—a signal that the writer might be ready to say goodbye and move on to something else.

But as I confronted the years reaching seventy, I found myself fighting the change in my own personal story or, more precisely, not understanding what it meant for me. I knew that change was inevitable and that I needed to come to grips with it as I got older. Unfortunately, it would take a lot of bad stuff happening before I was able to find a new perspective, to begin to accept the change and try to move on. It never occurred to me that I would someday end up immersing myself in myself, as I was doing now by writing this book, attempting to achieve the clarity and the "matterness" I had encouraged my students to seek and discover. It is so much easier to mine the mysteries of other people's lives than those of your own.

Immersing myself in other people's lives is not work unique to me; lots of writers do it. But I chose that line of work purposely to meet my own life mission then: not just to write and publish or to find a new direction, something new to learn, but to be accepted as a person, to fit comfortably, seamlessly, into other people's subcultures. This may well have reflected my overwhelming lifetime history of insecurity, but it captured who I was and what I have always needed to accomplish—and why my extended series of books about so many different subjects has brought challenge and psychic reward.

It was in the military that I began to find my way and strike this path. There, I was in a company of men ranging from eighteen to thirty years old from all parts of the country, with various backgrounds and levels of education. Laird was one of the few who were educated and well-read. The fact that I fit in with that subset provided great satisfaction. True, many of us were serving in the Guard to satisfy our military obligation—it was during the Vietnam War and the draft was in effect—and we would all go off at the end of our short enlistment, return to the lives we'd left behind, and maybe never see each other again. But this didn't matter to me; it was my innate ability to become a human chameleon that turned me on and clicked with me. Like I did with Laird, who thought I was a college man. And it wasn't that I didn't want to be my own person. To the contrary, connecting with others gradually helped me shape the person I thought I wanted to be. But I could also, at the same time, be what others needed me to be to belong. The two ideas, it turned out, worked in tandem.

Actually, it didn't take long for me to realize that I wanted to be a writer and write true stories by gathering material through immersion. Mr. Meyers planted the seed. But I never sat down and method-ically thought this out. I never said to myself, "I think I will become this or that in order to become a better, more well-rounded person, make an impact, get famous, be rich and whatever else came with it." It all just evolved.

Unlike the guy I wrote about some time later, after baseball and motorcycles, in what I now know was my character-shaping, life-changing book, *Many Sleepless Nights*. Dr. Thomas E. Starzl, the pio-neer liver transplant surgeon who played a key role in the book, told me that during medical school in the 1950s, he thought that his mis-sion in life was to cure cancer, but then he went to the library and read all about the research being done in the cancer arena, and the experts were saying that a cancer cure was around the corner, so he picked liver transplantation as his life's work because at the time, put-ting a brain-dead person's liver into another person dying from liver disease was considered pretty much impossible. But Starzl didn't see it that way; it was exactly the daunting challenge he desired. To de-vote his life to something overwhelmingly significant. Making the seemingly impossible possible.

I was not such a true believer. I did not feel a higher calling, not at first. For me, like I say, my mission just happened, one book, one milieu after another, each project a series of forks in the road, from choosing the subject to fitting in—an outsider permitted to be on the inside, a unique balancing act—to, of course, writing the book or ar-ticle in the end, and doing it, if not masterfully, then at the very least competently. I wasn't trying to save the world like Starzl; I was hell-bent on saving myself and becoming useful, somehow, making a con-tribution and learning about various aspects of life that I would never have been privy to without those immersion interventions and being acknowledged for that effort in one way or another.

While doing this kind of work, as you might imagine, you be-come intimately involved with people you are writing about; you make, in a way, close relationships. "Friends." I put this word in quotation marks because the reality is, when you jump in and out of people's lives, those friendships last only as long as the research and writing, and then, even if you try hard to keep in touch, they invariably fade away. Think about it. You hang out in a children's hospital or a zoo, two of my immersion books, day and night, live the life of your subjects, observe and often share their pain and triumph. And then, while these deeply involved people—your book friends—continue to treat kids with cancer or asthma, or anesthetize lions and tigers, elephants and goats, in order to examine their teeth or manicure their claws, you are totally and completely somewhere else, on another book. You are crawling under a weird robotic vehicle in the Atacama Desert in Chile, where it hasn't rained for one hundred years. Or learning how to write code from artificial intelligence engineers. These worlds do not intersect. Even when you try really hard to stay in touch with those with whom you have shared significant moments, sustaining personal intimacy and a passion for their work is difficult.

What I think the people I write about don't understand is that I am closer to them and much more involved with them than they are to and with me. And it will always be that way. During an immersion I hang out with them for two or three or four days in a row, day and night, and when I disappear from the scene, they might miss my presence and be excited to fill me in when I return a few days later, but while I am away, I am obsessively thinking about them, writing about them, trying to understand and portray them in a way that will be accurate, honest, and genuine. They live and breathe in my head, constantly. Until, of course, the book is over, and another book begins, and I become obsessed with other people in other places and situations, who are compelling for different reasons.

For a long time I found this in-and-out world a safe place to be. After all, as the outsider looking in, I was not usually part of the story I was telling. My job was to capture the scene and situation—and not be responsible for what happened. Just report and re-create it and find meaning in the experience. Usually I established a comfortable distance between me and those about whom I was writing. But the people I came to know and care about when I was immersing myself in the organ transplant world impacted me. Hanging out with them day after day was like being on another planet where all your friends and neighbors, and you yourself, are in constant state of psychic numbness. Even today, so many years later, my days of immersion in this high-intensity milieu, the people I met, the suffering they endured, remain a part of my life, like endless YouTube clips unraveling and replaying deep inside of me as I walk the streets, teach my classes, engage in conversations.

During those days I felt fortunate to be granted entry into the inner sanctum of their lives. And much more than just fortunate—a "lucky dog," as the saying goes, to not be facing the hanging noose that ceaselessly tormented and tantalized them. Life or death? Transplant or die? Or, perhaps, somewhere in between? Theoretically, their lives could continue without a transplant, but for how long? A day, a week, a month, a year? When the body is a time bomb, how could anyone know or plan or think ahead?

And then the next hurdle, should they be so lucky as to get a new heart or liver or lung and survive the surgery. Transplants could fail for one reason or another. Some recipients would have to be transplanted again—and again. And even if they made it for a year, or years, they were often debilitated by the antirejection medications that were essential to keeping them alive.

While I felt concern and compassion, there was always a reassuring disconnection—a safety zone—between them and me. I wasn't going to die next month or next minute or next year. Most probably, anyway. I had loads of time. I didn't need an organ transplant.

Now however, at seventy, my reassuring disconnection, my

safety zone, is evaporating. Not because of an organ diseased or out of whack, but simply because of wear and tear on what was then my pretty goddamn healthy body and my good fortune. In a way, and I realize I am being self-centered about this, I am facing now, or will soon be facing, what my subjects were confronting then. Gradually decreasing health, cognitively and physically, and the frustration and fear of isolation and irrelevance that comes with it. Maybe it is not like having cirrhosis of the liver or renal failure, but aging is a condition that can be, that is, pretty damn frightening and impossibly uncurable. And unlike these folks, I don't have, won't be getting, a second chance. There's nothing those brilliant surgeon-scientists can put into me, as far as I know—a vaccine? an elixir? a new brain?—that will slow down or eliminate the damage and disintegration of the years.

I am not talking only about facing the specter of death when I think about these people and those days and my transplantation observations. Or, now, old age. I'm talking more about the feeling, that state of being stuck. Trapped and helpless, out of control, waiting for something to happen and not even knowing what you want to happen. Except that you want to live. Or live longer. That's what life-or-death and organ transplantation is all about, I discovered. And also, goddamn it, old age. It doesn't matter who you are, what you own, who you know. A subtle sense of insecurity, an anxiety, emerges from time to time as the years creep up on you—and there's really nothing to do about it except to close your eyes, grit your teeth, and propel yourself forward and pretend to the world that it does not exist.

I will never forget an interaction I observed between an organ transplant surgeon, a colleague of Starzl's, and a patient who was slowly dying while waiting for a new organ. Paraphrasing Winston Churchill appealing to the British people in 1941, in the darkest days of the Blitz, the surgeon told his patient: "Never give in, never give up. Never. Never. Never. Ever."

The real quotation, which I later looked up, is a little different but says essentially the same thing: "Never give in, never give in. Never. Never. Never. Never. In nothing great or small, large or petty, never give in, except to convictions of honor and good sense." But with those words, the patient somehow responded; he managed to live a couple of days more—until an organ became available for transplant. The meaning of the message was clearly imprinted on my mind. I will never give in—and I will never forget how much I might achieve in my life if I continue to try and get better at what I am doing. Not trying, not working to improve, means capitulation.

I think about those words now, and the way in which those folks in the transplant community inspired me, and I am quite frankly embarrassed about my feelings of confusion and disruption at confronting old age. Or comparing them with me or my senior citizen brethren. At the very least, shouldn't I be thankful that I made it all the way to seventy? But to be honest, I have already lived that long without thanking anyone. I mean, I am not opposed to showing and feeling gratitude. If there's someone, something, out there I could communicate with, God, Einstein, Starzl, Mr. Skink, whomever or whatever, that I should thank, believe me, I'm all for it. I will google Hallmark immediately and order a dozen gratitude cards. The more sentimental the better. But, another idea, also maybe from Google: An algorithm or app that generates life extension. A modified reboot?

Getting old can make one's mind wander uncontrollably, contorting hope and reality, fantasy and fact. But just like the folks I bonded with while researching this book, I am stuck. And I know, and I honestly appreciate, that they were much more stuck then, in that transplant center or through life itself, than I am now.

I HAD TOTAL ACCESS IN THIS MEDICAL CENTER: I COULD GO anywhere, do anything I wanted, jetting through the night on organ donor harvests, as I had done for Lizzie, or observing in the operating rooms during surgery. More than once I saw Starzl in the parking lot behind the hospital, slumped over, drained and deflated after losing a patient, mumbling, shaking his head, smoking cigarette after cigarette. He recovered quickly, though, usually by the next day. He knew he had a larger and more noble mission in life than most of the rest of us. We were just trying to get by, while he wanted to save the world. He was a true believer—in himself. Each setback seemed to fuel his determination, and invariably he came back stronger. I wanted to be so obsessed, so consumed with such unflinching tunnel vision, although I knew I wasn't that capable or committed. I marveled at his dedication and drive. Nothing stood in his way. And he eventually proved his point.

I once asked Starzl if gaining acceptance for the procedure he believed in, after so many setbacks, had been a magical moment in his life—coming after a time when he thought he had been defeated, fired from the University of Colorado because his colleagues thought that liver transplantation was immoral, unethical, and downright impossible, and then miraculously rallying and turning it all around and making it work at Pitt. How had he managed to endure the criticism and defamation of his dream? Was this, I wondered, his rope test?

Not at all, he told me. "I didn't honestly pay any attention [to my critics] because I knew perfectly well that I was right, and I knew that there were some people who agreed with me, people who were quite creative and intelligent in their own way, and so I paid a lot of attention to them. I never felt like I was exactly alone in the whole thing."

I always wished I could feel that way, so sure I was doing the right thing and making decisions without doubting myself, just plunging right into whatever situation I was involved in, completely confident that I knew my subject, my approach, my brilliant objective, comfortable with who or what I was. No second, third, fourth thoughts. Just do it. In the end, I'd be right. I'm not saying Starzl did not suffer through bouts of insecurity, but following the Churchillian dogma of perseverance, not only did he never give up, but he also never stopped believing in himself.

I lost touch with that transplant patient who rallied with the Churchill quotation, and I don't know how long he lived, or what struggles he confronted after the surgery, for that was the rub and perhaps the real rope test of the liver transplant experience. While it is true that the surgery could be brutal and go on for many hours, and that people died all the time on the table, the surgery was and is, in many ways, the easiest part to endure, especially these days when the procedure has been perfected. Surgery is only the bare beginning of the quest for survival. It is not really the magical moment or the ultimate rope test. It is only the preamble to what can be an endless gauntlet of suffering, ongoing suspense, and heartache.

Nineteen

IN THE BEGINNING, IT HADN'T BEEN EASY TO GET ACCESS TO Dr. Starzl and his organ transplant team—he was pretty much unavailable for a direct approach—but I figured out a way to enter his inner sanctum through another door. I immersed myself in his subjects, the recipients of his transplants and the candidates who came to Pittsburgh from around the world to receive livers from the only team anywhere that had registered a modicum of success at that time. This was in the late 1980s. The subjects were mostly ordinary people—and a few famous folks, like the porn star Linda Lovelace—all stuck in a state of helpless limbo.

First, they were dying of incurable liver disease. They had a week, a month, a year to live. They stayed in residences around the medical center, clutching their beepers and waiting for them to explode with the news that someone had been killed in an automobile or motorcycle crash (motorcycles were referred to as "donorcycles," for riders usually died from brain injuries, leaving the livers untouched), a drowning incident, whatever. But not just anybody who died would be a match for the potential recipients. The donor had to fit—size, age, and blood type were among the many parameters—so it was a real game of chance. And even then, the grimmest fact of all, there was no guarantee of success.

But the stark reality of the situation didn't seem to matter to those who were so vulnerable, confronting death. The candidates came in droves. They looked terrible. You could recognize transplant candidates around the medical center instantly because their skin was a deep mustard-yellow from jaundice. Their bellies were bloated because their livers failed to process fluids, while the rest of their frames were skeletal, so seemingly fragile they looked as if they could break apart with a touch. I hesitated to shake their hands for fear that their fingers would crumble. And the surgeons, nurses, and others who comprised the transplant service, with an obsessed Starzl setting the tone, were so occupied with the actual procedure—jetting through the night to some far-off city, harvesting the organ and returning it to Pittsburgh in its Igloo cooler, and then finally transplanting it—that they didn't have the time, the desire, or even the heart to interact with these lost and desperate folks. I don't mean the medical staff was unsympathetic, but maintaining an objective distance from those subjects whose lives would soon be in their hands was an inevitable imperative.

Although I eventually gained access to the transplant units and the operating arena, and could hang out with the medical staff, including Dr. Starzl, my most meaningful interactions were with the families who had accompanied the candidates. There were few men, and those were mostly older and retired, their wives sick and dying. Most men had to work, to keep their jobs, to maintain their insurance coverage and support their families, to pay their escalating bills. More often, those waiting with candidates were wives caring for husbands, mothers caring for children, or daughters caring for parents. These folks had stopped their lives, quit their jobs, wrenched themselves from everything that was comfortable and familiar, to relocate with their loved ones, and then suddenly, in Pittsburgh, they simply had nothing to do but wait. It was agonizing. Day after day they watched TV, hung around the hospital cafeteria, or the smoking areas outside the medical center, or the rooms of the people they were supporting, cooling their heels, waiting for the surgeons to do their rounds, see their loved ones, and depart, each surgeon's visit no longer than five minutes, sometimes less.

But they weren't just waiting; they were, rather, waiting for someone to die in order for their loved ones to live. Candidates waiting near the transplant center were, in fact, in a bizarre competition with one another. Though they and their families, all in the same limbo, drew strength and hope from one another, they were still also often waiting for the same liver.

Once the size and blood type of a donor was determined, there was the other deciding factor: which matching candidate—man or woman or child—was the sickest? The selected recipient would be the person closest to death. So the mothers and daughters, family and friends, agonized, trying to decide how they should feel and what to hope for. Did they want their loved one to become so sick that they would inevitably die within the day or the hour? If so, then the next liver available, if there was a liver available, might be theirs. But maybe no donor would die for a day or a week. Or maybe something would happen along the way and the donor liver wouldn't be viable. Then there'd be no return—no possibility of waiting another day for another donor liver. This is what happened to Lizzie.

I remember Thresa Fortner, whose seventeen-year-old son, Mark, had been waiting for a year for a liver and was gradually weakening, going in and out of consciousness. "I don't know how I am supposed to feel," she told me, "about these people," referring to the other patients and families in the unit. "There are always two answers to every question I ask myself. 'Do you want your son to get sicker than he is?' And I answer, 'No,' because then he will be closer to death. But also, 'Yes,' because the sicker he gets, the more the transplant team will focus on his case and try to help him."

"Would you like to see a big automobile accident in front of the hospital with many fatalities?" I asked her.

"No, I don't want anyone to die. But yes, if someone dies, then maybe my son will live."

Thresa and the many other family members I interacted with amazed and impressed me, not just because of the love they had for their children and partners, but because of their dedication and commitment. Whatever had occurred in their families before liver disease undermined and often destroyed their lives, they were there, rain or shine, day in and day out, for their loved ones. Their sacrifice was overwhelming and seemingly never-ending. Which is not to say that all the candidates and recipients were covered by caring relatives and friends. One woman I wrote about, Rebecca Treat, a twenty-year-old soldier suffering from hepatitis, who arrived at the medical center in a coma, hours from death, had literally been abandoned by her husband, who was unable or unwilling to confront the responsibility that faced him. She was dying alone.

Mark Fortner finally earned his transplant, and as far as I know, he is alive today. So, too, with Rebecca Treat, who has been married and divorced three more times since getting rid of her first husband. I hear from her periodically, and I am Facebook friends with her adult daughter. That Rebecca would never open her eyes again after arriving at the medical center in such a sorry state had been a given to most of the staff at the medical center. But somehow she lucked out. Transplantation, as scientific and precise as it might seem, comes down, more often than not, to a roll of the dice. Like life itself.

Friends and relatives and loved ones, the connections you make and the emotions you engender, whom you end up with and whom you lose or become alienated from, are equally difficult to predict—very much games of chance. Who is going to win and who is going to lose? What is winning, as far as love and friendship go? Nobody knows.

Or if they knew, nobody was telling me.

Twenty

A QUARTER CENTURY AGO, I WAS YOUNG ENOUGH NOT TO think about who, were I in that similar life-or-death waiting situation, would sacrifice so much for me. My first wife and I had been divorced for more than ten years, and we hadn't said a word to one another since the day we signed our divorce papers.

I was out of touch with Burt, my old motorcycle partner who would eventually die of heart disease, although he tried to slash his wrists a couple of more times, most tragically and dramatically on the day of his wedding with his second wife, Patty. His weak heart eventually succeeded in taking him out of the agony of his life at a time when, ironically, his furies had subsided, and he really wasn't so anxious to die anymore. At the time, he was building aquariums for collectors and selling hobby fish in Chicago, where he and Patty had moved.

I had been very close to Susan and Iggy in Pittsburgh—Iggy was kind of like an older brother to me when I was growing up, helping me through my difficulties in school and counseling me about how to deal with my dad. But Susan and Iggy had moved to New Jersey years ago; they had two teenage sons and a business to run, and a life that was pretty much disconnected from my own day-to-day social activities and the few friends I had.

Iggy had once told me that the way to distinguish between a casual friend and a real friend was to ask yourself which one you could call in the middle of the night to bail you out of jail. But this transplantation thing wasn't a one-night stand—it could have been and usually was a forever situation. There were transplant candidates who were waiting in Pittsburgh for a donor for more than four years! Frank Rowe, a thirty-five-year-old engineer from Philadelphia, was a transplant candidate I was close to. He was accompanied by his wife, Joyce, who carried Frank's beeper, did the housework in their rented apartment, and served her husband and his increasing needs loyally without complaint over this very long haul.

I didn't think at the time about who would make such sacrifices for me. In my mid-forties, it wasn't necessary to worry about that, although the thought ran through my mind that if and when I was trapped in a similar life-or-death situation, I hoped someone would step up for me.

But at seventy, I was wondering who might care enough about me to make such a selfless sacrifice on my behalf. Not that I might need a transplant. My liver and heart were in pretty good shape, and besides, at seventy, you are probably beyond the age of acceptability for most transplantation. Why waste a good liver on a guy with maybe 5.1 years to live? But also, at seventy, any number of things could happen that would make me helpless—a paralyzing stroke, Alzheimer's, a crippling auto accident. Who would be with me were any of those things to occur? We all think about and fear becoming helpless. Who would take care of us? Or who would we want to put into such an awkward and untenable situation?

I won't say that my brother Richard would abandon me if I became unable to fend for myself. He has devoted his life to the public school system, first as a teacher, then as a principal, and finally as a supervising administrator—"an upstanding citizen," anyone who knew him would say. And although he is often unable to express his feelings, he has a good heart and always seems to try to do the right thing. But I'm not at all sure I would even want him to be the person upon whom I relied, not because I don't trust or even love him, but because it would be much too much of a burden, uncomfortable and agonizing, a yoke on his life that would weigh him down. Would it make him bitter and resentful toward me? I didn't want that. And relying on him alone would be a burden for me, as well.

When you are unable to take care of yourself, you want to be ministered to out of love, not just responsibility. At least that's the ideal situation, if anything can be considered ideal in that circumstance. Not that Richard did not love me. But you don't want to feel that the person caring for you is doing so just because they have to, because there's no other person or option. You want them to make a compassionate choice. But I guess that way of thinking is just idealistic nonsense. Joyce Rowe really had no choice. Frank was her husband. They had been married for half a dozen years. Responsibilities often negate choice. Unless you make the immoral choice, like Rebecca Treat's husband, who chose cowardice over courage.

Patricia, my second ex-wife, was a good possibility, because, in fact, she did have a choice. And she was a nurse and maybe my closest confidante, aside from my mother. But, a fatalist, she insisted she would die long before me. Her parents had both died young. And what if she found another partner and remarried or relocated? My son was struggling with, as it turns out, unsurprisingly, given his unpredictable actions, bipolar disease and a host of other "diseases." He had trouble enough caring for himself and making it through a week on his own. How could he worry about or care for me?

My ex-girlfriend, Michele, had her own serious problems—for one, a mother wasting away with Alzheimer's, to whom she was obsessively loyally committed—and thus didn't have a lot of time for me. Besides, although we remained in regular touch, she was no longer at that moment a significant part of my life. She would not be the devoted partner at my bedside in times of trouble, as I had once thought, and as she had once promised.

It is not fair to say that my relationship with Patricia was the reason I am no longer with Michele. I was the reason. Or my inability to learn how to live with and navigate interactions between two women I love. Or to learn how to let go.

Behind my house there's a small carriage house, and that's where Patricia moved when we divorced. Our son was six years old at the time. The plan was to make both parents, mom and dad, accessible to him. As a kid, he could skitter back and forth across a small red-brick courtyard from one home to the other, so that we could share custody without the traditional weekend/weekday division and the animosity that often arises during such artificial arrangements.

When we divorced, Patricia and I made a pact that we would never break: our disagreements, our inability to live with one another, would never affect our child. We would never fight in front of him, and every decision we made about our own lives and our own relationship would be analyzed and weighed based upon his needs and interests.

I'm not at all sure that we made the right moves regarding the raising of our son, considering his current state of mind and mood, but we did our best to work together on his behalf. Right or wrong, the results of anyone's efforts come down to that same roll of the dice, and with our son, there had been few recent jackpots.

Whenever I met a new woman, I was very up-front about my relationship with my ex-wife and our regular contact, especially after my son had started to unravel at age eighteen. Initially, the women I've met have been very supportive, endorsing my fatherly devotion, but invariably my closeness and regular contact with Patricia would become an issue. When my son went to high school, Patricia moved to another neighborhood, but our friendship and connection continued, and the separation between our homes didn't seem to make a difference. Now, with my son's mental illness, we are closer than ever.

Michele is a dark, glamorous Italian woman, very traditional, a one-man woman, she frequently assured me. I had no reason to doubt that; her loyalty and love were clear. I couldn't ask for any more. But with Patricia in the picture, my picture, she felt kind of trapped and perhaps misused, more like a mistress than a lover and partner. And she resented that, was troubled and confused. Despite my protestations and explanations that I wanted to be a good dad and make my son the priority in my life, and so maintain an ongoing connection with his mom, my relationship with Michele began to break apart. Michele used to say, "How would you feel if the situation was reversed? Would you tolerate my close friendship with my ex-husband?"

I replied that I would, if a child was involved, especially one as needy as my son. I believed that then. But I realized, as time passed, that this was probably not true. I'm not a jealous person, but I would not have liked it one bit. Maybe would not have stood for it. Whatever that might have meant. I can't deny my own insecurities. Which was perhaps a reason to hold on to and love both women, selfishly, I guess. I tried for a while to find a path back into my relationship with Michele. I didn't want to lose any more people I loved, especially as I grew older. And I felt empty, lonely, missing her presence. But what irony. Holding on to one inevitably meant losing the other.

I was feeling pretty much alone at my seventieth birthday, and I realized that I had to try to do something about it. You got to a stage in your life when you faced a turning point—maybe because of sickness or loneliness or retirement, or simply because you had run out of things to do. Run out of goals. You could settle in and make the best of the years you had left, as your choices dwindled down. This was fine, I guess. Dickie Diamondstone and his friends seemed pretty much okay with that plan of action—or nonaction. Or a focused fun-filled retirement action. I sure did admire how Dickie had transformed his life by trying to stay connected and relive his past—or re-create a different satisfying present from the roots of his past. It was his own personal immersion project. I gave him credit. He was practicing the art of hanging out. And I eventually came to believe that that's exactly what I needed to do. Hang out with myself. Or pretend I was doing an immersion and becoming a chameleon in my personal life, which would mean, I thought, stepping back from learning and growing from other people's lives so that I could learn and grow from my own.

Twenty-One

NEW RITUAL: MORNINGS AFTER STARBUCKS, I PLACE THREE eggs in a pot of water and turn on the burner, then climb up to my second-floor office to begin to write or answer e-mail. At that point I remind myself to return to the eggs in ten minutes because the pot I use is very small and the water boils away quickly if I don't pay attention. But I always seem to forget about the eggs in the pot and, at some point, will hear the "pop, pop, pop" as the eggs explode across the room. I will dash downstairs, clean up the mess, shards of shells and burnt yolk, floor to ceiling, and promise myself never to forget the eggs again.

For a while I considered ditching the eggs for breakfast and switching to oatmeal or Cream of Wheat. Or toast. But I hate the idea of being defeated by forgetting. I know I have short-term memory challenges. But we're talking just ten minutes here. In my own house, while I am in my office one floor above my kitchen. And besides, Cream of Wheat or oatmeal was what they served mornings at the assisted living facility where my mother was then living—perfect, the nurses told me, for the residents who don't have teeth or don't have their dentures in place in the early mornings.

I too have been having big trouble with my teeth.

Right now I have six new crowns for teeth that had until recently given me good service for nearly seventy years. Two shattered on hard pretzels and peanuts, deviations I should have avoided. The other four just turned against me, one after another.

My oral surgeon, a tubby, balding guy with a booming voice who always seemed to be talking as if he has memorized his patient monologue word for word, has been joking that I am making it possible for him to retire early. I don't think that that's funny. But we've been getting to know each other over the past few years. And as I sit there, captive in his chair, my jaw numb, he regales me with stories about his children, his grandchildren, his landlord, and the history, lore, and legend of teeth.

Now I know that the story of our founding father George Washington having wooden dentures was an enduring and totally inaccurate myth along the lines of the chopping down of the cherry tree. And who was to know that there was a National Museum of Dentistry at Mount Vernon? Perhaps learning this stuff about teeth and George was the positive side of aging and dental treatment. The other positive was that I don't have to answer; I can't answer because as he talks his fingers are in my mouth digging and pressing and pulling. Sometimes he struggles and grunts—my teeth are evidently obstinate. At least I can't hear the noises he makes, and his ongoing commentary, muffled by the brain-shattering cacophony of his drill. I do see his mouth move.

But oral surgeons and dentists are not the only doctors I have been making wealthy and getting to know. One day, out of the blue, these neat technicolor spots appeared in front of my eyes, zooming around, off and on, wherever I looked. They're called floaters, according to my newest best friend, my ophthalmologist, Dr. Oii (pronounced "Wee"). This is a guy I used to see every three years for a vision check. A new prescription for my eyeglasses, maybe. Or not. That was the routine. Now we get together for a chatty conversation, examination, an hour or so, every four months.

Dr. Oii explained that eye floaters are caused by changes that take place when the jellylike substance inside your eyes, called vitreous, becomes more liquid. The fibers within the vitreous clump together, casting shadows on your retina—thus the floaters. Not worrisome, floaters will come and go, and eventually you will learn to ignore them, but it is a symptom of upcoming or existing intraocular pressure, a primary risk factor for glaucoma. This happens when you get older, Dr. Oii told me, like all the other doctors told me, like everyone everywhere was telling me, a familiar refrain and a fact of life I didn't need to hear again and again. Everything happens when you get older. I've got what I call "falling apart syndrome."

Have I mentioned sciatica?

Sciatica is caused primarily by spinal degeneration—and often, I discovered by going online, for no particular cause or reason, except, of course, old age.

My chiropractor, another new best friend ("Call me Josh") explained that by squeezing and pinching me, he was disrupting the cycle of pain in my back and legs by "targeting hyperirritable spots—trigger points—and applying precise pressure to break muscles out of their pathological patterns of spasm and inflammation." This was gobbledygook, but I was all for it. I am for almost anything, in fact, because I sometimes can't walk to Starbucks or anywhere else for days, let alone run, when sciatica suddenly strikes.

Josh is not only a poke and pinch artist, he is also a devotee of cold showers. Just a few minutes once or twice a day would be helpful, he insists—an idea I totally reject. I did try it once, for maybe a second, and it might have triggered a heart attack. There are only so many compromises an old man can make, and giving up a soothing hot shower and freezing instead is not, for me, one of them. Josh has often suggested cold laser therapy to stimulate my muscles on a molecular level. It's an extra sixty dollars per treatment. But better than a cold shower.

My podiatrist informed me that he too could use a laser, for the heavy deposits of dead skin cells, calluses, that have been appearing over the last few years on the bottoms of my feet. Or cryosurgery—freezing with liquid nitrogen. He could also just cut them out with a knife called a curette, a small stylus-like instrument with a hook, scoop, or gouge at the tip. Although a laser eliminates scarring, the laser treatment costs about ten times more. Since the vast majority of the people I know will never look at the bottoms of my feet, including me, I opted for the curette.

I do know a bit about cryosurgery, however. My dermatologist has been shooting me with that stuff, liquid nitrogen, to eliminate the seborrheic keratoses, blister-like bumps that have been appearing on face and scalp over the past couple of years.

My dermatologist—her name is Dr. Noel—works quickly and efficiently. She's a handsome, tanned young woman with a brilliant toothpasty smile and glittering diamonds on her ring finger. She walks into the room, examines my face and head, seeking moles, which she will often shave, obviously with a curette, and send off to biopsy. Melanoma, at my age, is always a threat. For the keratoses she uses the cryosurgery gun called a cryoprobe, which looks a lot like a bicycle pump with a spritzer top. She's like a gunslinger with that pump with which she will invariably shoot me. It burns for a bit, remains sore for a couple of days, turns to scab, then usually disappears. Until they appear again, sometimes in different places on my head and scalp and sometimes repeat performances in areas that were treated. I also have to expect age spots, she calls them liver spots, as I get older. Everywhere. Has something to do with the lack of elasticity in my old man's skin. Not a lot to do with the liver.

Seborrheic keratosis is inherited, I learn. I do remember my father's many visits to his dermatologist when he was in his eighties, the red blotches and scabs all over his face after his cryo-squirts, month after month. Another reason to resent my dad, I think.

I have also been getting acquainted with a urologist—I mean really acquainted—because suddenly, over the past couple of years, my PSA has been seesawing up and down. PSA (prostate specific antigen) is a protein produced by cells of the prostate gland. The urologist, a rather inelegant guy who always wears a wrinkled white shirt (maybe the same shirt?) and an awkwardly knotted tie, is very technical in his conversation. A test determines the level of PSA in a man's blood, he says, as we huddle together in his tiny exam room. If the level is high or higher than normal, this may be an indication that you have prostate cancer. Or, on the other hand, it may not be an indication of anything. "Normal" depends on many other factors, including your age, race, genetics, or, for that matter, the presence of a urinary infection. Levels are determined by a measure of nanograms per millimeter of PSA in your blood, and the demarcation line—the magic number, the number you don't want to exceed—is 4.0.

There's also a big disagreement over whether PSA levels actually mean anything, for all men my age seem to have some form of prostate cancer, but when you get past seventy, he informs me, you will probably die from other causes before the prostate cancer gets you. This is not particularly cheerful news.

The conversation goes back and forth this way for a while. And then he does his dutiful dirty deed, a digital rectal exam (DRE). This is what I mean by getting really acquainted—up close, inside, and very, very personal. He wants me to come back again in six months for another visit, another intimacy to share together.

"Visit" is not the correct term for what was going on here, even though all of these providers are exceedingly polite and try to be accommodating. "Visit," the word, has a kind of a friendly, warm connotation. Like fireside chats, or afternoon tea, or cake and cookies and fruit punch over the holidays. Sessions with these guys—dentists, ophthalmologists, podiatrists, dermatologists, urologists—"visits" with them, are more like assaults, and not just on my body. That's trivial compared to how it all works on my mind, chipping away at my dignity, my feelings of self-worth and self-sufficiency.

A decade ago I didn't need, didn't even think about, any of these "providers"—another word, an insurance word, that is quite inappropriate to what was going on. "Providers" provided untold frustration, and information I was reluctant to try to process, and now these provider visits have become seemingly more crucial, indispensable, and numerous than my work. Facts of an untangling, disintegrating life.

One day, before starting to write in my office, after Starbucks, and taking my first sips of my venti, I looked at my calendar for the previous year and counted more doctor appointments, including follow-up checkup exams, than I had business meetings or classes.

I found them, those constant medical inconveniences and sacrifices, those "provider visits" related to my health and well-being, damn annoying. Although not, as I sat at my desk that morning, as annoying as the eggs.

First came the sickeningly familiar "pop, pop, pop." And then as I ran downstairs, the smoke detector detonated and the noise engulfed the house: "Bleep, bleep, bleep."

I extinguished the burner and opened the kitchen door to the back porch and waited until the stench was gone and the smoke alarm reset. Then, after cleaning up the mess, I went back up to Starbucks for a second venti.

Twenty-Two

IT WAS DECEMBER 14, 1964. I HAD MUSTERED OUT OF THE MILitary by then and had just started at Pitt in night school as a freshman, a few years before the Helium Centennial and Johnny Carson and Judo and Karate for Christ. I had recently settled into an apartment, my first on my own, and I had come over to the family's Beechwood Boulevard house to see my mother for breakfast that morning—something I would do from time to time, waiting until my father left for work, then showing up at her door, smiling sheepishly and hungry as hell. We were listening to the TV news—not watching; the TV was in the living room and we were in the kitchen—as the report of the mysterious leaper came on, the lead story. My mother ran into the living room to turn up the volume so that we could hear the details while I was eating.

The backstory, which I mostly learned later, was interesting. Construction on the Fort Duquesne Bridge, a double-decked arch bridge over the Allegheny River, had begun in 1958. It was meant to connect the downtown business area with the north side of town. The main span of the bridge was almost completed in 1963, but because of delays in acquiring necessary rights-of-way for approach ramps, the bridge would not connect to the other side of the river until 1969. The lack of approach ramps meant that the bridge—technically not yet a bridge—ended abruptly, frozen in midair, hanging naked over the river. It was referred to by amused and frustrated commuters with the tongue-in-cheek moniker the Bridge to Nowhere. Years later, this also became the nickname of another unfinished bridge in Alaska.

But the story that day, which absolutely amazed and tickled my mother, was about this mysterious, crazy guy who drove in his car, a Chrysler station wagon, and "leaped," the reporter said, off the Fort Duquesne Bridge, sailed 170 feet over the Allegheny River, and landed upside down on the dry riverbed on other side, unscathed. Literally crawled out of his vehicle and walked away without a scratch.

The guy who did the dirty deed was Frederick Williams, twenty-one years old, an undergraduate chemistry major, premed, at the University of Pittsburgh. He would eventually go through medical school at Pitt, serve his residency, and then leave town, moving to California. No one ever found out why he did what he did, which was one reason, maybe the main reason, the leap off the Bridge to Nowhere became a Pittsburgh legend.

But evidently the police back then did not know the identity of the leaper until a day or two later, because Williams wasn't named in the news that morning, which is why, on a whim, I had told my mother that the mysterious, unidentified Bridge to Nowhere leaper was me. I even conjured up some delicious details, like how I had rocketed through downtown Pittsburgh at ninety miles per hour, tearing onto the ramp leading to the bridge, crashed through two sets of striped wooden sawhorse barriers, and then was airborne across the water. I was guessing, imagining, just spontaneously inspired by the moment. And I wasn't far wrong; as it turned out, that's pretty much what the real leaper did.

I think, because of the way she glanced up from the eggs she was scrambling for me and turned in my direction, her eyes raised in exasperation, that she believed me, at least for a couple of seconds. I think she believed that I was perfectly capable of doing such a dumb wild-ass thing, which, at the time, may have been true. But then she knew almost immediately, by the way I was smiling back at her, my own eyes shining with mischief, that I was joking, baiting her. As she got older, I joked with her a lot. It was our way of connecting, me appreciating her easy laugh and her willingness to play her own game, she pretending to be peeved at her eldest son.

She was quite a simple, loveable soul. Once in a while, after my dad died, I took her shopping at the local supermarket, the Giant Eagle. Everybody knew her there. You walked into the Giant Eagle with my mother and the cashiers would yell out, "Hey, Mollie," or, "I love you, Mollie!" She was a friendly, easygoing lady, always polite, and interested in other people, no matter who or what they were. She had a way of being empathetic and sympathetic to anyone's problems and concerns, even if she did not always understand them.

For the next few months we had a running gag-dialogue about the Bridge to Nowhere leaper. We analyzed repeatedly how Williams had rocketed through downtown, sailed over the water, landed upside down in his car, and managed to survive. I don't know, can't count, how many times she said, in that way she talked, like the whining, high-pitched Jewish mother she was, "Why did he do such a dumb thing? He could have killed himself, that *meshuggeneh*." Yiddish for a crazy person. She went on and on about how stupid and *meshuggeneh* Williams was. What was Williams thinking?

Sometimes she would bring Williams up out of the blue, apropos of nothing. Maybe we were watching TV or eating dinner alone, and she would look at me carefully and say, "He could have killed himself."

And I would jump back on it instantly, getting into the spirit of the thing. "*Meshuggeneh*," I would reply.

By bringing up Williams, I think she was telling me she was afraid that if I didn't watch myself and settle down and get a job or finish college, do something respectable, I too would become a *meshuggeneh* maniac. She was probably right. In high school, I was constantly truant, put into detention, expelled for fighting or general misbehaving. I once hit my senior year English teacher on the head with a book when I was playing catch with a classmate standing behind her and miscalculated, and prior to that I had been kicked out of my bar mitzvah study class when I hit the rabbi in the head with a bagel. I meant to toss the book and bagel over their heads, but I missed in both cases. Another reason I was no good for right field.

It took my mother a while to begin to understand me, but down deep I think she tolerated and maybe even appreciated my *meshuggeneh* behavior, mostly because it made her laugh, and living with my dad was far from a laughing matter. And I think she recognized my outside-the-box antics as a way—the only way—her eldest son could distinguish himself, demonstrate his differences, rebel against where and how he grew up. She, unlike my dad, seemed to be able to picture, bring to life, the off-the-cuff spontaneity of the things I did. When I confessed that I hit the rabbi on the head with the bagel—and was expelled, permanently, from bar mitzvah studies—her first question was: "What kind of bagel?"

"Plain," I told her.

She persisted: "Was it a cream cheese bagel?"

And finally, after I answered, "No cream cheese," she replied: "Thank God. It might have made a mess on his suit and he would have made us pay for the cleaning."

Twenty-Three

FREDERICK WILLIAMS WAS NOT THE ONLY PITTSBURGHER MY
mom and I joked about, although he was her favorite. Pittsburgh has
changed a lot in many ways since then, but in the 1960s, 1970s and
even early into the 1980s, the city seemed to be engulfed in weirdos
doing outrageous things, mostly illegal, and for the most part getting
away with their crimes—at least for a while. My mother loved these
guys. It was all part of the Pittsburgh personality, we agreed, what
made the city unique and more than a little peculiar.

Like that guy who went downtown on a bus. He was six feet tall,
weighed more or less two hundred pounds, and wore a white shirt,
no tie, zippered jacket, and a baseball cap, and quietly handed neatly
printed notes to bank tellers demanding cash from their drawers. Sixteen robberies between 1961 and 1963 by this guy who, according to the
FBI, would have been on their Ten Most Wanted List if they'd known
his name. Pittsburgh embraced him. People all over the city were running around claiming to be him or accusing others of being the mysterious robber. He was cleverly branded by police and beloved by the
media as the elusive, uncatchable, legendary "commuter bandit."

Then there's Nicholas Perry Katsafanas, a.k.a. Nick Perry. Unlike the commuter bandit, Perry was a dapper dresser with an ebullient personality, whose early evening local TV show, *Bowling for Dollars*, beat out the national prime-time evening news. Perry was tapped as host of the statewide Pennsylvania Daily Numbers drawing. The daily number was determined by three machines in which Ping-Pong balls numbered zero through nine were shot around a Plexiglas container by puffs of air. In sequence, one ball popped to the top of each of the machines when a trap door opened, and together the three balls formed the winning number. One day in April 1980, every ball except those numbered four or six was injected, by Perry and a cohort, with white latex paint so they would be too heavy to come to the surface and pop through the doors. The idea, for Perry and those few friends he confided in, was to bet on every combination containing only fours and sixes. The winning combination that day turned out to be 666. No fours at all, which was kind of unfortunate for Perry, for it made the authorities suspicious enough to investigate.

Perry was proven to be the culprit and sent to jail, but in Pittsburgh he has been lionized. In fact, two decades later a movie was made called *Lucky Numbers*, inspired by the infamous "Triple Six Fix." John Travolta played the Nick Perry character, with Tim Roth and Lisa Kudrow as costars. Despite the excellent cast and the direction of a well-known comedic writer with deep Manhattan roots, Nora Ephron, it was a bust. But the movie continued the lasting legend and made Nick Perry immortal in his own hometown.

As Pittsburghers saw it, what Perry was doing was ripping off the state—so he was cool. No harm done. Pittsburgh is "someplace special," a slogan we cling to, while Pennsylvania was someplace else.

On the other hand, Sienna Miller—an actor who came to Pittsburgh to make another movie, *The Mysteries of Pittsburgh*, from Michael Chabon's first novel—was not so cool. In an interview with *Rolling Stone*, Miller complained to a reporter about her difficult life as a movie star, traveling all over, and not too many great places. "Can you believe this is my life?" she asked the reporter. Then she referred to the city as "Shitsburgh."

My mother loved this story the best, I think. Miller's scatological reference was over the top—to say that S-word, a word my mother would use in private, at home, all the time, and giggling and apologizing every time she did. But in public? A famous movie star? That was daring. That too was *meshuggeneh*. And my mother appreciated the idea of women breaking out of the mold, doing unexpected stuff, letting go for the hell of it. Like her crazy, rebellious motorcycle-riding son. Unlike the children of the women in her mahjong group, her every-Thursday-night-out event she never missed, whose kids were in law school or had started successful businesses and were making tons of money. Pillars of the community.

Not that my mother endorsed my antics, but she was never judgmental—at least not directly. Instead she would make broad worried-mother exclamations. When I returned to Pittsburgh after motorcycling the country, off and on—California, Texas, wherever—she'd say, "What the hell is wrong with you? You could have killed yourself!" Just like Fred Williams. Or responding to the way I was then dressing in leathers and big black boots: "Nice Jewish boys don't wear cleats!" Which was precisely the point. She knew that and so did I.

But then she always wanted to hear about what had happened to me, especially the crazy stuff. Even as I grew older and less apt to be so *meshuggeneh*, she was always ready for another story. Like when I told her about my plans to enter a peeing contest with a guy from New Jersey, Eddie Price. Eddie was in Pittsburgh on business—I had met him through Iggy and Susan—and he was constantly joking with me about how many times I had to stop at a casino to pee when I ran on Atlantic City's Boardwalk. Every couple of miles I had a preplanned peeing place on the Boardwalk.

"I bet I could pee more than you," Eddie once told me.

So when Eddie was in Pittsburgh, I decided to drive him back to New Jersey so that we could count how many times we each peed. We didn't bet anything—we just did it for the hell of it. And we never did define what a legitimate pee actually was, so maybe we would fake it a little bit. Didn't matter. By that time I had given up motorcycles and was driving a Porsche 911, a red convertible—the real reason for the wager for Eddie, so that he could drive the car part of the way.

My mother was tickled by this idea. And was quite frankly relieved that I had come to my senses and was now into sports cars with four wheels rather than motorcycles with only two. I remember that I called her a couple of times along the way to report our progress—which was slow. At Johnstown, 60 miles east of Pittsburgh, we had peed five times each, if I recall correctly. At Altoona, home of the famous railroad Horseshoe Curve, 110 miles out of Pittsburgh, we were at eleven peeing places and eleven pees each.

Usually it takes about three hours to drive on Routes 22 and 30 from Pittsburgh to Altoona, and maybe two and a half hours in a red Porsche, but at Altoona we were over the four-hour mark because we had stopped so often. Peeing and then subsequently fueling up, hydrating to maximize our peeing, took time.

I defeated Eddie in our peeing contest, my twenty-three to his twenty-two, but by the time we reached Philadelphia six hours later, we had pretty much given up, calling the contest an official draw. We were wiped out and just wanted to get to Atlantic City to report our adventure to Iggy and Susan. And pee, a legitimate pee for sure, one last time, like a ceremonial congratulatory toast—a nightcap after a great dinner event.

I telephoned my mother when I got to New Jersey to tell her that I had made it safely and that I'd out-peed Eddie Price, a goy, which seemed to make the story even better for her—Jews over Christians—

we Chosen People could even pee better than anyone else. That was saying something. A positive point.

I devoted a lot of time to talking with my mother about my travels and adventures, and I do think it delighted her, even though she constantly complained that I was not a doctor or lawyer. But invariably, wherever our conversations rambled, we came back to our old standby, Frederick Williams, and to wondering why he, a nice boy from a good family, a premed student with everything to live for, even if he wasn't Jewish, would take that daring wild and crazy and *meshuggeneh* leap.

As I got older and busier, married twice, I didn't see my mother nearly as often as I once had. Then my dad died, and suddenly she was living alone. Her old friends were passing as well. My father used to joke that my mother had lived with a phone in her ear, she had so many friends at one time, but gradually the phone stopped ringing in her house, and she became reclusive and afraid. Refused to venture out for nearly any reason, except for the Giant Eagle and her weekly hairdresser appointment.

I hated to see this slippage, and, selfishly, I feared what was going to happen to me without her. She was the only person I knew and would ever know with whom I could act, be, completely and utterly myself—silly, serious, confessional, hysterical. Maybe that's why I became so utterly paralyzed, and so embarrassingly and inexcusably angry and resentful, when I began realizing—although not completely accepting—that her demise was approaching, would happen sooner rather than later. I could sense that it was happening every time I talked with her on the phone or thought of her while I was traveling. A dissolving image in the camera of my eye, like in the movies. My mother here. My mother fading out. My mother gone.

Twenty-Four

IT WAS LATE, MAYBE TEN O'CLOCK, AND I HAD HAD A LONG DAY and was ready to settle down in front of the TV with my *New York Times* in my lap and not say a word to another living soul until 6 a.m. at Starbucks the following morning, when my phone vibrated. Ordinarily I ignore the phone at that time of night, but I saw my mother's number and knew she would never call me that late unless there was something wrong. Indeed, she was desperate, frightened, and in agony.

"Help me. I'm so scared. I don't know what to do." She was crying and clearly unhinged. "I fell," she said. "I'm stuck," she added. "On the floor."

"Did you call Richard?" I asked.

All our lives, Richard had been the good son. It was Richard who handled her finances, Richard who devoted his late Sunday afternoons to his mother, reading her mail with her, making out checks for her to sign, dealing with insurance and Medicare issues—available at every opportunity to service her account, so to speak. Every family seems to have that "stand-up" member of the clan who's around and available to do the everyday stuff, including the dirty work, being on the front lines, and ours was Richard. He was the first to arrive when there was trouble with my mom, big or small—from having issues with the cable TV remote to falling and not being able to get up. Except for now.

"Did you call Richard?" I said again. I was stalling. I couldn't quite bring myself to admit what I needed to say or do.

Richard was not answering his home phone or cell, she told me, so she tried my ex-wife, Patricia, the hospice nurse. Patricia had adopted my family as her own. My mother trusted her as a medical expert and a fellow woman she could confide in. But Patricia worked twelve-hour shifts, rarely answered her phone after 8 p.m.—she'd be sleeping—and didn't answer that night.

"The writing is on the wall," Patricia had recently warned us. "Soon Mollie will not be able to care for herself—she can't really do it now, truth be told. You need to face the facts and be prepared. She's ninety-three years old, after all." But despite what I knew in my heart was true, the last person in the world who was prepared to face the facts about his failing, weakened, soon-to-be-dying mother was her eldest son: me.

"But what about Richard?" I asked again, still stalling and trying to control the fear and anguish that was rushing through me.

My mother replied: "What should I do?"

"What do you want to do?" I countered.

She didn't answer. But what I wanted to do was bury my head under my bed and pretend that the phone call hadn't happened or that I was out of town or the country or the universe—totally and completely and permanently unavailable. What I wanted to do was cry, or scream at the top of my lungs, in fear and frustration—for my mother or for me, I wasn't sure which. "Okay," I said, "I'm coming."

What I really wanted to do was kill Richard. Why wasn't he available, that asshole?

I remained in my bedroom where I had taken my mother's call and tried his cell number about five times, and he didn't answer. Why wouldn't he answer? Isn't that the reason to have a cell phone? You carry it around wherever you go so you can be available when trouble occurs. When your mother falls on her ass and almost kills herself, you ought to be ready at a moment's notice. I figured he was walking his dog—and I found out later that that was true, and he had forgotten his phone. What the fuck was wrong with him? He was so damn lame. He regularly walked his dog and forgot his keys and then called me to open his door for him. We were next-door neighbors. I never did that: lose stuff. I was alert, smart, thorough. I was Mr. Lee Never-Make-a-Fucking-Mistake Gutkind.

What was wrong with me? I asked myself. I was standing there by my bed, half undressed, just as pissed off at my brother as I was scared for my mother and for me. What was I doing, frozen in place? Stalling? Just as I had on that morning at Starbucks with Tony down on the ground and me with my boots glued to the floor, fearing . . . everything. I was unable to face the reality of my cowardice and my own selfishness, especially regarding my mother, who had protected me countless times from my ferocious father when I was young. How stupid and despicable was I, I thought, as I finally, grudgingly, put on the clothes I had just taken off and hurried from my house.

I walked to Richard's house and knocked. No answer. So I jumped into my car.

But then, instead of rushing directly to my mother, I drove around the block a couple of times searching for Richard—maybe another five minutes of wasted time, because I was so scared to face her myself. To face what I knew was happening. She was losing it—and I, in turn, was losing her.

Finally I resolved to forget Richard and go to my mom. Fuck him. I could take care of my mother. For once in my life, I would show Richard how to be action-oriented, how to do the right thing, how to be the hero son—not so *meshuggeneh*, although in retrospect I was more *meshuggeneh* then than I can remember being in my whole life. I couldn't think, reason things out.

But then I took one more turn around the block. Just one more time. Cursing him aloud in my car and feeling panicked.

When I finally saw him walking into his house, I began to yell. "Where in the fuck were you? Your mother is lying on the goddamn floor of her house, and you are walking your fucking dog without your fucking phone, oblivious to the world, while she is almost dying."

He didn't say a word—at least I can't remember him saying anything. My heart was pounding so loudly as we drove over to Mollie's house, which was once my grandfather's house and the place where I spent several years of my life, in the second-floor apartment where we lived and in the basement in which I was periodically incarcerated by my rage-prone father.

We arrived at her house, scrambled up the stairs to the porch. Then I remembered that I didn't have a key to my mother's house, that only Richard and Patricia had keys. I stepped aside so he could let us in—but his key didn't work. I don't know if Richard was so nervous he couldn't turn the lock or fit the key into the notch, but just when we were about to give up and break in through a window, my mother opened the door. She was breathing heavily but was in control again, sort of. And we too were back in control once we saw her. She was clearly rattled and shaky. We helped her to a chair and learned what had happened. She had tried to stand up and go into the bedroom, but in the process she lost her balance, maybe blacked out, maybe even had a stroke, we theorized later. She collapsed on the end table next to the TV and woke up on the floor. She was okay now, but shaken and mentally scattered.

Not the first time she had fallen, we found out. She had fallen many times in the last few months, resulting in numerous bruised ribs, according to the X-rays when we took her that night to the Emergency Department. This was serious, we knew; Mollie could not go on indefinitely this way. The following day she became an in-patient at a facility for the elderly, a place called Charles Morris Rehabilitation Center, where her bruises were treated and she received physical therapy and learned to use a walker. Or tried to learn. She also received a total evaluation—mental and physical. She stayed at Charles Morris, recovering and learning, for one month.

Twenty-Five

IT WAS ALL-HANDS-ON-DECK FOR THE DREADED TEAM MEET-
ing at Charles Morris: nurse, social worker, dietician, physical therapist, and marketing director gathered around a table with my family for a powwow about what to do with Mollie. This was when the
family—Richard, Patricia, my other brother, Michael, who lived in
Philadelphia, and me—were attempting to make the decision about
putting my mom into the Weinberg Village assisted living facility.
I began calling it the *existing* living facility, because that is what it
was—a place to exist, sometimes barely, before she died.

When I arrived at Charles Morris that morning, my mother was
waiting in a wheelchair. She looked like an old man. One of the
nurses had washed her hair, and so it was flattened down on her head
like a dry, bare bush, steel wool gray. She had a one o'clock appointment at the facility's hair salon, which, when you live in a rehabilitation center for old and decrepit people, means they will come and
get you sometime, anytime, after one o'clock. It's not as if you have to
keep to a time schedule in a place like Charles Morris. You've got all

day, all night. There's nowhere to go. You are waiting all of the time—for nothing to happen.

I had never realized that my mother's hair was so short; it was always teased into wooly waves when I saw her, pumped and puffed up by her beautician. No matter how bad or isolated she felt when she was living at home, she always managed to find the strength to go to the beauty parlor and get her hair done. It was a shock to see her hair then; it was as if she was naked. Her entire head was wrinkled up like a prune; her wide nose, a family trait, was a bizarre tortured appendage; her teeth were a dirty yellow.

I saw myself twenty years hence, maybe less, sitting in the wheelchair, waiting for the what-to-do-with-Lee team meeting, my assisted living, existing, sentence.

For a moment she looked at me searchingly: did she know me? Recognition came in a few seconds and she smiled—and when she smiled at me, it was like I was her son again and not a nervous, crotchety, petrified caretaker.

We all sat around the long table, and the physical therapist told us my mother had two more weeks to get ready to get out—that is, to be released. She'd made some progress, had learned how to use the walker, but had not learned enough to be on her own yet. Her balance was the problem. The conversation went on and on, but the upshot was inevitable. Mollie would not be going home.

At the end of the meeting, the marketing person at Charles Morris—her name I forget—said she'd been wanting to meet me because she knew about my book and wanted me to give a talk at Charles Morris.

"You mean to your staff?" I asked.

"To everybody," she said. "The patients."

What the hell was she talking about? I tried to imagine giving a talk, a lecture, to a bunch of people like my mother. A talk about writing? That would be ridiculous, obviously. But worse, the marketing person told me she wanted me to talk about dying, like I was supposed to tell these semi-gorked-out people who couldn't walk, couldn't remember what they did an hour ago, couldn't hear for shit—nothing—about what it was like at the end of life. Shouldn't they have been telling me? I thought.

The book she was talking about was *At the End of Life: True Stories about How We Die*. It was a mix of personal essays about dying in different ways and under various circumstances, from diverse points of view: a 911 telephone operator, parents who have lost a child, a grief counselor, a physician losing a patient, on and on. It was an anthology: I didn't write it; I only edited it. And as an editor, I looked at it only clinically—that is, from a literary point of view—judging whether the pieces were good and compelling stories, whether they communicated interesting information, whether all of the pieces fit, flowing together, one after another from beginning to end.

What, I wondered, was this marketing person thinking? She wanted me to come and give a talk about dying or preparing yourself for the end? Me, who was afraid to get old, afraid to lose control, and worse, afraid to become feeble, like all of these residents of Charles Morris?

This would never happen.

Who the fuck was Charles Morris, anyway?

But while I certainly had no intention of giving a writing workshop or lecture at Charles Morris, I had done, of course, more research, mostly because I knew what was happening to my mother or would happen sooner rather than later. I knew my mother's many falls might have been avoidable, or her lonely life might have been more tolerable, if she hadn't spent so much time in her house, dozing, dreaming, and trying to get through the empty hours of every day by herself. Sometimes my mother had difficulty getting out of bed. I would call her at noon and she'd still be dozing, and I'd say, "Why aren't you up?" and she would answer, "What for?"

She did have visitors—two women we had hired who came to sit with her, to take her shopping or on other errands, or to lunch, at twelve dollars per hour. And of course Richard and Patricia, and I, and sometimes even Michele with her mom, Norma, came calling. But her basic problem was loneliness. No matter how depressed and disillusioned she felt on any normal day, if you could engage with her, my mother would come alive. Rally. She could have had more company by agreeing to be more social—she could have gone to the Jewish Community Center in Squirrel Hill for lunch and joined all of the other seniors. But Mollie had become very antisocial, a sad reversal from a time when she had so many friends, the phone lines hot with conversation and gossip. Previously, my brothers had wanted her to move to a place where she would have company—assisted living maybe. But she had refused. She said she wasn't going anywhere. Like so many other elderly people, she said, "I will stay here, in my house, until I die."

Gerontologists have a phrase for this state of being—"aging in place." It describes the experience of elderly people who choose to remain in their own homes rather than move into homes for the aged or live with children and relatives. According to an AARP survey, older people maintain that staying in their own homes solidifies their sense of dignity and integrity. "If bad health or economic insecurity forced them to move in with family or, worse, a nursing home," the study says, "this would be a devastating loss of face as well as privacy."

My mother owned her own home, which is essential for those who want to age in place. And women are more likely to age in place alone than men: thirty-seven percent of American women sixty-five and older live alone, compared to nineteen percent of men the same age. Women are better at cultivating and maintaining social ties generally, and as a consequence, they are less likely to be socially isolated. Interestingly, another study I found, funded by the Economic and Social Research Council, found that women over sixty who lived alone expressed more happiness with their lives than married women of the same age. Not my mother, who missed her Jack, after his burned-down Tryson's transformation.

The irony here is that, as I was reading these studies from AARP and other organizations about the elderly and "aging alone," as I was learning about my mother and her contemporaries, I realized that I was also part of the subset that had been studied. My mother might have been older, but we had more in common than biology and blood. We were both elderly, mother and son, and both "aging alone." This reality seemed weird, and I didn't like to think about it. But it was true.

With advancing age, it is inevitable that people lose contact with their friendship networks, that they find it more difficult to initiate new friendships, to belong to new networks. A study I read revealed that the presence of perceived loneliness contributed strongly to the effect of depression on mortality. Thus, in the oldest, depression is associated with mortality only when feelings of loneliness are present. In many cases, depressive symptoms, such as withdrawal, anxiety, lack of motivation, and sadness, mimic and mask the symptoms of loneliness.

We knew that Mollie couldn't take care of herself—she needed round-the-clock care, and her own house was simply too small for that to be comfortable. We wanted her to stay at Charles Morris longer to really familiarize herself with the walker and to give us time to decide what to do with her next. Or maybe it was just to give us time to process what was inevitably going to happen to her. But there was a Medicare problem. The hundred-day rule. The social worker, the marketing director, and the therapist together explained the situation. The patient gets one hundred days of rehabilitation and care at any one time. That's all they get—unless they can stay away from Charles Morris (and other facilities) for more than sixty days. If they make it out of incarceration for sixty days, then they get another hundred days. The thinking here was, the sooner my mother gets out, the more Medicare days she will have left, if she loses her balance, takes another tumble into a table, falls down a flight of stairs—who knows what. In this scenario, if she leaves soon, my mother will, precisely, have sixty-three days left, but if she can live sixty days without killing or maiming herself, she will qualify for another hundred days. It is all a juggle. It is like a savings bank—you get interest if you keep your balance and don't fuck yourself up.

"I am not sure I am ready to use the walker by myself," my mother had told me a few weeks before this meeting. "It scares me."

"But you can do it," I said, keeping positive.

My mother laughed. "Sure," she agreed, "as long as you are standing behind me."

I was shaken by my mother's inability to walk—a reality that seemed to have come on quite suddenly. Yes, she was slow moving at home and getting into a car was a struggle. But if we were all patient and waited, as slow moving as she was, she was quite able to manage. I had recognized that she was slowing down, but it never really occurred to me that she'd be stopping—or almost stopping, nearly immobile without help.

She was also not thinking too clearly anymore. Of course, neither was I—especially about my mother. That day I had visited, she had touched her gnarled arthritic finger to her lips and said in a whisper, looking around to see if someone was listening, as if maybe someone was hiding in the room, "I think I am going crazy."

"Join the club," I said, "you and me both."

"Don't tell a soul," she said. "It's my leg. My leg just keeps popping up."

"Popping up?"

She demonstrated by lifting her knee a couple of inches. "It jumps on its own accord. I can't control it."

"It just," I repeated, "pops up?"

"It's happened four times. The last time is when I was sleeping. Popped right up. I couldn't believe it."

"Then it happens in your sleep?" I asked.

"No, it woke me up one time, but the other three times I was already awake. Don't tell a soul," she repeated. "This is between you and me."

"You mean because people will think you are crazy?"

"No, it's because I want to make sure I am right. What if it didn't pop up? What if I am imagining everything?"

I understood what my mother was trying to say, this sense of confusing imagination with reality. I felt this same instability of memory, this lack of a balanced awareness—what's real and what's not, what happened and what didn't—every day. I don't know for sure if my knee clicks when I walk. I feel it clicking, comes when I least expect it, but when I walk and think about it, the click doesn't come. Is it clicking or not? I have sinus problems, my nose is sometimes congested, so I keep a bottle of Claritin beside my computer on my desk. But I can never remember if I have taken a pill. The bottle is there. But did I? I don't know. Maybe I take too many Claritins sometimes, just to make sure I have taken one. It is frustrating and mind-numbing when you don't know what you do and what you don't do.

These conversations with Mollie—I always called her by her first name, initially a privilege of her eldest son, then common practice in my family—were becoming increasingly challenging. Everything I said, whatever we talked about, I found myself shouting, sometimes connecting and sometimes not.

"Mollie, the sun is shining. The wildflowers are blooming everywhere. Mollie, it's a beautiful day."

"I didn't hear you."

"The Steelers lost a big one in Cleveland last night."

"I still can't hear you."

"Goddamn it," I would say. "Frustrating."

"Don't talk dirty. I'm not one of your girlfriends."

"How could you hear that?"

"Whadya say?"

"You think I have girlfriends? You know something about me I don't know?"

"I can't hear you."

"It doesn't matter."

Truth be known, it did matter. For I could no longer talk to Mollie, with whom I had once been able to converse for hours about the most personal of subjects: money, sex, my brothers, my wives and girlfriends, my fears of loneliness and abandonment, and, of course, Frederick Williams. It was only Mollie I came to for comfort for all that troubled me. No one else. It was Mollie who had fought for my release when my father locked me in the dark cellar for hours on end when I was a kid of five or six. It was Mollie who jumped between us on the stairs leading to our apartment when I was seven and too little and afraid to fight back, protecting me from my father's flying fists or swirling strap. Mollie was my beacon of trust and my safe-haven partner. My mother saved me; she shaped my life.

Now Mollie was leaving me. Her life was ebbing—she was waiting for her bus.

That was the metaphor Mollie employed to help me feel better after two failed marriages and more than a few unraveled relationships: that life was like a bus stop. If you missed the first bus, or even the second or third, there was always another one scheduled. And when you paid your fare and found a seat, you never knew what was going to happen, or, as she would put it, *what was going to be*. Something good could come of it in the end. "If one thing doesn't work, then there's always another."

This actually proved to be true, sort of, to a degree, in her case, for she found new friends, all of whom were living under the same handicaps and circumstances, at the assisted existing facility. True enough, they were all waiting at their last bus stop; the next time they got on their bus, it would take them to the end of the line. I knew, and she knew and accepted the fact, that this facility was no replacement for life as she had once lived it—as a mother and grandmother, going shopping and to the hairdresser, playing poker and mahjong, and indulging in the other joys she had once appreciated. And Weinberg Village, next door to Charles Morris, one of the best places in our town as far as assisted existing facilities go, was pretty pitiful in comparison to what she had enjoyed in her past.

But when I came to see Mollie during those last eight months that she lived after the all-hands-on-deck meeting, she mostly seemed comfortable and at peace with what was going to happen next, although she told me repeatedly she was getting damn tired of waiting for the bus.

"The days never end," she told me. "I can't sleep at night, so I lie awake thinking about what's going to happen to me, when I am dying. I can't go to the bathroom without someone helping me out of bed, so I ring my buzzer, and no one comes—until I fall back to sleep, and then they come and wake me up, and I go to the bathroom, finally, and then it starts all over. I can't go back to sleep again. It makes me crazy. I am always so confused. This is not a life," she said again and again. "This is not a life."

My mother, I realized, was more than ready to pay her final fare. Her bus, she would have said, was way behind schedule.

Twenty-Six

I ONCE GOOGLED AND LOCATED DR. WILLIAMS IN CALIFORNIA, telephoned him and asked him point-blank if he was drunk when he took his wild ride. He hung up the phone without a reply. I telephoned him a second time. He didn't pick up. I called the next day, but he was holding out, and I was frustrated. So I talked with him in my head, even if he didn't talk back. I pictured a dried-up old man with bronze skin, leatherized by the sun, and his eyeballs, whirling in response to my question, were yellow and fierce.

"You leapt off the Bridge to Nowhere. You flew in the air almost two hundred feet and smashed your station wagon to the ground. And then you got up and walked away, and you became a Pittsburgh legend and a mystery to me. Now, that is not kosher. I want to know why you did it and how you survived, and then I will leave you alone and you will never hear from me again."

He listened. I imagined those whirling, yellowed-balled eyes, gleaming in the sun. Then, after a too-long pause, he replied, "It's none of your business. It was something that happened a long time ago."

"Were you drunk? Were you running from the police? What crime did you commit?"

"Why are you tormenting me?" he said. His voice was like rolled-up paper, crackly.

"Why won't you answer?" I persisted. "It won't hurt you to answer the question. The police are not going to come after you; the newspapers aren't going to hound you and write bad stuff about you."

"What does it matter to you?"

"It's part of Pittsburgh history—the origin of the Bridge to Nowhere. The flying leap that became immortalized. Like the Triple Six Fix. Like the commuter bandit. Don't you understand? This is no laughing matter. Pittsburghers have a right to know. What's the secret of your survival? Look," I said, and now I was almost pleading, "you don't understand. This is serious business. Why did you leap, and how did you survive?"

"Why do you care?" he asked again.

"I need to tell my mother," I told him, "before she dies."

Frederick Williams did not answer.

I might have called him back, or reimagined another interaction, but it was way too late. My mother died on December 28, 2013, five days before my seventieth birthday, the Bridge to Nowhere question unresolved.

NOT LONG AFTER MY MOTHER'S DEATH, I READ A NEWSPAPER story about a driver of an SUV, a Kia Sorrento, who, speeding down Greenfield Avenue, lost control, crashed through a fence and the front yard of a house, careened from a brick wall, and went airborne, landing upright on his wheels on the roof of the Giant Eagle supermarket, an entire city block from where the collision started. This was my mother's Giant Eagle, where she shopped almost every week, until the assisted existing facility. It was also, this Giant Eagle, on the site of my old school, Roosevelt, where I had failed so disastrously in right field.

The police were everywhere that day, the story went on, along with officials from the fire department, Allegheny County's hazardous materials team, and the county's health department. The supermarket was soon evacuated when firefighters learned that gasoline from the SUV posed a danger to the building.

The driver was unidentified in the news story, but the reporter quoted a man whose rental unit was directly adjacent to the supermarket, who said: "I was sitting on the couch, and then I heard, 'Boom!' I thought my chimney fell. Then I looked out my bedroom window, and I saw a car on the roof of the 'Eagle.' And I saw a guy crawling out of the car and standing up on the roof, saying to somebody, maybe himself, I don't know, 'Yeah, I'm all right.'"

When I read this article, I said aloud to myself, "Just like Frederick Williams."

I wished my mother had still been around so that I could have told her about the SUV flip-flopping and flying onto the roof at the Giant Eagle. I would have taken her in my car to the spot. She would have been amused—fascinated, in fact. We could have had a great conversation, a vigorous dialogue and debate. The story would have ended the way all of our Frederick Williams conversations ended. The driver of the Kia was clearly *meshuggeneh*.

Twenty-Seven

STUFF CONTINUED TO HAPPEN TO ANNOY AND EMBARRASS ME as I lurched into my seventieth year, stuff that confirmed my aging, circling-the-drain insecurities and put me constantly on edge.

Like, after the Haitian Hospital benefit party at the downtown Bitz Building, I began chatting with this woman in the valet parking line, and she invited me to meet her for a drink at a bar, the Mardi Gras Lounge, around the corner from where I live. I knew many people at this bar, and so did she, and for a while she and I went our separate ways. But eventually we found each other, and we talked.

Huddled next to her at the bar so that I could hear her over the loud music, I listened to her cancer travails, her first and second husband travails, her job travails in Pittsburgh and in Texas where she grew up. She was forty-two years old. As the bar was starting to close, she said that she was sorry to have monopolized the conversation and that she didn't learn much about me, which, I assumed, was the perfect opening to ask if she wanted to get together again and talk more.

"No, thanks," she replied. "I prefer dating men at an age when the fun side of life is not so far behind them."

Like, recently at my health club, on a cross-trainer, an aerobic machine for legs and arms, in the final minutes of a one-hour computerized circuit, I was talking with my friend Susan. We were both philosophical, discussing forgetfulness and our attempts to keep our short-term memories intact.

"Sometimes I space out," Susan said.

"I work really hard to keep things together," I told her, now drenched with perspiration and exhaustion. Sixty minutes, nine hundred and sixty-two calories at level fifteen. I got off my cross-trainer after the cool-down, another five minutes, and more calories burned, wiped my face with a towel, and put on my jacket, catching my breath and continuing my conversation.

"I'm constantly monitoring myself," I told Susan, "I feel the pressure. I'm always fighting to focus. I don't want my son, anyone, to see—or to think for a moment—that I'm slipping."

As I headed to the door, I checked for my wallet, car keys, water bottle, gloves, making sure not to forget anything. But then I realized I couldn't find my cell phone. I searched the front pouch of my nylon jacket, where I normally keep it, and then the side pockets. I went back to the cross-trainer. Two weeks before this event, I had driven all the way home from this club and showered before I realized my phone was missing. I searched everywhere before retracing my steps to the club and finally finding it where I had initially put it—in the cup holder of the cross-trainer.

But today the phone wasn't in the cup holder, either. I stood, just for an instant, in the middle of the club, surrounded by dozens of aerobic and weight-lifting machines, men in sweats, women in Spandex, feeling a slight edge of panic welling up inside, while sympathizing with Susan as she rambled on about her own aging difficulties, when I realized, suddenly, that the phone I was now so desperately seeking was in my hand, against my ear.

————

AND THEN THERE ARE THESE SHIMMY-LIKE LEE-IS-SO-fucking-old scenarios that play out in my mind from time to time.

I am lost in the Panera at the Miracle Mile and I am wandering aimlessly in my Birkenstocks with black knee-length socks, downing refill after refill of dollar-a-cup coffee, pounding on the tables, *bum bum-bum-bum-bum . . . bum bum.* And then, next thing I know, I am in the hospital and an impatient nurse is trying to teach me how to use a walker and feeding me Cream of Wheat with a spoon.

I am in a wheelchair, my yellow teeth chattering, waiting to get my hair done.

I am booked to give a big-deal speech, maybe at Harvard, maybe even at the White House, and I stand there on the stage, holding a microphone, only to realize that my fly is open, and when I try to zip it up, I drop the microphone, which makes a loud blasting noise throughout the hall, and everybody in the room is staring at me. And meanwhile my zipper gets stuck as I try to pull it up, and the only way I can loosen it is to take off my pants. And then I am standing there talking to myself or, even worse, talking to Mr. Skink, in front of all those people, fighting with my fly and knocking my glasses to the ground.

At least, a saving grace to these imaginary aging humiliations is that I have never shuffled. Or not quite yet. Like my friend Ron, who started to shuffle when he turned eighty. I don't know whether he knows it or not, because he still walks fast enough, but now it is not a walk, it is a shuffle: he leans forward as he walks, the length of his steps has shortened, and he drags his feet on the cement. You can hear him coming a mile away, pushing his head forward, scraping his shoes on the sidewalk, dragging the lower half of his body behind him.

I can hardly look at Ron because I so much fear I am looking at myself a few years from now, shuffling like an old man. When we meet for a drink and he lifts his martini glass, his hand quavers. I lift my glass of Malbec, hold it in front of me and dare it to move, pleased that I can keep it steady but dreading the day when my own quake appears like Ron's. These are the signs and symptoms of sarcopenia: Sagging and wrinkled skin. Hair loss. Trembling of the extremities. Stooped posture and dragging feet—the fucking shuffle. And loss of coordination (probably while zipping?). I looked it up.

Twenty-Eight

FRANK AND I MET AT THE ADVERTISING AGENCY WHERE I WAS working promoting helium. He had been a high school English teacher for a dozen years after college but had joined the agency as a copywriter trainee just to try something different. We connected almost instantly, discovering in our first friendly conversation the one thing we had most in common: that we were both facing the vexing problem of how not to get married. More specifically, how long we could delay the inevitable.

Marriage was around the next corner for both of us—for me, with my first wife, with whom I was then cohabitating and who was under pressure from her conservative Presbyterian parents to do the "right and proper thing." It wasn't really that I didn't want to marry her; I loved her. But the idea of commitment scared me. If I couldn't decide what I was going to do in any given week—or even on any given day— how could I commit to one person, no matter how special she might be? I mean, to me, we were talking about a lifetime. That's what marriage was supposed to signify, right? Divorce happened, of course, but it was a much bigger deal then than now.

Before long a basic difference between Frank's situation and mine became evident: I knew that sooner or later, when I did get married, it would be to a woman, while Frank would also marry a woman, but deep down he desperately wanted his marriage to be with a man.

Being gay, openly, anywhere in the United States in the 1960s and 1970s, except maybe in certain sections of San Francisco and New York, was challenging, and this was even before the AIDS epidemic. But in Pittsburgh, then the blue-collar capital of the world, where the phrase "natural man" was plastered on billboards and cans promoting our homegrown Duquesne Beer, it was anathema. Back then and for years before that, Joe Magarac, a muscular, down-to-earth, hard-hatted giant of a steelworker, was a celebrated mythical local folk hero. Murals and sculptures of Magarac still exist today in municipal buildings and parks as a reminder and representation of what the Pittsburgh man's man was once supposed to be. And in 1974 when Robert ("Bobby," people snidely called him) Duggan, the local district attorney, surprisingly shot himself in the head, his political opponents attributed his sudden death to fear of humiliation that he would be discovered to be gay.

So, it was difficult enough being a Jew in Greenfield or an African American anywhere in the Steel City in the 1960s and 1970s, but if you were a homosexual at that time in Pittsburgh, you were, quite honestly, fucked. Especially if you wanted to live a relatively untroubled "normal" life.

Frank maintained his heterosexual façade before and during his marriage, but he and so many others, I soon discovered, were leading double lives in our town. District Attorney Duggan, by the way, was also married—to a woman—at the time of his death.

Frank was a character as charismatic as I had ever known. He was tall and handsome, an impeccable dresser—very Brooks Brothers in suit, tie, and button-down oxford cloth. He was a teacher, like I said, and according to many mutual friends, a damn good one. After his short stint at the agency, he would return to the classroom. But his real passion was singing and acting—musical theatre. He performed throughout western Pennsylvania and West Virginia for many years, and everyone who ever came into contact with him loved him and wanted to hang out with him. He was pure unadulterated spontaneous fun. He would sing anywhere, at almost any time—show tunes mostly—at the drop of a hat. Bars with pianos, and there were a few in Pittsburgh then, enticed him. He could drink anyone under the table. But he was a very likeable drunk.

I wasn't much of a carouser until I met Frank and his friends. He introduced me to a new world: judges, attorneys, car salesmen, physicians, TV executives, body builders. The men I would meet through Frank on Friday nights at bars and lounges around the city were "normal" on the outside, but they would talk to each other and gingerly touch each other in ways I had never witnessed before. They began their nights out by drinking double Beefeater martinis with chasers of Duquesne, the "natural man" beer, or Iron City, the other Pittsburgh homegrown brew. Invariably, after a couple of drinks, they would tease each other, veiled innuendo about what or who they really were and what they planned to do with—or to—each other that night.

Sooner or later they might break out in song. A favorite was the title song from the 1966 musical *Cabaret*. But they could also sing a variety of show tunes as the night wore on—almost anything from Broadway. Frank would begin with his beautiful baritone and we would all join in, sometimes so smoothly and spontaneously that our performances might have been rehearsed.

Invariably, some of the men disappeared into the men's room. Or wandered into the parking lot. They returned breathless and flushed. Sooner or later they would call their wives or girlfriends and say they'd be late, they were sorry, they were with Frank—and that, to the wives and girlfriends, meant drinking and carousing, boys being boys. I haven't the slightest idea if the wives and girlfriends suspected there was more to it than that. At least some of them must have. Frank's fiancée must have known . . . something. But they married anyway. I was an usher at their wedding.

None of those men ever touched me. I was Frank's private property. But they all wondered: on those nights after all the bars in Shadyside closed and the crowd of boys dispersed and staggered their way home—everyone except Frank and me—did he and I get it on together? The guys must have assumed I was with them in spirit and maybe in fact—that I was playing the same game they were, hiding my yearning to be "out" by being so masculine "in." How could they not? An ad exec weekdays and a leather-clad motorcyclist at night and weekends? After all!

Frank and I had a ritual after these wild drunken nights. We would meet at Mellon Park, a small patch of manicured gardens and fountains in our Shadyside neighborhood, and have a nightcap. Just a quick drink, a couple of cans of beer or sips from a bottle of whatever Frank had in his glove compartment, while we recounted the hilarious details of the evening and contemplated the alliances that had taken place in the bathrooms or parking lots while we were partying. We chose Mellon Park for those nightcaps because of the secret pact we had made when we first met.

As I said, we were both staving off the pressure to marry, but we knew we would soon succumb, and we decided that we would do something significant to mark the upcoming days of matrimony. We bought a bottle of cognac, and early one morning, after a wild evening, we snuck into the park with a shovel and, illuminated by the sunrise, selected an out-of-the-way spot in a corner garden and buried the bottle. A year later, on the night before Frank's wedding, we returned to Mellon Park, dug up the bottle, drank half of it together, and reburied it. Six months later we returned, unearthed the bottle a second time, and downed it, the night before my marriage.

I know this was a silly thing to do—juvenile, a shenanigan that men get themselves involved in because they are and will always be boys. But the closeness Frank and I shared on those occasions has never in my life been matched with a man since. For a long time I had feared that there was something in my personality, my DNA, that tainted me in a way that made significant relationships impossible, with a man or a woman. It wasn't my weight or my Jewish background or even my in-and-out immersions; this inability to connect and form meaningful, long-lasting relationships was a flaw that I suspected would always haunt me and preclude intimacy.

I wasn't able to do that with my first wife, obviously. Perhaps I had especially wanted to marry a WASP—with Villager sweaters and Capezio loafers; polite, mannerly ways; pale complexion and straight long blonde hair—because she was so different in background and orientation from anything, anybody, I had ever experienced. This was how I had been managing my life for many years since the rope test and the military—doing something different. Good for my psyche maybe, good for me professionally maybe, but clearly the wrong reasons for marriage, although I did not know then the right reasons for marriage.

My wife was a philosophy major and a pianist; eventually she became a high school English teacher, but she always had her head in the clouds, quoting Aristotle, John Stuart Mill, Bertrand Russell. I was always trying to figure out what she was talking about and continually making fun in defense, mostly because I was so clueless and, I admit, outclassed. I did learn a lot from her when I listened and tried. But that did not happen often enough to make a difference.

We remained married for six years. Frank and his wife stayed together a lot longer. It would take me many more years and another failed marriage to become the person I thought I wanted to be. Frank, as it turned out, found his way, found himself, much sooner than I did.

He told me about it later: One day, many years after his wedding, sometime in the 1990s, his wife was in the house preparing their dinner and Frank was sitting on his front porch when Jimmy, a total stranger, walked by. His shirt was off, for he had been walking in the park. Jimmy was bronze and muscular. He had rich black slicked-back hair and blazing white teeth. Their eyes met, and a feeling of relief and release surged through Frank, an explosion of yearning and emotion like he had never experienced before. All of Frank's fear and trepidation of being "out" disappeared in an instant. Leaving the porch and the upcoming dinner as if he was in some sort of trance—and he was—he walked down the steps and followed Jimmy. Two weeks later they were living together.

I often think about why and how I had fit in so well with these guys, closeted gay men living double lives, constantly fearing being discovered, outed and ridiculed like "Bobby" Duggan. Of course, it was primarily because Frank brought me into the fold and vouched for me that I became an accepted part, an outlier, in this inner circle. I would never, it went without saying, breathe a word of what I knew. And I think they liked and accepted me. I was with them—Frank and his friends—in spirit, and I could have been with them in fact, if I had been so inclined.

I don't mean "liked" in a physical-sexual way. They appreciated and respected the work I was doing, my desire to become a writer and make a difference. And with me they were willing to drop the macho-male façade that guys, especially in the 1960s and 1970s, broadcast to the public. You could talk with Frank and his friends about what you thought about, what made you nervous about the life you were leading. Defensive barriers melted when you stopped trying to explain the essence of who and what you were, which is what happened when we were all together. It was a circle of trust and intimacy.

And never having known a gay man before, or at the very least anyone I knew to be gay, I found these men fascinating. I often stood back and watched them interact, trying, completely unsuccessfully, to recognize mannerisms, traits that distinguished and separated them from everyone else. What was it that made them gay? And me not gay? What was it, I have wondered for many years, that Frank felt when he first saw Jimmy that sunny afternoon while the woman he had married was in their kitchen preparing their dinner? Did he feel the same desire that I felt sometimes seeing and becoming aroused by my first wife or later Patricia or, later yet, Michele? Or was gay love, gay lust, different? Better?

Whatever it was, it was that magical moment for Jimmy and Frank that Sunday afternoon, an amazing, unrelenting enchantment that I wished—and that perhaps we have all wished from time to time—I could experience and share. Man or woman, maybe it didn't matter. Just to feel something so electrifying for another human being.

I didn't think Frank felt that strongly about me, but he did feel much more than the deep spiritual, sentimental bonding and friendship we shared, I discovered. It had happened the night before my wedding, after we partied and celebrated with a bunch of the guys through half the night, and after our interlude at Mellon Park, digging up and finishing the cognac, toasting each other and reminiscing about the memorable events of our friendship, most of which had to do with how he and our not-yet-maybe-never-"out" friends fooled the world about who they really were and what they were doing with one another in secret. The fact that they could live two lives and get away with it was often as amusing as it was precarious to them. There was something incredibly intoxicating about the social-sexual tightrope they were walking, like the yearning and concealing of a drug habit, the passionate balancing of conflicting loyalties and desires.

Today I live very close to Mellon Park; it is exactly a mile from my house to the park entrance. I have calculated it with a pedometer, since it is the first mile of my regular running route. Sometimes I go around the park, but sometimes, depending on how I am feeling or what I think I want to feel at the moment, I will cut through and pass the little garden where Frank and I concealed the cognac.

Not that I stop to talk with Frank, like some people tend to do at gravesites or memorials, but that memory, the wave of our intimacy, wafts through me as I run by, and I experience simultaneously a sense of joy and a longing for the warmth and the fun we shared. I think that's what I miss most about Frank and our time together with and without the rest of the gang—the fun of it all. Their situations were serious and precarious, to be sure. They all had a lot to lose: reputations, families, friends and neighbors unaware of their double lives and perhaps, were those people to become aware, unaccepting. Times have changed, to a certain extent. We are talking a half century past.

But Frank and his comrades confronted that aura of threat on those Friday nights, cloaked in the glue of the group, with abandon and release—and I was tickled to be a part of it. So often, late at night, we were singing at the top of our lungs, being silly and, wherever we were in a bar or on a sidewalk heading for another bar, laughing loudly at our silliness. At the fun we were having with our ongoing, hilarious boys-will-be-boys charade.

I have done a lot of cool things in my life, performing as a clown for Ringling Brothers, climbing Kilimanjaro, biking across Tanzania, four Outward Bound wilderness survival treks, and all of these experiences and those I have documented in my books were exhilarating and satisfying, but they were never as much downright good old-fashioned fun as those Friday nights with Frank. Which is how I will always remember him, for such a goddamn good time he gave me, and most especially the affection he shared with me the night before my marriage, right after we emptied the cognac bottle at Mellon Park and returned to my apartment.

My first wife was staying at the hotel in which we were to be married the following afternoon; Frank, my best man, was responsible for making sure I would be at the wedding on time, and so he was staying with me. Sleepy and still half intoxicated from all that drinking, we made up the sofa bed in the living room for Frank and said goodnight. I went into the bedroom that my soon-to-be wife and I had shared for the past year, set the alarm, threw off my clothes, buried myself under the blankets, and immediately fell asleep until, at some point maybe not too long after, Frank crawled into my bed, draped his arm around my shoulder, and pulled me closer.

I can't say I was surprised. From the beginning of my involvement with Frank and his gay friends, I had wondered if an event like this might occur and what I would do about it. But I knew that if it did occur, the decision I made might alter the rest of my life and the friendship I so cherished with Frank.

I did not move after feeling Frank beside me, neither resisting nor cooperating, waiting and contemplating in my stillness what could happen. Knowing that I loved Frank and that he loved me, for he said so that night as he scrunched up against me; knowing that I could, and might, for the simple sake of our friendship, allow Frank to do to me whatever it was gay men do to each other when they make love; knowing that I did not really want that to happen, perhaps because I was unprepared to discover something about me I did not want to face up to; and knowing at the same time that there was something I was feeling in Frank's warm body that was different, not unpleasant, and piqued my curiosity; knowing that I did not want to offend Frank, did not want to do anything that would in any way splinter the friendship and the bond we shared; knowing that I was at the precipice of something entirely new I could experience—another immersion, I thought, for the chameleon Lee! A ridiculous notion that might have tempted me to move forward. Or was it a justification?

All these things ran through my mind as I lay there, wondering what Frank would do if I resisted, and also, of course, if I didn't resist; waiting, I think, to do in the end what my mother would always advise, except maybe she would not have advised it in this case, to see what happened.

I don't know how long I waited—it could have been thirty seconds and it could have been thirty minutes—but eventually Frank made his own decision. He removed his arm from around my shoulder, slid out of my bed, and retreated into the living room. In the morning, over breakfast, dressing in tuxedos and cummerbunds and black bow ties, we calmly discussed my upcoming wedding, went over the details of the night before in Mellon Park, laughing all over again, listened to the news on NPR, time passing by. But never that morning, and not ever throughout the many years of our off-and-on friendship afterward, did either of us ever mention, at least to one another, what had happened, what had not happened, what could have happened, between us in bed the night before I first married.

I am not saying that I haven't thought about it, wondered and speculated about it since Frank crawled into my bed that night and pressed himself against me. It is just one of those things in life that might have been that wasn't, that might have changed everything but didn't. One of those things that you find yourself rethinking and re-contemplating, those "what if" questions that will never be answered or resolved. And I think I am just as satisfied that it wasn't resolved. I like to speculate about what would have happened if I had been more responsive, the thrill—or the aversion—I might have experienced, and the amazing story I could have written about me and a night in the arms of a man.

I LOST CONTACT WITH FRANK AND JIMMY AFTER A WHILE, AS I stumbled my way through a second failed marriage. They found a new and very satisfying life with an increasingly emboldened and accepted gay community in Pittsburgh. But as I became more socially active after my divorces, I would run into them at bars and restaurants, and gradually we got reacquainted and got together frequently. Frank was still performing, so I went to many of his shows, and Jimmy, it turned out, could sing as well and loved show tunes.

There was one Frank-and-Jimmy production I will never forget, because I was a reluctant costar. Months before my mother's ninetieth birthday I suggested to my brothers that we have a party to celebrate such a milestone. We made a list of all the people Mollie might like to see—relatives, friends still living, neighbors, even Dickie Diamondstone. And Michele would be there, with her lovely mom, Norma. Then we decided that we needed a program, a special, original way to honor her life. "Let's commission Frank and Jimmy," I suggested. And we did.

For the next few months we met with Frank and Jimmy frequently, Richard and I and Patricia, briefing them about Mollie's past, the people who had accepted invitations to her party, so that Frank and Jimmy could write songs about Mollie and her friends and her long life. We rented a banquet hall in a private club—it was to be a long champagne lunch—with, of course, a piano.

We met once more with Frank and Jimmy a few days before the big event and we went over the entire program, perhaps thirty-five minutes long, including the lyrics to all of the songs they had written up, until the grand finale number, the closing song. "That's when you and your brothers take over," Frank said.

"What do you mean, 'take over'?" I said. "You mean, like, thank my mother for her love and support through all the years? Something like that?"

"No," Frank replied. "I mean you need to sing to her."

What was he talking about? I was not a singer. I mean, I could sing "Cabaret," emboldened by Beefeaters and beer, with the rest of the guys. But sing a solo? No way.

"Not a solo," Frank replied. "You and Michael and Richard will sing to her together."

"No way," I said. "Totally out of the question."

"You gotta do it," Frank said. "This is your mother. It's her ninetieth birthday."

"No," I said.

"I thought," Frank said, "that you were the great immersionist. That you would try anything to have a new experience. The guy who sparred with world wrestling champion Bruno Sammartino, who motorcycled America, performed as a clown for Ringling Brothers. You can't perform for your own mother?"

I could, and did. We all did, the three brothers. The funny thing is, no matter how hard I try, I cannot remember the song we sang together. Neither can Michael or Richard or Patricia. All I can remember is standing side by side with my two brothers, decked out in shirts and ties and our best suits, shoulders touching shoulders, crooning to a startled and clearly nonplussed blue-haired old lady, as those three men she had brought into the world, nurtured and protected, serenaded her.

There was a stark silence, a frozen second, when our song was over. Maybe we sounded terrible or maybe my mother and everyone else in the banquet room thought we had gone *meshuggeneh*. But I have never felt closer to my two brothers than I did at that moment. The intimacy was profound, although in the end not so long lasting.

Jimmy and Frank were long lasting, however. They remained together, sharing a life and performing, for twenty years, until Frank, my Mellon Park boon companion, died of cancer, nine months before I turned seventy.

Twenty-Nine

MY RELATIONSHIP WITH FRANK OVER THE YEARS DID NOT PRE-
cipitate a change in me or my personal connections with others. I
had remained distant and sometimes defensive with most everyone
else, except for Iggy and Susan and my mother. Maybe it was because
Frank was living a double life that we were so deeply connected. He
was practicing a personal immersion during the day—being whoever
he had to be, teacher, actor, singer, bon vivant—and living the life he
longed for and belonged in on Friday nights. It wasn't at all too different from what I was doing as a writer, although it never occurred
to me back then.

When Frank died, and I was so close to seventy, I began to realize
what I was missing or losing—the history and longevity and connec-
tivity that real sustained friendship can bring. Frank had been suffering and wasting away with cancer for nearly a year. And I had been
grieving for him and missing him from the moment I knew and accepted the fact that he had incurable cancer.

Not that it was an easy task; the sadness and grief and impending
loss becomes an inescapable weight in your heart and your conscious-

ness. You walk around knowing that something terrible is going to happen to someone you love, is already happening, and there's nothing you can do about it except let it all play out. I had the same feeling about what was going to happen to my mother, as each day ticked by. You do not accept it, but you resist thinking about it because it is so hopelessly depressing, and you try to adjust to what is inevitable.

But when Iggy died, only months after I turned seventy, I was flummoxed and horrified and petrified, for suddenly, without warning, I became terribly alone, empty and confused. I had for many decades had two good male friends to rely on. And then, in less than a year, I had none.

It honestly never occurred to me that Iggy would die, at least not so soon and suddenly; he had been part of my life since I was twelve years old, the father figure I needed because of the real father I never quite had. He was certainly old enough to die; he was eighty. But he had been a vital part of my life for so long, a friend to trust. No matter that he was three hundred miles away in Atlantic City. I knew he was there, someone to reach out to in times of trouble. He would, as he had promised, bail me out of jail in the middle of the night. And more.

In Pittsburgh, Iggy had owned a business that distributed beer and soft drinks to stores and private customers. After school—or even, when I was truant from school, in the middle of the day—I got into the habit of walking down to Iggy's and becoming a part of his amazing milieu.

He was a simple man, self-educated, but he had an aura and a way about him that made me feel important and special. He listened to me and accepted me for who and what I was. Which didn't mean he didn't want me to change, but that he never criticized me; he simply asked questions about whatever I told him about my life, questions that made me think a bit about my ideas and actions. And sometimes change my mind when his questions led to reevaluation. Which was all I really wanted at the time.

He too was quite charismatic, but in a different way from Frank, who was appealing because he was an entertainer, a bon vivant with an incredible earnest enthusiasm for life and good times that was infectious. Iggy was quiet and restrained, more of an engaged listener than a talker and performer. But he seemed to be wrapped in a kind of magnetic aura that made you want to get closer to him, be enveloped by his presence. And it was not just me feeling that way. That's how he affected most men who knew him.

I remember once meeting Iggy for coffee at an outdoor corner café. I chose a chair next to him at the rectangular table. A bunch of other guys we knew came along, all men as it happened, and joined us. Which was fine. But they all wedged their chairs at the table pushing in between Iggy and me, just obviously to be closer to him. Eventually there were maybe six of us, bunched up together as close as we could get to Iggy. Our chairs and elbows were touching. There was plenty of room to move and spread out more comfortably at the other end of the table, but none of us was willing, seemingly, to give ground and lose that cloak of comfort and trust that Iggy mysteriously provided.

When I was young and lost during high school, Iggy had introduced me to Harry Coke, Paul Pepsi, and Buddy the Squirt Man, truck drivers for the bottling companies licensed in the area to manufacture the beverages they delivered to Iggy to sell at his beer and beverage distributor store. I loved being with Iggy and his friends, and to my great relief and surprise, none of those men ever referred to my weight or my voracious appetite.

I always tried to arrive at Iggy's for lunch, even if sometimes this would be my second or third lunch of the day. Iggy's desk was spread with bundles of orange-brown butcher paper, which, when opened, exploded in pungent aromas of corned beef, pastrami, pickled tongue, and pickles the width of your fist. Conversation focused on women, how to seduce them, what to do when you succeeded, how to save face when rejected. Other subjects included adventures from World War II and the Korean conflict, and sad stuff about divorce, debt, and death—the "3Ds." Frequently Ray Riddle, the Canada Dry driver, brought in "stag" films and showed them on Iggy's ancient projector in the basement. It was unfortunate that such activities were programmed around lunch—I didn't really need to eat—but the sensory gratifications, the tastes and smells, were enhanced by the excitement of the sexual adventures on film. Sharing baskets of French fries smothered in ketchup and chicken salad sandwiches squishing with mayonnaise while watching oral sex was titillating and hilarious; we all screamed and moaned with nervous pleasure.

There were many times during my high school years when my father went after me and I ran away—or times when I felt alienated and alone and needed to talk to someone—and Iggy was always there. Or Susan, with whom I became closer in later years than with Iggy himself. The thing I loved most about Susan, what we shared together, was how much she and I loved Iggy, no matter what he might have done to annoy her—or me. Which was plenty. Iggy was chronically late to every dinner or social event that he had ever been invited to. He couldn't ever seem to be on time. We often joked, Susan and I, that there was real time to deal with and Iggy time.

But no matter how late he was, how many dinners Susan prepared that were warmed over and sometimes not so edible, when Iggy finally arrived, Susan lit up the room. All was forgotten; Iggy was home and then everything else was fine. Iggy and Susan opened their home to me and to many others who were like me, alienated and confused, employees who seemed lonely or out of sorts, or people just burdened by life itself that Iggy might run into. You never knew who you would find at Iggy's house—strangers he met in grocery stores who were troubled or just had a good story to tell. They would invariably tell their stories at Iggy's house, and Susan would cook for them, wash their dishes, and if necessary do their laundry.

Iggy lent them money—often just gave them money. Found them jobs. Connecting with and helping those who might be down and out, socially alienated, had always been a near obsession with him. Maybe that's why he had befriended me.

After the military, when my soon-to-be first wife was sneaking out of her dorm to be with me, we would take refuge at Iggy's house in the suburbs. Their two young sons were like little brothers. My then future wife's parents, who were clearly wary of me, perhaps because of my religion and, even more, my hippie persona, frequently telephoned Iggy and Susan in search of their daughter, accusing them of hiding us, which Iggy never denied. "They are two nice kids who love each other and want to be together. What's so terrible about that?" It was a question they could not answer, except to say that she was truant from her dorm room, to which Iggy answered, "I know."

Unlike Frank's slow wasting away, Iggy's death occurred in a horrendous instant, sudden and tragic and ironic—so true to the spontaneous unpredictability of life. Iggy was going to his favorite neighborhood restaurant with Susan and their granddaughter Rebecca to celebrate Rebecca's acceptance into medical school. That night, the restaurant's parking lot was full. They circled a couple of times without success, so Iggy dropped the two women at the door, and they went into the restaurant to get a table. Iggy parked the car across the street. They would meet inside.

It was dark, and the street was poorly lit as Iggy began to cross. According to a bystander, Iggy waited while two cars passed him, and then suddenly a third passing car hit him. Susan and Rebecca heard the sirens, saw the lights, and came out of the restaurant to investigate. They heard Iggy choking and saw him shaking, lying on the ground. Then he was dead. The bystander did not think the driver of the car had been speeding, and a Breathalyzer later confirmed that the driver had not been drinking.

Did the car swerve into Iggy? Did Iggy not see the third car and decide to cross? Did Iggy see the car and try to engage it in a race to cross the street? Did Iggy have a heart attack—he had a heart condition—and fall into the moving vehicle? No one will ever know. Even the driver was unable to provide information or explanation. Iggy had just suddenly appeared out of the darkness, in the middle of the street, illuminated by the headlights. There was a sound, a muffled but unmistakable heart-wrenching crunch, and then he was gone. Many questions and few answers—and numbness and pain forever after for those who loved him.

I remember the phone call from Susan late that night, 10:45 p.m. Hard to forget. Her voice, usually energetic, liltingly musical and lovely, was cold and flat. "Lee, Bob's dead." When he moved to New Jersey, he had lost his Iggy nickname and become Bob.

"What do you mean, he's dead? He can't be dead." I knew that was a stupid thing to say. But I was dumbfounded.

"I know," she said. "Come quickly."

I was at their house the following morning with Patricia and my son in tow. I was okay, in control, first with my elegy at the funeral, recalling his early days in Pittsburgh and the way he befriended and helped me and others, then as a pallbearer, sliding Iggy's casket into the hearse, and then throughout the long drive to the cemetery, which was in another town a half hour away. But when we lowered him into the ground, my body began to shake, and I was convulsed in tears and moaning, the shock of his *goneness*, who he was to me so definitively wiped out. I remember grabbing onto Eddie Price, the guy with whom I had had the peeing competition, and we held each other, he too moaning and crying until Iggy's casket was covered with dirt, shovel by shovel, disappearing from my view, each shovelful stabbing my heart.

Iggy's death made me feel more than a bit unhinged. What the fuck, I thought, is all of this about? First you are all right, more or less. You've got stuff to look forward to—granddaughter's exciting future and perhaps precious great-grandchildren who might follow and enrich your life even more. Your business is going well. Your sons have become very successful adults with their own families. And then? What? Annihilated, squashed, plastered in the middle of the street at the height of a celebratory moment? This was not right. It made no sense. It should not have happened. But, of course, it did.

Iggy was dead. Frank was dead.

These days, I think of Frank from time to time, especially when I run through Mellon Park; he was such a warm companion, a male love of my life. But Iggy is always with me, inside me, his bleeding, choking image, when I am walking up Walnut or crossing any street, anywhere, anytime, night and day, haunting me and reminding me, cautioning me, that my life, like his, could stop in a mangled instant, and I would no longer have a future. Not a second or a breath or a prayer. It could happen. It had happened to Iggy.

That year, from the late fall of 2013 to the late fall of 2014, with my seventieth birthday right smack in the middle on January 3, 2013, I lost my mother and my two best friends, three vital personal connections I had had almost forever; they had impacted my life, shaped my history. And I also lost, during that same time—or said goodbye to, or struggled relentlessly with the agony and regret of saying goodbye to—a new friend, the man whose life and work I was certain would help me fortify my legacy as a writer.

He was the subject of a book, a big book, a significant book that would turn heads, cause conversations, represent and bring together all of my efforts over the years to create and re-create a never-before-told true story that would always be remembered and would always matter.

Until it didn't.

Thirty

I FIRST READ ABOUT MENACHEM IN THE *NEW YORK TIMES* IN 2008. His story read like a spy novel.

In 1939, three nights before the Nazis arrived in the town of Oswiecim, Poland—which they renamed Auschwitz and turned into a death camp for Jews and others—a sexton, an assistant rabbi, buried his synagogue's Torah in a secret place known only to him. The Nazis, he knew, would otherwise certainly defile and destroy this sacred treasure.

A scroll inscribed by hand in Hebrew on parchment derived from a kosher animal, the Torah consists of the five books of Moses—Genesis, Exodus, Leviticus, Numbers, and Deuteronomy—considered the Word of God by Jews, Christians, and Muslims alike. For Jews it represents their covenant with God. By venerating and protecting the Torah, Jews show their appreciation for being the Chosen People.

After the war, the sexton dead, an informal group of Auschwitz survivors began a quest to locate the lost Torah. After decades of fruitless searching, the man known as the Torah Hunter was approached for help. This was Menachem Youlus, a middle-aged Orthodox rabbi and a scribe, a sofer, trained to write Torahs and to fix damaged ones, make them kosher. Over the years, Menachem (his preferred moniker) had found and restored more than a thousand lost and desecrated Torahs snatched by Nazis and Stalinists during World War II, often risking his life to do so. He would, when at all possible, return those rescued Torahs to the original owners or their families.

Menachem made two trips to Auschwitz, the first in 2001, when he scoured the area where the synagogue had been located and the cemetery adjacent to it with a metal detector. Survivors had reported that the Torah was encased in a metal box for the purpose of preservation. Menachem failed in his first attempt, but in 2004 he expanded his search to areas adjacent to the original cemetery, and within a few hours the metal detector started beeping. Menachem began digging and found the metal box. When he opened it, the Torah was there, but it was missing four panels. The entire scroll, stitched together from many panels approximately three yards in length, when unfurled may be as long as a football field.

"The obvious question," Menachem told the *Times*, "was, why would the sexton bury a scroll that's missing four panels? I was convinced," he added, "those four panels had a story themselves."

They did.

Menachem placed an advertisement in a local newspaper, saying he would "pay top dollar" for old parchment with Hebrew letters. Soon he received a reply from a priest who said, "I know exactly what you're looking for, four panels of a Torah."

The priest explained that the farsighted sexton had removed the panels before burying the scroll and given them to four congregants, who later, after the Nazis had taken over, smuggled them into the camp so that prisoners might feel closer to the word and heart of their faith. The panels were handed over to the priest before the prisoners who hid them were put to death. Menachem bought the panels from the priest. Unable to transport antiquities legally from one country to another without proper documentation, Menachem smuggled his treasure into the United States inside the linings of his suitcases. He then reintegrated the panels and repaired and refurbished—made kosher—the entire Torah.

Months later, a wealthy businessman purchased the Auschwitz Torah for $35,000 and gifted it to Central Synagogue on Lexington Avenue in New York on Holocaust Remembrance Day, 2008. That was what the *Times* story was about.

I was quite taken with this story, and I discovered, in an internet search, many other amazing Menachem Torah-hunting stories in other publications, like the *San Francisco Chronicle*, the *Jerusalem Post*, and the *Washington Post*. And both the *Christian Science Monitor* and *Washingtonian* magazine, chronicling his adventures, had dubbed him "the Indiana Jones of the Torah."

Menachem had unearthed a Torah in the Bergen-Belsen concentration camp under a floorboard in the rotting World War II barracks—overlooked by historians, caretakers, and thousands of tourists for a half century. In Estonia he stumbled upon a church that had purchased dozens of Torah scrolls from a Russian general at the end of World War II. The sacred panels were used to upholster chairs and benches. In a small village in the Ukraine, he bought a rough hand-drawn map from a farmer who had approached him "out of nowhere" at a convenience store. This led to the discovery of two hundred and fifty Jews buried in the farmer's field, the shreds of clothing wrapped around their fleshless bones still bearing the rotted remnants of the yellow Star of David with which the Nazis had branded Jews.

And what about the story in the *Washingtonian* of the former Nazi who threatened to burn a Torah for all the world to see on YouTube if he did not receive a significant ransom? Menachem contacted the Nazi, negotiated a price, secured a bank draft for the agreed-upon amount, and immediately traveled to Berlin. But when he arrived at the Nazi's apartment, the Nazi insisted the payment be in gold. He did not, he said, trust Jewish banks. Overnight, Menachem somehow converted his bank draft into gold, and the following day he handed over the ransom.

That day, Menachem exchanged the Torah, which he had wrapped in brown paper, for a package of the same shape and size with one of his associates in Berlin, who was hiding in the lobby of the Nazi's apartment building, waiting for him. They each jumped into hired cars and drove off in opposite directions, Menachem ostensibly on his way to the airport.

Not long after, Menachem's car was forced off the road by two men in another car, who grabbed the package and ripped it open—only to discover that it was filled with rolled-up newspapers. The men began to punch and threaten Menachem. When he opened his eyes minutes later, his attackers were gone, and his face was a bloody pulp. But by this time his confederate was on a plane headed for the United States with the rescued Torah.

I was excited about this overall Menachem story, all of his incredible adventures. This could be a book, a big book, a best seller, a chance of a lifetime, especially for a writer like me, pushing seventy. I mean, how many books, especially immersions, which take years and years to research and write, did I have left in me? As I was reaching the end of my career, I so very much wanted an opportunity to write a book that might hit a home run rather than just, like most of my other books, getting me to first base.

But more than that—more than just making a splash—my motivation was also personal. I wanted my work to be remembered and appreciated, not just by those interested in the topics about which I wrote but also by people on Walnut Street and in Pittsburgh and absolutely everywhere. Maybe that was selfish and self-centered. George Orwell once noted, in discussing the reasons people become writers, "sheer egoism," including a wish "to be remembered after death" and "to get your own back on grown-ups who have snubbed you in childhood." I could relate to that. And Menachem seemed to be the ideal subject to help me accomplish my desires.

I worked fast, reaching out to Menachem the day after the *Times* story was published. I didn't want any other author with a book in mind to read the *Times*, jump on the Torah Hunter story, and beat me to it.

We met at his place of business. The Jewish Book Store of Greater Washington on Georgia Avenue in Wheaton, Maryland, a DC suburb, was like an old-fashioned dry goods store in lower Manhattan, with dusty paraphernalia piled and crammed into every open space. Not too different from the shabby shop my grandfather Isadore once owned, I imagined, when my orphan father was growing up. The front room was jammed with books on Jewish history, the Holocaust, Yiddish humor—175,000 titles in all, according to advertisements. The rear area was packed with gifts, menorahs, jewelry, prayer shawls, and more. The store's motto: "If it's Jewish, we have it."

Menachem's small cluttered office was in an alcove in the back of the store, surrounded by floor-to-ceiling shelves containing dozens of Torah scrolls, some waiting to be repaired, others to be sent to new homes. The mailing labels revealed the destinations: France, Russia, Belarus, North Dakota, Montana, Australia, even Uganda. He was exactly the nerdy nebbish of a rabbi I had imagined—a perfect portrait of the most unlikely and loveable hero type. Pale and slight, he wore the traditional *kipa* or yarmulke on the back of his head, covering a spreading bald spot. He was five foot seven, with a soft protruding paunch. The shoulders of his black suit jacket were flecked with dandruff. A real character to re-create.

Immediately, he regaled me with stories, not just telling them but acting them out, jumping up and down, re-creating the dialogue, capturing the mannerisms of his characters, and altering the tone and volume of his melodious voice so that it seemed almost like background music in a movie. Not just the stories I had reviewed when I googled him, but other intriguing and dramatic adventures, like the day he crawled into the rubble at the Pentagon after the 911 disaster to identify and bless the bodies of the casualties who were Jewish. "The first body I identified was actually a customer of my store." Or when he rescued Torahs immersed in the New Orleans floodwaters days after the devastation of Hurricane Katrina.

He knew people in high places. Rahm Emanuel, Joe Biden, and Bill Clinton were confidants. Not just politicians but admirals, generals, movie stars; he knew everybody who was anybody, and had counseled many. Then, after a flurry of nonstop story hours in his bookstore, when we broke for lunch at a kosher pizza joint, he revealed to me his secret and ambitious plan: an expedition to Iraq.

Soon after Iraq fell to coalition troops in 2003, Menachem had been dispatched by the U.S. Defense Department on a confidential mission to Baghdad to assess the Jewish antiquities in the once-illustrious Baghdad Museum. Up to and during Saddam's tyrannical reign, the Baghdad Museum had held more Middle Eastern treasures than any other repository in the world. Some had been spirited out right before Coalition troops marched into the city. But other antiquities had been simply ignored or unnoticed by the throngs of hasty looters, too ignorant to understand their importance or value.

"Three hundred and sixty Torahs are there." Menachem was breathless as he described the scope of the treasure. "We found them strewn on the floor of the subbasement, floating in dirty sewer water and being picked at, gnawed, by giant rats! Some of these Torahs are four and five hundred years old," he added. "We lifted those Torahs up, and we put them on metal tables and encased them with plastic."

From his jacket pocket Menachem whipped out a grainy photograph of what looked like tables with scrolls on them, and another of himself wearing a flak jacket for when he went out in the city with Defense Department bodyguards. "That day, I vowed to rescue these

Torahs and devote the rest of my life to restoring them back to their original condition."

And then he said to me, in a hushed voice, exactly the words I wanted to hear. Or thought I wanted to hear. This Iraq story, he said, would be my exclusive, the one story only I would have the opportunity to write, "a real scoop," and to be on the scene, from start to finish, as it played out.

To be honest, I was surprised. I had assumed that I would have to work hard to persuade him to allow me to hang out with him, meet his collaborators, and observe his Torah-hunting adventures. To the contrary; I was in! Just like that! And then he stretched his hand across the table, placed it on top of my hand, and leaned forward.

"As soon as I met you, when you walked into the store today, I thought, immediately, How perfect! How wonderful! God always sends his angels."

Over the next few months, as I traveled back and forth to Wheaton, I began drafting a proposal for my agent to offer to publishers. This is standard procedure in nonfiction/journalism. A proposal captures the essence of a book in forty or fifty pages, so that publishers will provide a cash advance for a writer to take time from his or her day job to research and write. Most of my previous books had earned contracts with modest advances, but when my agent offered up my Torah Hunter proposal, many publishers were interested. Very interested. And the proposal was purchased, after feverish bidding, by a distinguished publishing house for, to me, a generous advance, much more than I had ever received for my other books. This was a writer's dream, my dream of the one book that might constitute a lasting legacy, come true.

Thirty-One

I BEGAN MY RESEARCH BY CONDUCTING IN-DEPTH INTERVIEWS with people for whom Menachem rescued or found Torahs, and they told remarkable, tearful stories of appreciation and respect. The dentist Ian Shuman told me about his grandmother Minna, who had escaped the Nazi takeover in Poland by the skin of her teeth in 1939 and found her way to a cousin in Baltimore. She returned to her village, Dubrowa-Bialystocka, years later, then a widow, discovered that the old Jewish community's cemetery was in shambles, and financed its restoration.

One day, according to Menachem, he and Ian Shuman met at a local *shul*, and when Shuman mentioned Minna, who had died the previous year, Menachem told Shuman that Minna had, a few years ago, visited the bookshop and asked him to find a Torah from her village. He had the Torah now and had been waiting for her to contact him. Shuman purchased that Torah and dedicated it to his synagogue in honor of his son's bar mitzvah. Shuman said that Menachem, bringing him this Torah from his grandmother, had given new meaning to his life, and to his grandmother's memory. In fact, they were planning an excursion. When Menachem had visited Dubrowa-Bialystocka, he had come across a secret bunker that had belonged to Minna's family. The Nazis had been afraid to open it because they believed that there were Jewish demons inside. Menachem and Shuman would, he said, soon visit Poland to blow up the bunker with dynamite and "deal with the demons." He invited me to go along.

And a woman I interviewed, whom I will simply call Hannah, voiced the same effusive appreciation. Hannah's parents were concentration camp survivors. But most of their extended family from Poland had perished—more than three hundred blood relatives on her father's side alone, murdered. One day Hannah visited the bookstore to find something to read. As she browsed the dusty aisles, she saw Menachem meticulously repairing the script of a Torah, lifting old and broken letters off with a scalpel-like knife and rewriting them with a feathered quill. She said, "I wonder if you have ever run into a Torah from Tarnow. My parents lived there."

Menachem told her, "What a coincidence! I know of three Torahs from Tarnow available at this very moment." Hannah was excited and instantly responsive. "It was a *mitzvah*"—a good deed. Hannah had tears in her eyes. She had cried repeatedly throughout our interview as she relived her tragic family story, as did all of the men and women I talked with.

Every person I interviewed over an entire year or so had similar stories of how the Nazis separated and murdered their families, and overwhelming appreciation for how Menachem uplifted their spirits with a Torah and most especially with the story of its discovery and rescue, how he and his stories helped them find some resolution and closure to their losses.

All the while, as I conducted and transcribed these interviews, I periodically hung out at the bookstore, interacting with many customers who added more depth to the Torah Hunter legend. Menachem was active in helping handicapped children and their families, fighting with the government and insurance companies to get them coverage. Menachem repaired Torahs free of charge for synagogues in financial distress. Menachem gave free calligraphy classes for those who desired to write their own Torah. Menachem mediated marital and legal disputes voluntarily. And Menachem was revered by women in the Hassidic community. Most rabbis do not pay attention to women; they actively avoid them, especially in public. In Orthodox synagogues, women and men may not sit together; they are separated by a wall or curtain called a *mechitzah*. During celebrations, bar mitzvahs or holidays, men dance and drink and party, while women watch from the background through windows and doorways. But among the female customers in his bookstore, the women say to one another about Menachem, "He will shake your hand."

Menachem's stories and those of the people he had helped—and all this Judaism stuff—deeply affected me. Although my grandparents on my father's side were ultra-Orthodox, I had pretty much abandoned my religion. I had married two non-Jewish women and I had not, except for an occasional wedding, walked into a synagogue since my own bar mitzvah. My relationship with Menachem gradually drew me back into the fold. I attended Torah study groups and High Holy Day services. My son and I read aloud together the first five books of the Hebrew scriptures, the Torah ascribed to Moses. I thought maybe I would regain my religious and cultural roots and share them with my son. Menachem loomed in my mind as a symbol of strength and honor—what a good Jew could be. And, of course, there were the many stories and experiences I was gathering that would pepper my book with drama, and humor, and outright astonishing bravery.

There were times, I have to say, that I did question some of the stories Menachem told, first, because I had heard him relate the same stories to customers who visited the bookstore with various differing embellishments, and second, because his stories didn't quite reflect the stories others were telling about their interactions with him. Ian Shuman had no recollection of the coincidental conversation Menachem had described at their local *shul*. He clearly remembered approaching Menachem at the bookstore and inquiring about a Torah from Minna's hometown. But when I quizzed him about the conflict between his recollections and Menachem's, he brushed it away. And after all, they were soon going on an odyssey together to blow up the family bunker!

But my skepticism was assuaged when, one day, as we huddled together in his office, Menachem told me about the secret meeting he was about to have with Samir Sumaida'ie, the Iraqi ambassador to the United States. A very important and vital meeting that would lead to the dream project—rescuing the Torahs trapped and wasting away in the Baghdad Museum. I was to come along.

Thirty-Two

IT WAS NOON IN THE LATE FALL OF 2009, AND MENACHEM and I were standing at the entrance to a suburban synagogue in Maryland, about thirty-five miles west of Washington, DC. After a few minutes of nervous silence, Menachem pointed in the direction of the main road and said in his high-pitched, singsong voice, "Wait! They are coming." We watched the procession—a black Mercedes limousine bookended by two shiny though somewhat less ostentatious black Benzes—cruised down the winding drive leading to the synagogue and pulled up at the curb directly in front of us. "Get ready," Menachem whispered. He added, quavering: "Oy! This is it!"

Two burly men in suits emerged from the lead car. They approached, scanning us up and down with MRI eyes, and then positioned themselves beside us at the door. Two men, similar in dress and stature, climbed out of the third car and walked slowly to the limousine, all the while glancing warily left and right. Then the curbside door of the limousine opened, and two more men stepped out. The first was tall, young, in a suit with an open shirt. There was a slight bulge in that suit near the left breast pocket. "They will be armed,"

Menachem had warned, "but you will not see their weapons—unless, of course, they are necessary."

The second man emerging from the limousine was in his middle fifties, impeccably dressed in a perfectly pressed gray silk suit, white linen shirt, and fashionable blue-and-red-striped tie. His hair was gray, wavy and combed straight back, and almost iridescent in contrast to his dark complexion. I recognized him immediately—I had done a thorough internet search—the Iraqi ambassador to the United States, Samir Sumaida'ie, formerly the Iraqi ambassador to the United Nations and the most powerful representative of his country then in the United States.

Menachem and the ambassador were evidently on a first-name basis, and Menachem was, as usual, effusive: "Samir," he sang in his singsong way, grasping the ambassador's hand, "how are your handsome sons, your beautiful daughters, your wonderful wives?" Samir, Menachem had told me, a Muslim, had nine children and two wives.

The ambassador flashed a tight smile, reserved, but friendly: "Menachem, good morning."

The tall man in the suit with the bulge in his pocket was introduced by the ambassador as "my secretary," while Menachem nodded in my direction and said simply, "This is my man." Meaning, supposedly, that I worked for him and my job was to make certain the men would not be disturbed during their meeting. "Samir should not know you are a writer," Menachem had briefed me. "We are meeting in secrecy, talking business behind our governments' backs. So, don't utter a word."

The meeting between Menachem and the ambassador lasted about forty minutes. Menachem had told me that he had been permitted to bring a severely damaged Torah back to the United States when he had surveyed the destruction of the Baghdad Museum years before, and he had restored it to display his skill and commitment—an example of the work he could do if given the opportunity to repair

the other Torahs in the museum. This Torah, now here in the synagogue, was what he was showing to the ambassador as evidence of his
intention and skill.

The ambassador, although quiet and soft-spoken, seemed sin-
cerely engaged. He told Menachem that he was skilled in calligraphy
and had used over the years many different inks to write on parchment with quills made of reeds. Menachem said that he had learned
from an Iraqi sofer how to write with a reed and that he found it
much more challenging to use than the more traditional quill.

During the conversation, the ambassador's secretary took scads of
notes, and photos of Menachem and me. Menachem had alerted me
about the photos and warned that I was putting myself in jeopardy.
"You may be a marked man with the Iraqi secret service," he told me.
I didn't know what he meant by "marked man," but that wasn't the
time to ask for clarification. It was exciting to be there watching this
drama playing out, and also, I admit, a bit troubling. But even that
added to the intrigue and, of course, the story I would be writing.

As the conversation continued, Menachem outlined his plan and
proposal to the ambassador. He wanted the Iraqi government to allow him to collect the Torahs from the subbasement of the museum
and ship them back to his workshop in Washington. He would repair
and make them all kosher, as beautifully and carefully as the same
Torah he was showing the ambassador that day. Then he would return half of the collection to the Iraqi government—free of charge—
and distribute the remainder to synagogues and Jewish families in
the United States who had lost Torahs during the Holocaust. But not
to any Israelis—of course not, Menachem assured him. The Iraqi government wanted nothing to do with Israel.

Meanwhile I kept myself busy, looking like I was a person with a
job to do, by walking back and forth to the door, checking to see if it
was locked—it wasn't; there was no lock—and peering up and down
the aisles, ostensibly to make certain there were no interlopers, spies.

I felt rather foolish doing this, but I figured I had to do something. Otherwise, how could I explain why I was there if anyone asked? I had no idea what Menachem's "man" was supposed to do. But I was really delighted to be a part of this event, and I couldn't wait to re-create it for my book.

The ambassador continued to listen carefully throughout Menachem's presentation, nodding and asking a few clarifying questions, and assured Menachem he would seriously consider his proposal. But the ambassador had a final question as he and Menachem shook hands in farewell. "Who will be your representative—the person sent to Baghdad to coordinate the arrangements and assure the safe transport of our treasures? Someone must supervise, and you will be needed in your workshop."

Menachem hesitated for only a brief second, before turning and pointing to me. "He's my man. He will go to Baghdad on my behalf."

I was astounded by this bit of news. I had no interest in going to Iraq, one of the most dangerous places on Earth at the time, and still not a great place to visit today, especially for a Jewish writer, even if it was for the book of his lifetime. But I said nothing. I nodded. After all, this was the book of my dreams. What I had been waiting and hoping for. A book that solidified my legacy. Or provided a legacy where, perhaps, if I was to be honest with myself, none had existed. Nothing I had ever done before, baseball umpires, robotics, motor-cycling America, could in any way equal what my Menachem Torah Hunter book might achieve. Maybe I was starry-eyed, deluding myself. Maybe those stars were like floaters—shadows without substance that don't really exist.

But a month or so after the meeting with the ambassador, Menachem telephoned me. I was surprised by his phone call. Previously it was always I who reached out to him. He got to the point quickly, asking if I knew anyone at National Public Radio or the *Washington Post*. He had mentioned on a couple of occasions that two writers working for the *Post* and NPR had visited his bookstore, asking questions. Now he asked, could I influence reporters in both organizations to stop bothering him? He was feeling harassed.

Menachem knew that I had worked at NPR for two years as an editor and story consultant, had even been on the air, reporting, a few times. And that I had also written articles and essays for the *Post*. I told him I still had some contacts at the *Post* and NPR, but that they were incorruptible. I could not and, in fact, would not try to influence them.

"All right," he replied after a long pause. "Maybe," he mused as we said goodbye that day, "it will blow over."

It didn't.

Thirty-Three

ONE SUNDAY, LATE IN JANUARY 2010, A WEEK AFTER HE TELE-
phoned me, Menachem's photo was on the cover of the *Washington
Post Magazine*. The photo captured Menachem behind a stack of Torah scrolls, his arms folded, his head tilted warily, his lips locked, his
eyes narrowed and seemingly glaring into space. Maybe he was un-
shaven. If the photo was grim, the story was brutal. It detailed in an
irrefutable eight-page revelation that Rabbi Menachem Youlus was a
complete and utter fraud.

For the next few days, I felt numb. I had difficulty reading the story
from beginning to end. I would scan through a page or two, then put it
down and walk away, resisting the gruesome facts pouring out by the
paragraph and by the page about Menachem's devious conduct, his inability to document his stories and adventures, the contradictions in
his explanations, and his lack of accountability for the income he had
generated by selling the Torahs he had allegedly rescued and restored.

Right away, I received many e-mails from the people I had interviewed and from colleagues I had discussed the project with. "Is this
all true?" they asked. "What will you do now?" Some made jokes:

"Never trust a Hassidic rabbi who works for free!" I didn't know what was true and what wasn't, but I can assure you, I wasn't laughing.

What happened after the *Post* story was heartbreaking and disillusioning—and precipitated a flood of additionally devastating revelations. Prominent historians and Holocaust experts began weighing in with details demonstrating that many of the stories he told were downright impossible. Like his astonishing discovery at Bergen-Belsen concentration camp in Germany, when Menachem had tripped over a cracked floorboard and discovered a Torah that had been lost for more than seventy years. But after the *Post* story, historians realized that the building in which Menachem claimed to have discovered the Bergen-Belsen Torah had burned down ten years before he had visited there—or not visited.

For, as it turned out, Menachem hadn't visited Bergen-Belsen at all. Menachem hadn't visited Auschwitz, Ukraine, Germany, Poland, Russia, or anywhere else where he claimed to have discovered and rescued lost and desecrated Torahs. Passport records dug up by investigators at the United States Postal Service, on the case as soon as the *Post* article was published, revealed that Menachem had not left the country in a decade. He did take frequent trips to New York City, however, where Orthodox Jewish antiquities dealers sold him the Torahs about which he had conjured such amazing and remarkable tales.

Soon thereafter, the respected publisher who had bid so aggressively for my book cancelled my contract. I felt like a fool and a victim, as I did when I learned how Dr. Mason and the rest of my classmates had bamboozled me into believing that WWMG was something special and not a ruse or a sham. But much, much worse. What had I done to deserve this? I had wanted this book to be the crowning glory of my career, and I had harbored the vague idea or hope that Menachem's story would somehow lead me back to my heritage—my religion and roots. But then all of this excitement and anticipation and optimism collapsed on me in an instant.

Thirty-Four

IT'S NOT LIKE I GAVE UP ON THE MENACHEM BOOK. NO WAY.
For one thing, I couldn't believe that the publisher had cancelled the
contract. I mean, I believed it all right—what's not to believe?—but I
was more than a little surprised and disappointed. The original rabbi-
as-hero story was damn good, the kind of stuff that would resonate
with media. I had already fantasized about my appearance on Oprah
or Letterman. But wasn't this rabbi-as-hero-*and-charlatan* actually
a better, more intriguing tale? There were so many divergent story
lines to follow. Readers and viewers would eat it up. Or so I thought.

How had Menachem scammed the *New York Times* and most of
the major media throughout the world, over many years, for one
thing? I have written for the *Times*, and their fact checkers are relentless. How did they not fact-check Menachem? Or how did Menachem manipulate them? How did Menachem pull the wool over
the eyes of prestigious PhD historians who had validated all those Torahs? Or spin tall tales to the very well-connected Iraqi ambassador
to the United States? And his incessant blatant name dropping? So
downright ballsy, I guess, that no one thought to question. Would

you say that you knew Bill Clinton, were friendly with the family, or Rahm Emanuel, and had given them advice and counsel, if you weren't and hadn't? This subterfuge was remarkable. Cool, in fact. A story you can't make up—all about made-up stories! Which was a wild and incredible story in itself.

All this stuff ran through my mind constantly, a continuous looping tape, asking and answering to myself the same questions again and again. What was my publisher thinking, cancelling a contract? I had worked with them for years. They had published many of my books. If there was anything I knew about, it was what makes a great story—and this had everything. So I thought.

I approached the cancellation of my book as another rope test—a "never give in, never give up" Winston Churchill-like moment. My agent circulated an amended proposal to publishers—a number of different versions, in fact, one comparing the Menachem Torah Hunter story to the Frank Abagnale *Catch Me If You Can* best seller, which became a Steven Spielberg movie, and another to the Bernie Madoff Ponzi scheme. But there were no takers. Then I tried to turn the book into a novel, but I guess I am not much of a fiction writer, because I couldn't seem to make up anything more bizarre than the true Menachem story. I even sketched out a fictional version in which Menachem was a woman—Minna, in honor of Dr. Shuman's grandmother. Neither male nor female version worked.

The rejection of my efforts made me try even harder. "Never give up . . . never give in." My faith in Churchill's words never wavered. I had all kinds of other things to do in my life: completing other writing assignments; putting together anthologies, like my *End of Life* true stories collection; editing *Creative Nonfiction*; and teaching and creating nonfiction story projects for Arizona State University, where I had become a faculty member. Not that I bagged my responsibilities because of my Menachem obsession; I did what I needed to do. What choice did I have?

Besides, there were other things happening in my life that were just killing me. I am exaggerating, but that's the way it felt. My son had not only stopped taking classes at that prestigious university with only a semester or two to graduate, but, unhappy and unsatisfied with the care and attention he was receiving from social workers and psychiatrists, he was self-medicating, using the internet as a major resource for the experimental chemicals he was ingesting. He was in and out of hospitals, rehab facilities. He was invariably angry at me, at his mom, threatening terrible scary stuff to us and to himself, and quite literally out of control.

I don't want to say too much about this; my son deserves his privacy. The stigma of being mentally ill is a pervasive and destructive reality in this country today, unfairly blemishing the lives of people who cannot help themselves for their feelings, fears, and behaviors. But observing the person you most love and cherish in your life self-destruct, and not being able to do a damn thing about it, is the ultimate of all miseries. Each night you go to sleep, your phone beside you at bedside, hoping that it will not ring, for you know exactly what it might mean if it does detonate in the middle of the night, and each morning you wake up, wondering, first thing, what might happen to blow up your day or, in fact, destroy your life. You are, to say the least, obsessively wary, sometimes feeling as if you are about to burst.

I know I am not the only parent in such a state of frozen and helpless limbo. I have done my research, as usual. I have even written a book about childhood mental illness and the problems with which the children and their parents are confronted. There are, in this country right now, more than 17 million children and young adults with a mental illness diagnosis, rendered frozen and helpless by a system of care that is totally dysfunctional. No matter how hard I tried, there seemed to be nothing I could do to make a difference in my son's life. Even with the knowledge and insight I had gained researching and writing my book, I had no control over a person who had no control, which is maybe why I could not seem to give up on Menachem and his story. It seemed to me, then, that I had to keep going—on something, anything—to keep myself and my life afloat. So I focused and obsessed about my Menachem book to make myself feel productive and useful, in control of something.

I half remembered a line from a Tennessee Williams play I had read long ago: something about how everyone is trapped in their own lives and beliefs, and it is hell to get yourself out. Williams's actual line was even more depressing when I looked it up: "We all live in a house on fire, no fire department to call; no way out, just the upstairs window to look out of while the fire burns the house down with us trapped, locked in it."

After my seventieth birthday, during my struggle with the Menachem story over the following years, many remaining links to my very skimpy personal world were disintegrating. Not just my mother and my son, but my friend Susan was also lost to me, and to herself, after Iggy's death. No longer could we commiserate and share life and aging stories and dilemmas. Crushed and heartbroken over the loss of her husband, all she could do when I called her on the phone was weep. I sat there listening, receiver pressed against my hot flushed ear, trying to make her feel better with inane comforting comments and bad self-deprecating jokes, wishing all the while I could hang up and proceed through life as if Iggy was still alive or if I had never known him. Gradually, we stopped telephoning. It wasn't working. Then we texted periodically, but texts leave a lot to be desired in terms of intimacy. It's kind of like tweeting, isn't it? Little substance, less passion. The texting ended, too, after a while.

I once wrote to a friend that the deaths of Frank and Iggy and my mother, and my breakup with Michele, and my son's issues with mental illness, and my loss of the Menachem book all happened in the same year, my seventieth. Because that's how it felt, I guess. When I wrote that e-mail, I thought it was true. Much later, I reviewed the dates of all of this disappointment and turmoil, only to realize that this had been an inundation of awful years. Not just one. But to me, it seemed that seventy was a tsunami.

Thirty-Five

I HAD TO GET MYSELF TOGETHER. MOURNING MENACHEM—and banging my head against the wall with editors and publishers—was not helpful. And the only way I had ever gotten myself together in the past was to do what I did best, to do what had always grounded and settled and focused me—to write.

But for a while, I couldn't. Couldn't write anymore. Or write anything that made any sense. There was nothing coming out of me—about Menachem or, for that matter, anything else. Day after very long day, I would find myself sitting at my keyboard, staring at a blank display, eating toast smeared with real butter, cookies, whatever, waiting for inspiration, ideas, and a fresh spin, which would not come. This wasn't what people call "writer's block." I wasn't blocked; I was beaten. All I wanted to do was cry. This was so stupid, so unlike me, the rope test kid, but all I wanted to do was weep and sob and let myself go. Such a strange and nagging feeling, thinking about and feeling like crying. Giving up and giving in—to what? I didn't know. I couldn't even give in to crying.

And what would that accomplish anyway? At my age, for God's sake. I was seventy years old, more than seventy now. I wasn't getting any younger, and the way I was acting, I wasn't getting any smarter, either. Time to face the facts: all these people who were an integral part of my life were, in one way or another, history, or in very shaky territory. And my book, this Menachem book, my writing life, which had kept me going, was also history. Or if not history, then in the most painful limbo I had yet experienced.

During that time I walked Walnut incessantly. Walnut Street is the main drag in Pittsburgh's Shadyside neighborhood. I've lived a couple of blocks from Walnut, off and on, for forty-five years—in many different guises and disguises. When I first came to Shadyside, I was a beatnik—young, seeking pot and poetry, and hungry for cool conversation about Kerouac and Ginsberg. Walnut Street teemed with wannabe beats and bearded men and sinewy, lazy-eyed women encased in black. I was still in Shadyside when I became a hippie a decade later, raunchy with outlandish sideburns, cultivating grass in my backyard to tempt the coeds. "Free love! Kill the pigs! Fuck the Establishment." And then, a few years later, I was walking Walnut as a tweedy college professor.

Walnut Street had these unique stores, like the leather shop, infamous for porn and pot, run by a ponytailed beatnik named Ringo. The best jazz in America came to the Encore. Keith Jarrett, Chick Corea, Stanley Turrentine. The Encore served great steaks and was dark as a dungeon; you could do almost anything with a date or someone you just groped, who groped you back, in the squashed-together crowd. The Encore was open until the early morning. You could get a martini at 3 a.m. Or go across Walnut to the Gazebo for the best pastrami omelet from New York to Chicago.

Walnut has changed since I first wandered that street, as have I. It is newer, glitzier, younger, while I have gotten older, much older.

The Encore is now the Steel Cactus, serving nachos-and-cheese cuisine. There's an honest-to-God steel cactus—a gigantic prickly penis that you have to dodge—near the middle of the sidewalk. It lights up at night in lime green. The days of jazz and pot and sex at the Encore are long forgotten, except by us old folk, once the beats and later the hippies. Sometimes I still feel like I belong. I recognize a few people who are still walking Walnut, hanging on, remembering what it used to be, like Ringo. Or maybe just pretending, imagining that, in some ways, it is still the same.

But I also feel like a ghost or a shadow as I walk the streets, rather than a person in real time and a native, among so many graduate students and the hordes of millennials who don't seem to notice me and wouldn't know what to say to me or how to relate if, on the off chance, we did make a connection. Like one unusually friendly young woman at Starbucks recently who leaned over my shoulder and asked me what I was reading. And when I said, "Mailer," she replied, "I never read direct mail."

TIME PASSES, AND IT GETS EASIER TO STAY IN YOUR HOUSE and live with your memories and, alas, your resentments, to drink red wine and watch *Law and Order* reruns, which is how I lived for a while.

Law and Order was perfect for my state of mind. (I am talking about the original TV series and not the spin-off *SVU* and *Criminal Intent*; the original was prime time on NBC for a record twenty-four years.) The show had great characters, who stayed long enough in their roles that you could get to know them and recognize their personalities and motivations. Like, on the "order" side, Jack McCoy (Sam Waterston), the crusading executive assistant district attorney who could and often did tightrope legal and ethical boundaries to win his cases. He had a bevy of women assistants, who were intelligent, forceful, dedicated to justice, and loyal, including Angie Harmon, Jill Hennessy and Annie Parisse.

Jerry Orbach played the lead senior detective, Lennie Briscoe, on the "law" side, along with junior detective Chris Noth (later "Big" on *Sex and the City*) who remained with the series six years, followed by Benjamin Bratt and Jesse L. Martin. Their superior, Lieutenant Anita Van Buren, played by S. Epatha Merkerson, on the show for twenty years, is especially memorable because of her calm demeanor and incisive analysis of each investigative step of the case. She persevered despite the ways in which her superiors would take her to task and block deserved promotions; African American women supervisory personnel were not, as you can imagine, particularly popular at the NYPD then and maybe now.

What I like about *Law and Order*, what drew me to it day and night, is, basically, the reliable structure to every episode. It would begin almost always with a scene in which passersby or uniformed officers discover a homicide. Then the detectives arrive, scope out the crime scene. Invariably the senior detective (Briscoe was the best) ends the first scene with a clever or cryptic remark. After a series of commercials, the detectives are back at headquarters discussing the case with Van Buren. Many investigative fits and starts and a few surprises follow, and more intervening commercials come and go until a suspect is apprehended and the lawyers take over.

For McCoy and his assistants there are almost always many legal turnabouts and complications in and out of the courtroom until they (usually) convict the suspect, often on the strength of McCoy's brilliant and passionate final argument. There are other moments I expect and appreciate, like the subtle yet forceful music that emerges preceding a dramatic confession, when the suspect realizes that McCoy has the goods on them. And who can forget the legendary *Law and Order* "dun-dun" sound, the signature of the show?

I watched those episodes repeatedly—I still do, in fact—because I knew exactly what was going to happen, scene by scene, episode after episode, and even though I had seen most, all 364 of them, I think, maybe as many as three or four times, I continued watching and watching because there would be no surprises. All that would happen I expected and anticipated from start to finish, and all those characters like McCoy and even Briscoe, who died in 2009, would keep coming back, in the game, episode after episode, ad infinitum. Just like I wished my life was—totally and completely and utterly predictable. To put it bluntly, I was damn unhappy. And, except for McCoy and Briscoe and the rest, pretty much alone.

During this period I thought a lot about a novelist I knew and admired. Theodore Weesner's first novel, *The Car Thief*, a coming-of-age tale about an alienated teenager on the run from society, published in the 1970s, had been praised worldwide: "a literary gem," according to many critics. Other than in literary circles, however, the book was never a hit. Nor were any of his other books, including his fifth, *True Detective*, which in the late 1980s received a scathing review in the *New York Times Book Review*. Whereupon Weesner answered the *Times*'s editors with a letter the paper published verbatim. Weesner scolded the *Times* because the review was too short and placed "inconspicuously." Petty grievances. But the last few sentences were unforgettable, words that tens of thousands of writers wish they had had the courage to confront reviewers or readers with. "I cannot deal with this," Weesner wrote. "Your reviewer did not even understand what he read. I repeat: Your reviewer did not even understand what he read. And you printed it. You broke my heart. You owe me so much more than an apology."

This—*You broke my heart*—is what I wanted to say to Menachem, and to my publisher, who had taken away a project I had given my days and nights to, my working life to, my faith and *my heart*, for years. Many years before and after my contract cancellation!

Don't you know what writers do, how they give themselves to

their work and their stories in isolation, how they/we squeeze every last idea and emotion onto the page, day after relentless day, rethinking, revising, living with the book inside our heads while going through the motions of the world whirling around us, shopping, teaching, selling shoes, whatever? Don't you know, understand, empathize? Weesner was imploring the *Times* and its readers to understand and appreciate our process and our misery. *You owe me so much more than an apology.* And perhaps they did, which is also perhaps why the *Times* published his unusually candid letter.

Which leads to another aspect of writing and being a writer. If we die by the book, we also live by the book and the process of writing. Because no matter what we confront in the world day to day—poverty, tragedy, alienation, abandonment—we always have our outlets, the books or essays or stories to which we give all we've got, alone in our rooms or in coffee shops, wherever. The words on the page we eke out can in the end destroy us, but they will also save us if we don't give up or give in to despair.

I remember reading an introduction to an edition of the autobiography of Johann Wolfgang von Goethe by the British writer Humphrey Trevelyan. I'm no Goethe scholar, but he was a pretty amazing guy, a poet, playwright, novelist, scientist, statesman, theatre director, artist, you name it. So was Trevelyan, for that matter—a diplomat, once ambassador to the Soviet Union, and a prolific writer and biographer, who was quite taken by how Goethe had continually reinvented himself. Trevelyan observed that to achieve greatness, an artist must "never grow complacent, never be content with life and always demand the impossible." And, he added, when he—the artist—cannot achieve "the impossible," he "must despair."

I know what Trevelyan is positing. Even though the impossible may not be reachable, let alone practical, that shouldn't impede efforts or ambition or dreams. But the consequences of not achieving what you so desperately desire—that despair thing—really got stuck with me. What an awful word, a connotation of hopelessness and defeat that I did not want to associate myself with. Even when my father lost his store, pulled a gigantic Shimmy, he may have despaired, but he too in some ways reinvented himself. At the very least, he reevaluated, unstuck himself, and moved on. As did my mother in her assisted existing facility. As did Dr. Starzl. But could I? I knew in my heart that I must, that the Menachem book was dead and buried, that I should drag the Menachem folder from Dropbox into the backup files on my Time Machine—or maybe even press "delete" and eradicate it and him from my life.

Just because I could not write any more about Menachem and his Torah capers didn't mean I could not write about the important subjects and ideas that affected lots of people around the world. Like aging. Like loss. Like fear of loneliness, fear of being alone. About me and about knowing where I want to be grounded and where I want to go for the next four or five years. Or maybe many more, if the promise of my genetics means anything. I've got to keep trying. Not crying. I cannot, I decided, I will not, I vowed, continue to allow myself this dismal and destructive paralysis.

I don't regret the path I chose as a writer who immersed himself with strangers, but who could rarely hold on to them as friends. This is the life I pursued, the fork in the road I took. But as time passed, I began—slowly—to force myself to understand, to realize, that I was more fortunate than many of my contemporaries. It is such a cliché, but true. I had my health, and I had my sense of person. I mean, I knew who and what I was—and what I was not. And what I was missing. Regret was a waste of time. You can't do anything about what you have done. Better to do something new than nothing instead. But it took me a while, lots of *Law and Order* limbo, lots of walking and thinking up and down Walnut, to come to grips with this truth.

Thirty-Six

MENACHEM'S SENTENCING HEARING—HE HAD, IN THE END, confessed and pled guilty to mail and wire fraud—took place at the Foley Square Courthouse, the U.S. District Court for the Southern District of New York, on Pearl Street in downtown Manhattan. He was represented by a stocky middle-aged man in a wrinkled blue suit, Benjamin Brafman, who had previously defended Sean Combs, Michael Jackson, and, most recently at the time, Dominique Strauss-Kahn. It is enough to say that he was a real hotshot defense attorney—one of the best, according to *Esquire Magazine*, in the business.

That afternoon I listened to Brafman plead his case for leniency in a courtroom packed on one side with reporters, observers, and a few detractors, and on the other with black-clad men and women supporters—grim and somber, swaying and praying for their beloved rabbi and Torah-hunting savior.

Attorney Brafman made an emotional plea. The rabbi's family would be destitute. The rabbi's charitable work should be considered, and his frail health—he had recently suffered a heart attack. Brafman cited case after case in which the U.S. District Court had shown leniency to men who had committed white-collar crimes but had helped their communities, as had Menachem. And this was the clincher: the rabbi was giving back all of the money he had misappropriated and concealed. Menachem had not vacationed with the money, gambled it away in Atlantic City, or bought a fancy car. He had many bank accounts and stock funds with three different brokers but had only touched the principal of any of them to send his eight children to private schools.

From the outset, however, there had been a catch to the rabbi's offer to return all the money. State and federal investigators had gradually amassed information that showed how calculating Menachem could be. At first Menachem denied having any money, but as evidence mounted against him, he said he would give back $200,000—that was all he had. Then, after more evidence was uncovered, he agreed to give back $500,000; *this* was the extent of his wealth. Finally, as even more illustrations of his deviousness came out, he agreed, after nearly a year of frequent denials and damning admissions, to return the complete mother lode: $1.2 million.

"What was that all about? What motivations were behind this confused mix-message man?" Brafman asked the packed courtroom in his summation, basing his case on Menachem's unbalanced mental state, his psychopathic behavior, and his poor health.

"Only God knows," the judge, the Honorable Colleen McMahon, replied after Brafman had rested. "He was crazy—and he suffered from the evil of greed."

In rejecting his appeal for leniency, Judge McMahon, a devout Catholic, continued: "For a member of the clergy to prey on the religious sensibilities of these victims is, frankly, a crime that turns my stomach in the way that few others do."

Menachem began his four-and-and-half-year prison term later that year, after the Jewish High Holy Days, at the Federal Correctional Institution in Otisville, New York, a medium-security facility housing male offenders. There he would be permitted to keep kosher.

Brafman, clearly and unusually conflicted, told the court before the sentence was pronounced, even as he pled for leniency for his client: "I did not want to be in this case—this is, in thirty-seven years, one of the worst three or four moments I think I have ever had to spend in the well of a courtroom."

I found out later that Brafman had only agreed to defend Menachem because his father persuaded him to do so. And why was that? First because his father, a Holocaust survivor, had once "rescued" a Torah and smuggled it out of Poland in a shroud. When questioned about the contents of the shroud by border guards, he told them it contained the body of his dead son. A worthy, Menachem-like story, for sure. And much later, years later, Brafman's father had purchased another Torah for his own synagogue—from Menachem.

Thirty-Seven

I WAS COMING BACK TO PITTSBURGH ONE FEBRUARY NIGHT from Arizona, where I had been teaching at Arizona State University for the past few years.

I got on a plane on what I can only describe as a diamond of a day, bright and sunny, with a refreshing breeze, mid-seventies . . . and landed in the Burgh in an icy windstorm at 2 a.m.—plane delayed because of weather, ten degrees below zero—and headed home from the airport.

Pittsburgh is the second gloomiest city in the country, behind Seattle and Buffalo, which are tied for first, according to the Dreariness Index. Arizona is different, obviously, sometimes better, but lots of weather downsides. While delightful in the winter months, the heat in summer is intense, worse even than that old furnace I had labored in during my boot camp days, before I passed the rope test. During July and August, especially, you try to go out of doors to exercise or do errands in the early morning or after sundown. It's so hot at midday—115 degrees not unusual—you can't, according to my students, wear flip-flops walking across campus. If you stop for a moment to say hello to a friend, the rubber will melt and adhere to the pavement. Fortunately, I am rarely on campus then. And I never wear flip-flops.

But this Arizona gig had opened a few new and fascinating doors for me. Previously, for nearly thirty years, I had been part of the University of Pittsburgh's creative writing program—the creative nonfiction guy among a dozen poets and novelists. Pitt in many ways was a good place to be for me, in my hometown, where I had been discovered, sort of, and encouraged by Mr. Meyers and others. The university that had allowed me to achieve a full professorship with tenure despite my having no advanced degree. For a long while I had not imagined that I would be anywhere else through my teaching career. But in 2007 I was invited to become a visiting distinguished writer in residence for a semester at ASU in Tempe and, just for a change of pace, I jumped at the opportunity.

Since its inception nearly a century ago, ASU was known best as a party school, populated by locals mostly, with a large influx of students from California unable to satisfy admission requirements to the many prestigious California institutions like Stanford and UCLA. Scholarship was not their thing, good times were. But because of the appointment of a new president, Michael M. Crow, previously a provost at Columbia University, the place was rapidly changing. Crow had coined the phrase "the New American University" and was restructuring traditional academic departments and establishing interdisciplinary knowledge centers, focusing on strategic partnerships and entrepreneurship to reflect the way in which science and technology education needed to interact with the real world, and in the process changing the face of higher education. Or so he hoped. Because of Crow, ASU was quickly transformed into what *USA Today* called the most innovative university in the country, with outreach platforms linked with Google and Apple, as well as an ingenious arrangement with Starbucks that allowed all employed baristas to attend ASU online for free. I wasn't involved in the Starbucks program—although I loved the idea because of my Starbucks attachment. Made me feel right at home.

As a visiting professor at ASU initially, I taught pretty much the same writing-workshop-oriented courses I was teaching at Pitt in the creative writing program. However, because of an immersion book I had recently published about robotics, I had a number of opportunities to interact with grad students and faculty in the interdisciplinary centers related to science and technology. One talk I gave about the power of stories to students at ASU's nanotechnology center, using nonfiction narrative to communicate difficult-to-understand subjects and concepts to the general public, led to a conversation with an audience member who was director of a science policy think tank. It had a mouthful of a name: the Consortium for Science, Policy and Outcomes (referred to on campus as CSPO, pronounced "Seespo"), but the director was frustrated with the fact that the public did not understand science policy or policy generally, and the scholars in their group, a wonky bunch, had no real interest in reaching out to people like us—the naïve and uninformed—to explain and highlight what they did. The director wanted this to change.

Opportunity happened quickly, as things tend to do under the leadership of President Crow, who had lured Nobelists and other prestigious scholars and scientists to ASU, and I soon accepted a generous offer to become distinguished writer in residence in CSPO and a professor with tenure.

It's not that I had never considered leaving Pitt. But I did not want to be part of another creative writing program. There was nothing that I could achieve teaching the same courses at another university that I wasn't already accomplishing in Pittsburgh. But with my creative nonfiction books about robotics and about healthcare—transplantation, pediatrics, veterinary medicine, mental illness—I had come to see that there was a lot about such crucial subjects that the public did not and would never understand and appreciate unless scientists, engineers, physicians, and policy professionals—the people who knew all of this vital changing-the-world stuff—would take a different approach to communicating their visions and knowledge through storytelling. And President Crow and the think tank leaders wanted new ideas and programs, not just the traditional graduate courses with the traditional workshop atmosphere. So I jumped at the chance to do something different and stretch my story-writing and interdisciplinary credentials.

Within a few years, I wrote a proposal to the National Science Foundation and received support for the launch of an international program bringing creative nonfiction writers and science policy wonks together to collaborate and teach one another what they knew. The program was called Think Write Publish (TWP). The wonks taught the writers how they researched and analyzed the future to design and fashion policy, while the writers showed the "thinkers" how to transform their ideas and research processes into story. Think Write Publish has had larger and more expanded iterations over the years, most recently bringing together writers and scholars to write creative nonfiction about the intersection between science and religion. The fellows selected for the program, who came from as far away as Afghanistan, were to eventually publish books and articles, which led to radio interviews and TV appearances and featured speaking engagements at prestigious conferences, exactly the way in which universities establish and gauge influence and prominence.

I have to say that I was way behind the curve with all of this policy stuff, the concern with reshaping the future in a safe and well-defined way—what my new colleagues were calling "responsible innovation." But I learned a lot and was excited and invigorated by how I could open new avenues of communication between the experts and those who would be impacted by their ideas and achievements, through what I had been practicing throughout my life: writing and teaching true stories. Creative writing programs traditionally focus on craft or story-writing technique and not so much on the message inherent in the story—the reason for writing, actually. Not that craft and technique are unimportant or less important. But a better balance between message and technique, what you are saying and how you say it, would make writers more productive, provide more employment possibilities, and allow their words to make a greater impact.

Besides, I appreciated the opportunity to do something different—a new kind of immersion for me—for I not only had to be the chameleon at CSPO, to fit in seamlessly, but I had to be part of the program as well. I could not so easily distance myself as a rebel, outcast, different-drummer, Cleat kind of guy.

And I liked my new colleagues and the people I met in the Phoenix area. They are good people with a keen respect for their environment and the beauty and value of the desert. And there's a combined casualness and grittiness about the place. It's true that the politics suck; the only place other than Arizona and some areas in the Deep South where Sheriff Joe Arpaio could become a hero might be Pittsburgh. And I also like the fact that few people at ASU are born and raised there. They come from all over, some for the great weather in the winter and spring, but most for the opportunity. The place is exploding with activity, especially in the Tempe-Phoenix area, where the university dominates the landscape and the culture. Everyone you meet is trying in a way to reinvent themselves, it seems—including, to a certain extent, me.

At the time I started at ASU, Frank and Iggy and my mother were still alive, my son in school, my Menachem book still in play, and *Creative Nonfiction* in the black because of the excellent staff I had put together and my dogged fundraising. Things were okay in Pittsburgh. So even though I would be out of pocket a lot in the sun-drenched Southwest, I assumed that I could come and go in Pittsburgh with some confidence that the little secure world I left behind would remain intact. And despite having this obligation in Tempe, where I was energized by what I was doing, I did find myself returning to the Burgh more and more often—sometimes weekly, in fact, especially as my mother began to fade and the eventual loss of my Menachem book continued to torture and tantalize me. Even when the delights of spring and summer turned into the nastiest of winters, as I experienced that night getting off the plane.

One thing about Pittsburgh that I really admire is the city at night, especially as you see it when driving in from the Greater Pittsburgh International Airport. You will ride twenty or twenty-five minutes through a dark and desolate parkway and then go through the Fort Pitt Tunnels. The view is not too impressive. Gloomy, littered with cheesy billboards and half-finished road renovation projects, often leading to sporadic detours. But when you emerge from the tunnels, all of the office buildings explode with eye-blinding light, along with the two open stadiums along the rivers—PNC Park, where the Pirates play, and Heinz Field, home of the Steelers—also lit up. Not to mention a glittering newish Three Rivers Casino. And Pittsburgh has its Point, where two rivers, the Allegheny, which made Frederick Williams famous, and the Monongahela, converge to form the Ohio. There's an illuminated fountain there. All of these lights, alive at the same time, their sparkle magnified by the rivers, cause an explosion that sets the city aflame. It's quite astounding, especially in contrast to the shabby gloom you left behind at the entrance to the tunnel. It's the most impressive view of most any medium-sized city I have ever seen. This always cheers me, despite the awful Pittsburgh winter.

But as soon as I got home that night, as soon as I stepped through the doorway, I knew something was wrong. I could hear it. I went down to the basement and saw the brown water gushing from a pipe that had burst in the subzero cold. The entire basement was flooded. I picked my way through the icy water, waist deep, found the shut-off valves, then retreated to my bedroom, dried myself off, and went to sleep. In the morning I walked the four blocks of Walnut to Starbucks for my venti, planning to return, wait for a reasonable hour, and then call the plumber.

On the way back, I slipped on the ice. The venti went up in the air as I went down on the ground, and then, quite ridiculously, landed on my head. It was like I was playing right field again at the old Roosevelt School playground. I was slightly singed and nearly drenched. I felt stupid and sore—landed right on my ass—but it was too absurd to do anything other than gather myself up, falling a few more times on the ice in the process, and slip and slide back up the street for a refill.

That morning I stopped at the table where the Starbucks regulars usually gathered and told my stupid story, with the special twist that I had left an absolutely glorious day in Arizona to be back in the "Pittsburgh refrigerator." I rarely took the time to talk to these folks at Starbucks; I usually grabbed my venti and headed to the door with a "see-you-all-later-have-a-great-day" wave and a mumbled "goodbye." But this story was funny and dumb, so I guess I wanted to share it with folks who would understand how Pittsburgh-weather-typical it was.

After listening to and laughing with me, one guy wanted to know why I'd been in Arizona. Was it vacation? And another guy—I did not remember either of their names, but they were very familiar faces, part of the Starbucks regular group—changed the subject slightly and asked about my classes at Pitt.

I looked at them both, and everyone else who was part of this interaction, maybe a half dozen people, and for an instant I didn't know what to say. A couple of these folks I had known for many years—sort of. They'd seen me walking Walnut and coming and going at Starbucks for as long as I could remember. Harry, whiskered and somewhat slow-moving, was an architect who had helped design many of the houses and businesses in the Shadyside area; we once shared office space side by side in a building where my magazine was then located. And Michael, the leader and convener of the group, retired now, had owned a popular delicatessen located in an alley right off Walnut. I had hung out there from time to time in the old days. And there was also Betsy, who sold fine wrist watches and jewelry at a shop on the street.

And yet they, or some of them, didn't know why I was in Arizona? As often as I had made my Starbucks entrance and exit and sporadically shot the breeze with them, I had never mentioned that I had changed jobs, leaving the University of Pittsburgh for Arizona State? That I had been commuting?

I quickly got myself together and replied, somewhat curtly, "I was there on business." That was all I could figure to say right then without getting involved in long explanations. And then I took my leave, walking back to my house much more carefully. One icy slipping incident was enough for one morning. And besides, there was the plumber and the dirty brown flood in my basement to deal with.

Thirty-Eight

I DIDN'T GIVE THAT INTERACTION AT STARBUCKS ANY THOUGHT until later. And when I did think about it, over a glass of wine that night, with my water back on and my basement gradually draining, I realized that the reason they didn't know even the barest details of my life was because maybe I'd never told them very much, maybe not anything—and that was on me, not them. How would they know about me if I didn't tell them?

It's not that I never talked to people at Starbucks and elsewhere on Walnut. I did chitchat—I was a good chitchatter when I wanted to be—but never in any depth. I always purposely held back. What was that all about?

Did I not want them to know much, anything, about me? Did I want to be considered mysterious, anonymous, distant? An in-and-out, slam-bam-thank-you-ma'am shadow character? The answers, I concluded, were yes and no.

Yes, because the main reason I went to Starbucks was for my venti, and the main reason I walked to Starbucks or somewhere, anywhere, on Walnut Street so often was to break away from my keyboard and contemplate what I was doing, saying, writing on that day. I did not always go into Starbucks; I was often just walking the street to breath some fresh air and review in my head what I had been writing, or trying to write. Mostly, when I walked, I kept to myself.

And even when I did run into people and did in fact engage, albeit momentarily, I was always careful to not be sucked into a conversation that would distract me and make me eventually regret losing time. Invariably, even if I found myself enjoying the interaction, I would cut it short; I got itchy, like there was a time limit or something for socialization, because then maybe they would expect me to do this, chat on aimlessly, every day. Which might interrupt the focus on my work. Or what if I just simply didn't want to talk that day, and if I demurred, would I come off as rude? And that, either way, would suck.

And also, most—not all—of the Starbucks regulars in the morning, those who were sitting around, were in my general age range, some retired or nearing retirement. I was afraid that they would start joking about how they, *we*, were old and decrepit and maybe would be dead soon. I am not sure that ever happened, I have no reason to assume it did happen, but if by chance it would, I wanted in advance to avoid it.

So I guess, when I thought about it, I actually didn't want them to know too much about my life. I had established a carefully controlled distance between me and them, or even perhaps between me and the rest of the world. Maybe that's exactly what I wanted. Or maybe I just wanted them to wonder about me?

On the other hand, I was walking Walnut, when in town, maybe ten times a day, shopping and stopping at various places—at Starbucks at least three times in the morning and once in a while in the afternoon when I needed a caffeine hit, or a bit of company. What "company" then meant to me, evidently, was seeing people I recognized and waving to them. Many days, embarrassingly enough, this up-

and-down-Walnut habit was my main social activity. And there were many other people around, not just Starbucks folks, that I could run into, could have talked with—younger people, working people, not to mention some very attractive women who, if I allowed my imagination to run away a bit, and if I took the time to probe, I might discover were widows, divorcees looking for conversation or more. Or maybe even better, science policy wonks!

So, no, maybe I was working against myself, maybe if the Walnut Shadyside folks knew more about me, I would have more friends. Maybe have some fun and company. Maybe I was going about getting a social life in the wrong way. If I wanted a social life, that is.

But the situation, my dilemma, my back and forth, my yes and no, was complicated.

I had this problem talking about myself. I knew it had to do with the fact that I was a professional listener and listening was what I did best. In my social interactions, I invariably sat back and waited for people to tell me whatever the hell they wanted to tell me. And then I would jump on what they told me and probe, asking follow-up questions, like any good reporter. This could take a long time, go in many different directions, and all the while I would be safe; never a word about me. This was the easiest way to socialize, if that was in fact what I was doing. People liked other people who listened.

And listening worked pretty well with men. Communicating with men, most men, is generally easier because they really don't want you to share a lot of a personal nature. It seems to make them uncomfortable. Sports, politics, money, harangues with bosses and clients, that's the stuff to get deep—if you want to call it deep—with guys. But it is not that easy with women. Women want to be more personal, sooner or later—and super-detailed. Generally, I had a lot of trouble in my relationships with women because I resisted telling them anything about myself—unless, of course, they asked. And even then, I only answered their questions; I rarely elaborated, unless I was pressed.

"How was your day?" Michele used to say to me.

"It was okay," I would reply.

"What did you do?" she would persist.

I never knew what to say because, in some ways, my life was so complicated, dealing with my son, writing about Menachem or something else, Arizona and CSPO, my magazine, Frank's death. Iggy. It took such an effort, and I didn't want to hear myself talking about all this stuff. What would it accomplish other than just plain exhausting and annoying me?

So I would reply, "I worked."

Not too satisfying, quite annoying and frustrating for her.

I realize now, I even knew it then, but I guess I wasn't willing or smart enough to deal with it, that I was being selfish, stupid in fact, and that Michele especially and a few others who asked those questions really cared about me and wouldn't be asking if they didn't. They really wanted to know. And I sure wanted someone, more than just someone, lots of people, to care about my health, about my life, the ups and the downs, how I was feeling about anything and everything. About the loss of Frank, Iggy, Mollie, my Menachem humiliation and defeat. My deflections clearly worked against me. So self-defeating.

And it's not as if I didn't want to talk about myself. I did. But I couldn't quite force myself to spit out any of this news, bad or good. It was difficult to depart from my usual stoic, distanced façade and talk about stuff that might unmask me. Even if I wanted, down deep, to be unmasked.

And I didn't want my age to come into those conversations, any conversation, especially with folks I hardly knew and didn't trust. I did not want to hear those "When will you retire?" or "How old are you?" questions that people inevitably seem to ask.

It wasn't because I didn't want to think about those Iggy-Menachem-Frank-Mollie-retirement answers and respond—or even

CSPO or *Creative Nonfiction*. I was thinking about them all the time and probably talking about them aloud and alone in my head as I walked up and down the street, maybe even discussing this stuff with Mr. Skink. But bringing them out into the open made me feel so damn vulnerable. Not to mention old and on my way out. Dwelling on them is not what I wanted to do.

What I wanted to do was write, exercise, eat with the teeth I had left (and replace them), see whatever it is I could see through all those appearing and disappearing floaters—and not think about what was happening to me until the last possible moment. I was not even doing what my mother had invariably told me whenever we were faced with decisions. I was not, in this case, waiting to see what happened. I was finding ways of not quite confronting or realizing what was happening, or at least not dwelling on it overmuch.

But if I didn't want to be personal with people—and I wasn't sure that that was true—why not talk about my work? Work is what I most cared about, work is how I distinguished myself from others. Work is what kept me going in the face of disappointment. And I didn't have to talk about Menachem if that got me down or embarrassed me for being such a sucker for a story. It was not as if I was a one-book pony. For God's sake, I had been writing and teaching and editing throughout my adult life. But, of course, I had an answer for that, too.

I didn't want to come off as a braggart and a blowhard by starting to tell people, especially people I did not know too well, all that I have accomplished and everything I did on a given day. And besides, it was difficult for me to explain "science policy think tank," not to mention CSPO—or Seespo. Sometimes I had to say "Consortium for Science Policy and Outcomes" half dozen times for people to remember it, let alone get it, if they ever did get it. And creative nonfiction? I can't count how many people thought they were being clever when they told me, "That's an oxymoron."

God knows, I was/am impatient. But trying to explain what I did was difficult and, if you were really going to do it justice, required long and probably boring explanations. And could I actually do it justice? Do people really care about the intersection between science and religion or, for that matter, liver transplantation? Half the time when I did try to elaborate on one of the things I was doing or writing, I could tell that I was quickly losing my audience. Eyes glazing over. People, it seemed, wanted sound bites, 140-character tweets.

Sometimes just telling people that I was a writer turned out to be really deflating. Not at all worthwhile. Responses, to say the least, were unsatisfactory, embarrassing, and discouraging, like:

"Oh man, you should write about me. My life is a book."

Or worse: "Have I ever read anything you've written?"

I never know what to say to that.

Once, a guy stopped me on the street and said he had heard I was a writer. I told him I was.

"Do you do book signings?" he asked.

"Yes!" I was ready to invite him to my next event. This was encouraging.

"Would you mind," he then asked, "signing my copy of *Slaughterhouse Five*?"

Not that I believed that people were being snide or nasty; they just mostly didn't know what to say to a writer, young or old, let alone about a science policy think tank—or creative nonfiction. So they searched for something, anything clever, and sometimes they babbled. Or were, without realizing it, downright hurtful and dismissive. And I invariably felt like a jerk, explaining, listening and trying to respond, even though I knew that they meant absolutely no harm.

And most writers don't talk about what they are writing, anyway. If you talk it out, then maybe you won't write it out. Once it's out, it's out! That's the danger of being friendly and open, at least from a writer's narrow and sometimes rigid viewpoint. Or my narrow and rigid viewpoint. I know writers who do talk about their work, going on and on, but that's usually in the company of other writers. And even then, I admit, they often bore me to death. Or make me jealous.

Understand: If people asked me a question, I would answer it. If they asked more questions, I would answer some more, whether professional or personal. I would give them what they indicated they wanted, but how do I know how much they really want to hear? Where should I start? How deep do I go?

Why not just send them to my website? Or hand them my card?

And yet, as I thought this all out, considering, weighing, debating, seemingly ceaselessly, I began to slowly understand that I was being unrealistic. I couldn't blame other people for my insecurities and my ongoing struggle to bolster and enforce my outsider image. It was too easy to blame other people. Other people would not change just to make me feel better or accommodate my eccentricities. Maybe I had good reasons to act the way I did, but they weren't good enough reasons if I wanted a better and more fulfilling life. So what if they didn't read my books? To be honest, hardly anyone does. Maybe I had to do the changing myself. If so, how much was I willing to change? There was no easy answer.

The thing is, I liked the image I had presented my entire life of being a loner. A totally self-sufficient dude, a guy doing his own thing. I didn't need to be picked first or second at Roosevelt Field and I didn't care anymore that I was shuttled off to right field because I was so lame I could not catch a fly ball. Who the hell wants to be part of WWMG, a group of insecure unimpressive boys who bonded together based upon a joke and a lie, one of whom had to change his name just to function as a professional? I was not like any of those guys; I was a stand-alone, go-it-alone "meshuggeneh with a mission."

I was Sal Paradise cruising the country, doing whatever the hell I wanted without worry or concern for what other people thought about it. I was like Art Williams throwing myself into the racist national pastime trying to make a difference despite ridicule, or even Dr. Starzl, who cared not a whit about commentators or critics and who knew in his heart that what he was doing was goddamn right, looking neither to the left or right, but plunging full steam ahead focused on his mission. Those were the guys I wanted to write about, the lives I most admired, and the way I wanted people to perceive me, true or not.

And professionally, in many ways, I had succeeded in that quest. I had pioneered this genre, creative nonfiction, since the nineteen-seventies, when lots of people in publishing or in the academy were dismissive of the label and what it meant. But on a personal level, that achievement, I realized, hadn't done me any damn good at all. I had worked so hard to accomplish what I thought I wanted. And then, when I got it, achieved my goal, it didn't really provide nearly the satisfaction I had anticipated.

Don't get me wrong: I was not backing down. I had no intention of making a radical change; that would have been stupid, not at all me and, well, not even possible. But it was time to make, let us call it, an "attitude adjustment."

I am not saying that I sat down and thought this all out one night over a glass or two—or three—of wine and then magically had an epiphany. But I did gradually come to realize over many days and nights and glasses of wine, and endless self-probing, how goddamn intractable I had become. And how my intractability was working against me.

Age—aging—does this to you. While it is true that the older you get, the more you know, it is also true that as you get older you know what works for you, how to conduct your life to get through every day and make it work with as few unnecessary roadblocks or detours as possible. Life becomes one day at a time, one step after another, just to get by, to hang in and hang on as long as possible, which is pretty much okay, if "okay" is enough for you. If "okay" is what you want the rest of your life to be all about, then there's really no reason to change at all.

Thirty-Nine

I ONCE HAD A CONVERSATION WITH A GUY I KNEW, LET'S CALL
him Phil, about the ways in which one might become successful as a
writer. It all had to do with climbing a flagpole—symbolically. And
it began in Nantucket, while we were waiting for the ferry to take us
back to the mainland.

Phil and I were both writing short pieces of prose at the time, Phil
mostly fiction and me mostly nonfiction. But in those early days,
we might have gone either way if some editor or publisher had responded favorably to the work we submitted. We would have jumped
at the encouragement and altered our direction in hopes of being
"discovered."

Phil and I were around the same age and pretty much at the same
beginning stages of our careers, having published very little. We
were both hopeful and enthusiastic, but at odds, completely oppo-
sites, in the way we approached our writing careers. Looking back, I
often think of Phil and me as tortoise-and-hare guys. Or maybe the
hi-lo duo.

Because here was the difference between the two of us, how we were mapping our careers. After Phil wrote an essay or a story, he would send it immediately to the *New Yorker* or *Harper's* or *Esquire*—the three most prestigious magazines a writer could ever hope to be published in back then, and maybe now.

While it is not impossible for writers in the early stages of their careers to be discovered by such exclusive publications, it is highly unlikely. For one thing, the competition is intense. Since these are the best (and some of the highest-paying) magazines in the world, you are up against the elite writers like, in those days, Updike or Roth or Joan Didion or Tom Wolfe, to name a few.

And for another thing, even if you were, in fact, very talented, a budding Hemingway, your work would probably never make it past the slush pile—hundreds, maybe thousands of essays, articles, stories, poems, sent unsolicited to magazines by newbie writers hoping to be discovered every month. The slush piles were usually screened by interns, college students on summer break, secretaries, even the mail room staff, who might have no way of recognizing whether the work they reviewed was that of a genius, a loser, or somewhere in between. So your work would probably not reach the desks of the editors who made the decisions and mattered. The system is not any different today, although easier in the sense that you can often submit your work online—which, on the other hand, makes the competition more intense and the possibility of being discovered perhaps even more unlikely. It was and is a depressing and unsatisfying situation. But Phil persisted.

At the time I appreciated Phil's confidence but not his approach. Hardly anyone was published immediately in the *New Yorker*. This was the pinnacle, the top, what you worked for and hoped for as a writer—and certainly not where you would expect to be at the beginning of your career.

Unlike Phil, I rarely even considered submitting my work to these publications. It was, I told him that day in Nantucket as we debated the pros and cons of our conflicting approaches, a waste of time. I had no interest in being buried in the slush pile hoping for a miracle that would never happen, when I could submit my work to smaller publications like newspapers, niche magazines or what were then called "littles," literary magazines not unlike my own *Creative Nonfiction* today, and maybe get some satisfaction and earn some credits as I worked my way up. Phil countered by insisting that that "process" of working your way up was self-defeating—no satisfaction in starting small. He would aim for the top. And if he never got there, at least he would be trying and not settling for something that would not, in the end, be fulfilling, what he wanted and dreamed about.

As we sat there waiting for the ferry and debating, quite heatedly, the merits of our conflicting ideas, I pointed at the flagpole at the end of the pier where the ferry would soon dock. "Look," I said, "you want to get to the top of that pole as a writer, where the flag is flying, which is exactly where I want to be, as well—someday. But you can't just shoot up there in one bounding leap. No one is going to raise your flag because you are Phil. You've got to climb it, from the bottom to the top. It takes time and effort. You pay your dues. Publish small. Make contacts. Get yourself recognized. Build up a list of lesser publications. The goal you aspire to and work for is not going to be reached in one fell swoop."

Phil was not interested in climbing the flagpole. Phil was going to make it straight to the summit, where the flag was flapping vigorously that day in the wind; he was not going to start at the bottom and work his way up. It was the top of the flagpole or nothing. And—this may have been implied, not said—he would get there before me with my tedious workmanlike way to make it big as a writer.

At the time, I did not think about or mention my rope test experience, but at some point, not right away, in the back of my mind, the rope test resonated. And then, years later, as seventy came and went and I began reliving and reevaluating my own narrative, I recalled the flagpole discussion and metaphor and what it signified, as I contemplated and confronted my dissatisfaction with where I was, in a personal sense, after seventy.

Perhaps it is more than coincidental that the rope and flagpole metaphors are so similar. They both represent hard work and possible achievement of a difficult sought-after goal. But it was interesting to me and impactful because of the circumstances with which I was confronted when I was eighteen, compared to years later when I was more than seventy.

I had approached my enlistment and the rope test somewhat blindly as a kid, consumed by hope and youthful ambition. I needed to leap—like Phil—to get to the top. If I failed one week, I would be faced with the same rope to the top the following week until, sooner or later, I would get there. And if, on the off chance, I didn't get there, well, then, I guess I would have spent the rest of the time in boot camp with the other losers I had been categorized with, doing odd jobs, nasty chores, throughout my enlistment. But now, I realized I was beyond the rope test as a metaphor and as a way of approaching this more personal challenge I was then confronting. Facing seventy, old age, fading away, more or less alone.

For one thing, I had already passed the rope test first and most significantly in boot camp—and then in various other ways over more than a half century. Back then, I was insecure and untested and had no realistic idea about what I might accomplish on a rope test day or any day thereafter. The whole thing was a shot in the dark. But climbing the flagpole was a more thoughtful and measured exercise, which was exactly, I concluded, how I would have to plan and orchestrate my improved connection to other people. The circumstances were entirely different because, in contrast to my basically know-nothing state of being and mind when facing the rope test challenge, I was, at that moment, very aware of my potential and my capabilities. And lack thereof. I needed to start climbing—from the bottom.

The loss of Iggy and Frank and my mother and my Menachem book, and my son's troubles, combined with coming to terms with my age, had stunned and wounded me, frozen me in place and forced me to evaluate and contemplate and regroup. And to look at things with a certain perspective that would have been impossible at eighteen simply because I had not lived long enough.

That's one of the good things about getting old. You know what you know. Or, to be more precise, you know what you remember. And I remembered Phil and his blind quest to reach the top of the pole—the symbolic summit—which, at this point in my life, was, for me, impractical if not downright absurd.

I could not, I realized, become Mr. Popularity in Pittsburgh. I could not expect to walk down Walnut or any street in any city at any time, day or night, and suddenly be hailed as an artist, a hero, a stand-up super citizen of Shadyside or anywhere else. And I could not expect magically to come face to face with the woman of my dreams. I did not even have a woman of my dreams. I did want a woman, though. Or I should say that I wanted the company and pleasure of women. Just because I was now past seventy didn't mean that I no longer felt longing and desire or that I lacked the ability to have a physical relationship. Just because I had not had one in many months didn't mean I couldn't or wouldn't. Besides, I missed Michele and I wanted her back in my life. But as much as I tried, I couldn't convince her that I had changed—or maybe that I had changed enough. Or maybe she had changed and no longer was interested in me.

But I wanted the company of men as well. Those wild Friday night experiences with Frank and friends, or hanging out with Iggy and his beer and pop cadre, and even those very old days with Dickie, Boo-Boo, Tooth, and the gang were precious bonding experiences I will never, obviously, because here I am writing about them now, forget. Later, as I went from immersion to immersion, motorcycles, baseball, transplantation, robotics, I had enjoyed and appreciated the company of other people, men and women, sharing ideas and the challenges of their missions—and of mine. At least for a while.

But on my own, between books and immersions, I was tired of being a lone wolf, a guy so obsessed with work and climbing the goddamn flagpole of achievement that I had lost touch with other aspects of life. The comparison I had made between Phil and me, that he was the hare and I the tortoise, rang true in another way. I was the tortoise ensconced—hiding its head and heart—under its shell. That was silly. I had nothing to be afraid of. Not even the unlikely possibility of pulling a Shimmy, making a big mistake.

In fact, I felt kind of foolish looking back and imagining or allowing Shimmy's catastrophe or my father's miscalculation at Tryson's to haunt or in any way intimidate me. What could happen to me, I thought, except for my own sickness or death, that hadn't already happened? Would I lose the prestige or the self-image that had sustained me for so long, my record of publication, my distinguished CSPO writer in residence title, my literary magazine—my life of immersions and books—just because I tried to have, to orchestrate, a more satisfying personal life? None of what I had so far achieved could be taken away from me. It represented who I was—what I am. But I wanted a little bit more.

And I was now not at all at the bottom of the flagpole, or at the bottom of the rope, as I was at eighteen. I had climbed a long way already. I was maybe as near to the flag in many ways as I might ever get. I was certainly closer, as it turned out, than Phil ever got, unfortunately. After many years of trying to climb to the top, he has explored other ideas and goals and has achieved a great deal. More than me in many ways. And he has not given up his quest to become a successful writer; he continues to pound away at his keyboard every day, but now with lower and more practical expectations. I've seen him a couple of times since that day at the ferry. And he has been very supportive and gracious about all I have achieved. I never did mention our flagpole conversation. Perhaps he doesn't remember it. But for me it was one of those rare and spontaneous moments that we never forget, and it has brought me clarity and direction so much later in life.

Forty

I CAN'T SAY THAT MY NEW AND IMPROVED LIFE HAPPENED RIGHT away, in a flash. It was a gradual process and sometimes a struggle up the social flagpole.

I did not have a plan; rather, I was just trying stuff out. Kind of like what I do in an immersion, just probing in one direction and then another, discovering what worked for me and for those I was hanging out with, and what didn't.

First, I began to try to loosen up and not be so intense and introspective—or seem to be. Little things. I began looking at people, making eye contact when I walked by them, mostly those with familiar faces on Walnut Street. Instead of staring straight ahead, engrossed in myself and what I was writing, I might say, "Hello." And when I did that, sometimes they would say hello back to me. And then, sometimes, I would figure out something else to say, lame stuff mostly, stuff I had in the past criticized and mumbled derisively about— the Steelers, the Pirates, the weather. But I got conversations going, quite easily in fact, when I wanted to, and sometimes people told me things that surprised and delighted me. Like books they were reading or wines they were drinking. Or where they were traveling. Or the work they were doing. Or stuff about the neighborhood.

It was amazing, I discovered, how many people leave Pittsburgh and go to other countries—China, Australia, Tibet—places I've been. Just because they were walking Walnut like me didn't mean that I was the only person in Shadyside who left town or had jobs in other cities. Of course, I knew that; I wasn't oblivious. I was simply all caught up in who or what I thought I was, and maybe never really considered or cared enough about what they were doing or thinking. And there was always, in the back of my mind, this caveat about being a silver top, an old gray-haired guy, who was trying to be friendly, just to pass the time. Who would want to talk with an old man, a guy who, it seemed, had nothing to do but while away the hours looking for conversation and company? What would they think of me? Would my aura of independence and purpose, if indeed this aura actually existed, be shattered? But okay, I concluded, if so, so what?

I began reaching out to strangers, too, or almost-strangers—wait-people in restaurants, clerks at convenience stores. I was . . . nice. Not that I had ever been not nice. But I became more open. I isolated things, distinctive things, that I had noticed about them, and I commented. New hair styles, sharp boots, unique tattoos. It wasn't that I hadn't ever noticed this stuff before—I am, after all, a writer, keen on cool details—but I had kept my observations to myself. Now I shared my admiration for them, their style and demeanor, and my efforts were appreciated. Next time I saw them, they reminded me that I had praised or, for that matter, just noticed them.

Funny thing is, I soon discovered that people were or had been noticing details about me as well. "Nice blazer," they might say, or, "You got a haircut!" At Starbucks I was no longer just the venti dark roast guy; especially after I shared the fact that I taught at Arizona State, where many of the baristas were receiving a free online education, I became kind of a celebrity. They still had no idea what a science policy think tank was, and they couldn't take classes with me because I did not teach online, but they sure appreciated what a free degree in history or English meant. I responded by bringing them T-shirts or other ASU swag from the Tempe campus. Now when I walk into Starbucks, I am not just the venti dark guy, I am "Lee!"

I ran into a guy—Steve, maybe ten years younger than me, an acquaintance from the old days in Shadyside—who told me he had been writing a memoir for the last twenty-five years and didn't know what to do with it, or whether it was any good, or how to make it better. He asked if I would read it and help him. Lots of people seem to be writing books secretly, without having the slightest idea how to write a book or what to do with it after they finish, and many people over the years have approached me for help. I have invariably demurred, politely. I was having trouble enough writing my own book—this memoir—and dealing with all my other books and projects, including Menachem. But this time, I told him I would read it, and I did read it and tried to help him. He has been appreciative. I have since helped others, mostly old friends, who were trying to write. And it didn't really take too much time or cause me to lose my focus after all. It was okay, I discovered, to help someone else do something that I knew a lot about.

Meanwhile, I took a big chance and told Steve that I was feeling somewhat isolated and alone now that Michele and I were no longer an item, and that on-and-off travel made having a Pittsburgh social life kind of difficult, which in part was true. I did not mention—maybe he sensed this—that my own standoffish attitude and reluctance to engage was also at fault. But "coming clean"—or partially clean—was cathartic, and he was responsive.

Steve introduced me to some nice people, friends of his, and invited me to parties and openings. He owned an art gallery. It was interesting to me that most of the people he introduced me to were people I knew, or kind of had known over the years. But I had never really talked with them, had conversations, or at least not for a long time. Obsession with my work and self-image had left me more than a little disengaged from a life I once knew.

And instead of drinking and eating alone with *Law and Order*'s Lennie Briscoe as my best friend and most intimate companion, I popped into neighborhood restaurants that I knew more mature people might frequent and talked to customers who sat beside me, often also alone. One place, Casbah, became a regular hangout. When I worked late at my keyboard, I would wander into Casbah an hour or so before closing and have a nightcap, talk with the bartenders who were winding down and cleaning up after a long evening, or with the few stragglers who, like me, had wandered in before facing home and alone. The Casbah bar is dark—you need an iPhone with a flashlight to read the menu—but when I brought my laptop, my display would light up and I could answer e-mail. Which made a boring task somewhat more tolerable. And often I could skip the e-mails because I might meet someone I knew or used to know—or someone new entirely. I had no problem just turning to my left or my right and engaging a stranger. Another connection for the chameleon, if not a friend.

There were other regular hangouts and connections I eventually discovered. On Tuesdays I could go down to the Elbow Room, where old Shadyside ex-hippie types like Ringo, the ponytailed guy who had the leather shop years ago, or P.J., a local radio personality, a guy called "the voice of Pittsburgh," hung out. Other old-timers showed up there periodically. I tried not to get annoyed, held my tongue, when they talked about old age and retirement and people who were now sick or dead. In fact, I had known some of these folks they were discussing; I joined in with my own thoughts and recollections, and it wasn't so bad. I appreciated the interaction. And even the memories.

Other groups emerged. When—a sad event—the Elbow Room, founded in 1947 and thus almost as old as me, closed down, I started meeting with Steve and some of the other guys he had introduced me to, a contractor, Will, and a designer, Todd, and a few others, on Tuesdays. This group was really kind of cool—or cool in the sense of how we came together. No plans for Tuesdays were ever made in advance, and usually nothing happened until maybe late afternoon. Then one of us would send a group text saying something like "Where are we going tonight?" or "Are you in or out?" And then the banter would go back and forth about where to meet and when, and invariably some or all of us were together, somewhere, by 7:30. Nothing much happened at these tiny trysts, just a couple of hours of connection, which was enough. Whatever I had been missing, or thought I was missing, was not nearly as awesome and enlightening, or on the other hand as difficult or awkward to manage, as I had imagined. Not in any way mind-blowing, just a bunch of guys getting together, drinking a bit and eating, like normal. It had been quite a long time since I remembered normal, though. I had once rejected normal. Now it was exactly what I had been missing, and I embraced it.

Tuesday wasn't my only big night of the week. There was happy hour on Fridays at Casbah, with more new people or old acquaintances renewed. I rediscovered Phil—not the Nantucket Phil—whose nonprofit foundation had brought social services and critically needed healthcare to hundreds of thousands of Pittsburghers for many decades. And Tasso, the architect who among other things designed the Greater Pittsburgh International Airport. Both of these guys were nearing ninety, and they were still showing up and making waves. Maybe they traveled by Uber instead of in their own cars. Maybe they had canes and hearing devices, and maybe they even neglected to trim their nose hairs. But they were still pretty damn smart and productive, writing op-eds for the local papers, helping out-of-work acquaintances in midlife find new jobs, and generally dishing out valuable guidance and advice to anyone who asked. They were neither disillusioned nor debilitated—far from dead. They were making their wisdom and experience matter. And Charlie: not just a former alternative newspaper editor and rock musician, but a changemaker who had established cultural and arts institutions Pittsburghers tout, nationwide, today. In some cases he had saved them from extinction, working pro bono when support and funding had played out. Will and Steve, from Tuesdays, were on the scene as well.

This sounds silly, maybe, but Friday happy hour at Casbah, maybe just ninety minutes from start to finish, seemed to all of us somewhat electrifying, a highlight to end the week. We couldn't miss it. Or we tried like hell not to. And there were always newcomers who wandered in or folks we had invited to change the tone and infuse new energy: Stuart, a designer; Jean, who owned a chain of coffee shops in town; Bob, an anesthesiologist—you never knew who might appear. This was much like my Friday nights with Frank, except that there were no secrets and no real plan, more like an ongoing explosion of spontaneity and camaraderie. I often walked home with Will on those Friday evenings, and all we could do was marvel at how terrific and special that Casbah time was.

I had heard from men and women my age how difficult it was to find new friends, and I had certainly assumed throughout my years of isolation that my personal world would continue to shrink as I aged. But instead it had expanded and been enriched, just because I had become more proactive and emboldened and more aware of my opportunities and options.

I even took up golf. Me? The Cleat, batting around a little white ball that seemed to have a mind of its own and went everywhere it was not supposed to go? Who would ever have imagined? Yes, I had been playing a bit of golf before with Michele. But Steve and his friends were avid golfers, and this was another potential bonding experience, so I attacked the game with a bit more gusto, although, I admit, not a lot.

And that thing about Pittsburgh that I had constantly complained about—that it was a large small town and everybody knew everybody else, turned into my advantage. I discovered that lots of people knew me or of me, what I had accomplished, and they were incredibly generous in our interactions. Former students from Pitt, and even people who knew my students and had heard them talk about me, the professor who was The Cleat, the creative nonfiction guy, often appeared out of nowhere and, now that I seemed to be more available, reached out to me. And then there were those folks who knew my mother and my brothers and my former wives.

I can't tell you what a great feeling it was when, on a Tuesday or Thursday or Friday evening, I could from time to time make what, to me, was the momentous decision to not do anything—to stay at home and be at peace with myself and, of course, Lennie Briscoe. Yes, I had been missing company, folks to hang out with, for a very long time. But I also realized, as time went by, how much I enjoyed—and needed—to be alone. Having the option, connecting with other people or not, not only eased my anxiety but was uplifting and reassuring.

I also did a bit more research, and rather than pinpointing stuff that would obviously depress me, I looked for positive and optimistic viewpoints about aging and loneliness. Or should I say aloneness? Like, people are happiest at the beginnings and endings of their lives, I found out in one study, and people with more positive attitudes about aging are less challenged by memory loss. These folks not only live longer, a half dozen years longer on average, but they have better handwriting. This last was something to really aspire to.

I ran across another heartening observation from a scientist who runs an "AgeLab" at MIT and had this really cool eight-thousand-day riff: There are about eight thousand days from the day you are born until your twenty-first birthday, he said in an article I read. And by your forty-fifth year, midlife crisis time, you've lived another eight thousand days. If you get that far once more and live another eight thousand days, past sixty-five—and I had indeed crossed that barrier—

then there's a 50 percent chance that you will live to eighty-five. Or another eight thousand days, more or less. Now, according to Google, on the day I was born, my potential life span was sixty-eight. So if I was in the lucky 50 percent, my life had gained an entire fourth quarter, gratis.

Loneliness, by the way, isn't only related to aging. A survey I read suggested that men and women from their late teens to mid-thirties were lonelier in life than their parents and grandparents. The Brits were taking the loneliness problem super seriously. England's National Health Service had recently created a loneliness job—a Minister of Loneliness, who connects folks like me, or those hotshot millennials, with one another. While I don't think I'd want to do an immersion with a Minister of Loneliness (it could be a very lonely job) or with a millennial, all of this information was helpful.

What I alluded to at the beginning of this book but haven't mentioned again until now is the fact that, over the past few years, I had put on weight—thirty pounds. But with careful attentiveness to diet, I have melted back to "slim" again—and not the way my Roosevelt School classmates would have described it. Which doesn't mean that I no longer deviate. I suspect that a little bit of deviation, nervous eating, is something I will always have to contend with. It calms me down. But instead of cookies and chips, I gorge on spinach, cauliflower, broccoli, healthy stuff. Few carbs and calories, and it seems to satisfy me enough and does not contribute to a bulging belly. Today I weigh almost exactly what I weighed when I was discharged from the Coast Guard.

I felt the change in myself physically in other ways. I could sense it in how I walked; my body language was more open. No longer did I hunch and glare. I had never even realized that I hunched and glared until I stopped doing it. And I wasn't rushing around so much; I learned to stroll. I have photos of myself from a few years ago, looking serious and intense, like a defensive lineman on a football field, but in more recent pictures, I am smiling more often, naturally and easily. I may sound like I am going overboard about all of this, such small things to exult about, but believe me, it was a revelation and a relief. Sometimes, more often than not, talking with other people, especially somewhat spontaneously, out of the blue, cheered the hell out of me when I was down and a bit depressed. In fact, when I was down and depressed, I would purposely walk Walnut looking for people with whom I could engage, which was often terrifically therapeutic. Who needed Dr. Mason?

I had the funniest thing happen one time when a woman came up to me, someone who owned a shop on Walnut, but who I knew only in passing. I was ready to greet her and pass on by, but she stopped and smiled and said: "You always look like you are having so much fun. You must have a great life." I was taken aback. Her observation seemed ridiculous, compared to how I had not too long before felt. But it downright tickled me.

Another thing: My expanded social parameters, as I walked Walnut or went elsewhere, did not in any way affect my work. I could stop to engage, interrupting my focus and concentration, and return to my keyboard and dig right in wherever I left off. Maybe there was a time in the past when I was so unsure and uptight about my writing that I needed to crawl inside my tortoise shell, but that seemed to be no longer necessary.

And I should say that few of my new friends asked about my work, or to my knowledge read any of my books, and they seemingly had no idea or any curiosity to learn what a CSPO was all about. But I didn't really care anymore—or not a lot. Maybe it was just too difficult for them to get there with me, ask about my writing or my teaching, maybe they were happy enough to be in a writer's company, or maybe, just maybe, they liked me not because I was a writer, or in spite of my being a writer, but because I was me.

One thing I realized—and this was quite mind-bending, I am embarrassed to say—was how important, vital, the people I had distanced myself from, those Starbuckians, were, in fact, to me, even though they remained to a certain extent distanced. Whether I talked with the Starbucks regulars or not, as I came and went for my venti, I really wanted to see them. Their presence was reassuring, the way they sat at the same table every day, seven days a week, inside in the winter when it was cold and outside in spring, summer, fall, also the same table. They even had their own rigid seating arrangements. Michael, the deli guy, always assumed the commanding position, his back to the wall, so that he could view his minions, take stock, and lead or oversee the conversation. And Betsy, the jeweler, always opposite Michael, never beside him, listening intently, leaning forward, nodding. And those who straggled in a bit later, Harry, Tamara, others, gathering around Michael, much the way those men I remembered meeting for coffee had surrounded Iggy.

As I walked Walnut in the morning, I anticipated seeing them, and when someone was missing, I couldn't help wondering what had happened to them. And this thought just came to me one day: Maybe I was also an anchoring element in their lives. Maybe they waited for me to walk through the door and grab my venti and give them a cursory wave. Maybe I was as much a part of the music of their mornings as they were for me.

Why were they at Starbucks, at the same time, day after day, coming together, connecting and seemingly enjoying? Maybe because they were seeking the same measure of stability and connectedness as I was? Just like Dickie Diamondstone, Boo-Boo, and our classmates? Just like Frank and his friends on Friday evenings so many years ago? Like Will, Charlie, Steve at Casbah? A reliable, solid, anticipated coalition of camaraderie? We were all, in one way or another, looking for the same thing, weren't we? These groups were building blocks, the glue of who and what we were, integral to our routines and the puzzles of our personalities. And the older we get, the more we lose—people we love, ideas we believed in, expectations, opportunities—and therefore the more we need these regular routine connections, those attachments that help us stay active and feel vital. Or just normal.

But didn't I know this all along, down deep? Who wouldn't? I knew it in high school, in the military, through every book, every trauma. But for a long time before this, I couldn't seem to make it happen, couldn't cross the line between them and me, couldn't climb the goddamn rope. Because of stubbornness or pride or stupidity.

But something had indeed happened early on in my transition to help me manage my change, to get out of my own way, to leap-frog my abhorrence of aging and the disappointments that might come with it. A symbolic breakthrough had occurred, beginning with something very silly and seemingly superficial that had bothered me, threatened me, limited me throughout my life. Coming to terms with what I regarded as my "unmentionable," my most deeply held and ridiculous, outlandish, ludicrous secret, had, at the very beginning of my efforts to change, helped me turn the corner.

Forty-One

"BUNION" IS A WORD DERIVED FROM THE FRENCH WORD *buigne*, meaning bump or hump. I looked it up a long time ago because I hated the flaw of mine that it divulged. "Bump" and "hump" are words that don't do my bunion justice, however, for my bunion shoots out of the side of my right foot in a point like a shark fin— at least that's the way Patricia described it. Patricia found my bunion fascinating, especially in cold damp weather when the bunion turned red and blinked like a stoplight or, if you prefer, like Rudolph the Reindeer's nose. (It also aches and pulsates while blinking.) Years later, Michele too expressed a great fondness for my shark foot.

I didn't get it, did not understand their attraction or attention to something so ugly and deformed, so contrary to the way in which I wanted to show myself to the world. Maybe these two women who loved and understood me, albeit in different ways, recognized in my bunion the real Lee—the damaged, insecure personality I was.

My entire life I have worked diligently to conceal my shark foot from everyone. I have declined invitations to pool parties so that I didn't have to take off my shoes. While I owned a house in South Jersey quite near Iggy and Susan for years, I rarely went to the beach, and on those rare occasions when my feet touched sand, it was with shoes on. I didn't shower in locker rooms at my club after working out because I would be revealing myself and my awful flaw. When lucky enough to lure a woman into my bedroom, during the periods when I was single or unattached, I undressed with the lights off or kept my socks on until we were in bed. My bunion—my big fat shark pulsating bump hump—has been my dirtiest, darkest secret.

Bunions represented, to me, my fatal flaw, the fallacy behind my façade, which I could not control. And besides, who gets bunions? Old people, decrepit people. Only God knows why I have been bunioned-up for my entire life. My feet were old and ugly before the rest of me was.

While surgery was an option, all the surgeons I consulted—and there were many—advised against it. After all, my shark foot wasn't hampering my activities. I could walk, run marathons, bike, whatever. So why fuck up your foot with surgery? And besides, my shark foot could be hidden by shoes and socks—and big heavy boots with cleats. Those boots with cleats were my camouflage and subterfuge. They called attention to my feet, demonstrated that I was not afraid of anything, for I was booted for battle. I was making a statement. Nothing could be wrong with my foot—a shark was the last thing anyone might imagine. Impossible. And, of course, those big black motorcycle boots had round toes, so you had to look carefully to see the shark foot indentation on the inside of my right boot. My left foot also had a shark, but not nearly as prominent and obtrusive as the blinking Rudolph on the right.

Like I said before, my attempts to become more social and available started gradually and were, in the beginning, trial and error as I groped my way back into the world and regained some social confidence and a sense of community. But I overheard a conversation one day about hot yoga—yoga practiced in ninety- or hundred-degree heat, so hot you could barely breathe or think of anything other than the stifling humidity and the agony of getting through the vinyasas, a method in which movements and concentrated breathing form a flowing sequence, ninety minutes of torture and total self-focus. In yogi language, you were leaving the real world behind and giving yourself to the practice, but the torture aspect was what appealed to me then. And the challenge of doing something new, testing myself in a different way. And I wanted diversion. The last thing I wanted at that point was to think about the things happening to me and my loved ones during the time in which, in my seventies, I was supposed to be "smelling the roses."

I had always made fun of yogis. To me they were a weird cult, walking up and down the street with their flip-flops flapping and clutching their mats and water bottles—round-eyed, like zombies. The last thing I imagined was that I, Lee Gutkind, the tough-guy motorcycle man, the hotshot loner, writer of true stories, The Cleat, would ever walk into a yoga class. And yet I had overheard that conversation, had watched that daily procession of yogis with their mats and their towels as they entered the yoga studio—and seen their sweat-soaked T-shirts, tights, and shorts as they departed an hour and a half later, glassy-eyed with peaceful elation—and the idea and the challenge became very appealing to me.

I should tell you that the yoga studio was on the second floor of my Starbucks building. You could, I soon discovered, as you reclined on mat and towel waiting for the torture to begin, detect through the floorboards the tantalizing odor of a morning venti dark.

I don't want to go into the various satisfactions I have discovered with yoga or even the fact that I could connect my favorite Starbucks with my vinyasas, which was indeed symbolically meaningful. I want to talk about what I had to do—what I continue to have to do—

to practice yoga. This was the most significant action I had to take: I had to take off my big bad boots and, worse, my socks. I had to "out" my bunion, my *buigne*, my terrible secret—my fucking shark foot.

And I did.

For the first class, and for every class in the years since beginning practicing, I have removed my boots and socks. Two or three times a week. Sometimes more. I expose my flaw—my shark! And guess what? Nobody looks at it, or says anything about it, or, as far as I can tell, thinks less of me because of my shark foot.

I am not saying that people never noticed, but evidently they didn't really care or care enough to stare. Or maybe they just didn't want to be rude. Of course, I have always understood that all of us have flaws, every last one of us, things of which we are ashamed or that make us feel uncomfortable, and some of the stuff is pretty stupid—like my shark foot or my age. But understanding human nature is one thing, and accepting and dealing with what you imagine might happen if you expose yourself is an entirely different matter.

I have talked more than a little bit about magical moments in my life and in the lives of others: how events, little or large, can influence who and what you are for a lifetime. I've had quite a few, beginning with the rope test. And my mom not recognizing me when I came home from basic training because her not-too-loveable roly-poly boy had slimmed down to manhood. Or my night with Frank. Or my Phil flagpole revelation. Becoming seventy was more like misery, more like black magic, but even that event seems to have become a positive turning point, as it has played out.

In all of these and other events, something happened that can be pinpointed and tracked forward. You follow its trajectory from magical moment to insight, discovery, surprise, disappointment, whatever. And usually these tend to be big moments—significant, triumphant, the crossing over from tipping point to sudden realization. A transformation occurs. But sometimes, in other instances, you don't know that the transformation has taken place or what will occur or did occur until something else happens that ignites your realization—like the conversation I had with a guy I met in yoga class a year or so after I began to practice and unmasked or "unbooted" myself.

The yoga I have become comfortable with is power flow yoga—very athletic and fast-paced and, of course, hot—so invariably I am twice or three times or maybe even four times as old as anyone else in the studio, perhaps with the exception of this guy we will call Truman, who also attends fairly regularly. Truman, who is a couple of decades older than most of the "kids" in class, although not nearly as old as me, is clearly fit, muscular in fact, and kind of cool. He's got some nice tattoos, elaborate depictions of dragons in bright colors entangled with snakes. He's a forensic pathologist in real life.

To this point I had, even though I had been changing, avoided mentioning my age to the yogis I met, or anyone else. Since forty and my escape from that decrepit crowd at Klein's Restaurant, I had kept my galloping years close to my vest. Of course, I had eventually accepted my age—to myself. Which was different. I could even say it aloud—"Seventy-Seventy-Seventy"—a painful self-inflicted chant when I was alone. But admitting it to other people, going public, was more than a little problematic. Once my secret was out, the reality would *really* be real.

Anyway, just as I have used my boots to camouflage my shark foot, I have always used humor to divert attention away from how old I am. So, in the past, maybe since I reached sixty or so, when people asked my age, I automatically made up obvious bald-faced lies. "I'm forty-seven." Just old enough that people would stop and think for a minute: *Could this be true? He looks much older.*

The comedian Jack Benny did this regularly, and it became a trademark riff for him—he was always thirty-nine. Even when he was in his eighties and had been on radio and TV for far more than thirty-nine years, a regular routine would consist of people running into him and asking his age, for one reason or another, and Benny would pause—and his audience would be waiting for this riff, expectantly, hoping for it, in fact; they would start to laugh even before he provided the predictable answer: "I am thirty-nine."

So whenever someone asked my age, I would say, "I'm forty-seven," and the questioner would look at me, surprised and confused, not knowing how to respond. What could they say? That I looked good for forty-seven, which would be a lie? Or that I looked a mite older than my age, which would be an insult? And then I would add, like icing on a cake, pointing up at my silver head, "I dye my hair this color to seem more mature. So people will be nicer to me. More respectful."

This always took people aback—they hesitated for a moment—and then they got it eventually and laughed, and if I was lucky, the conversation moved on to other subjects. I did this especially with women, because I didn't want them to write me off. I've still got a little bit of life in me, and desire. No matter how old he is, a man looks at women and sizes them up—at least I do—wondering if they are possible soul mates or partners, in bed or otherwise. Not that you really want them all the time. Maybe you just want to know whether they might want you.

After practice one day, as I was leaving the studio, Truman was chatting with one of the yoga teachers, Catherine, a slender blonde in her late twenties. I had already sized Catherine up—she was attractive, petite, and always friendly. I would, I thought, if I could, which I know I couldn't, take her out. Talk with her. Kiss her. As I was passing, Truman said to me, "We were just talking about you."

"Oh," I replied, "what about me?"

"You are in such good shape," Catherine said. I knew she meant "for your age," but she was polite, didn't say what she was thinking. Although she added, "I wish my grandfather would take yoga. I told him about you, how terrific and fit you are."

Her remark made me feel uncomfortable. This labeling, categorizing, pigeonholing of me and people my age was exactly what I had been fighting against and resisting. But I knew that what Catherine was saying to me, comparing me with her grandfather, who I assumed was not in the best of shape, was meant as a compliment. Making it through ninety minutes of hot flow yoga, or for that matter running a half dozen miles regularly, was an accomplishment even for a guy half my age—hardly something to be ashamed about. Feeling demeaned was wrongheaded and self-destructive. Was I not invoking that ism, ageism, that I had been fighting and fearing for so long, on myself?

I hesitated as I thought about this, and smiled politely at Catherine. But Truman was continuing the conversation, pursuing more information. "I hope I look and act like you when I'm your age," he said. And then, being more persistent, "Can I ask how old you are?" He added, "I'm fifty-one."

There are things I could have said, or might have said in the very recent past, and I paused and contemplated them: "No, you *cannot* ask how old I am. What the fuck business is it of yours, anyway?" or, my regular rejoinder, adapted for this special situation, "I am forty-seven—four years younger than you!"

But something held me back. Suddenly it didn't seem appropriate or useful or meaningful or even worthwhile to respond with my regular deflections. What was the point anymore? I thought. Who would I be fooling—aside from myself? Maybe people would laugh, and I could, as usual, joke my way through an awkward moment and escape. But escape what?

I stood there, still in my bare feet, parading my bunion—my blinking, red-nosed siren of a shark foot—and listening as they were telling me what I realized was the truth: I looked pretty good for my age. My bunion was not so disgraceful. It was, perhaps, a badge of courage, a sign of survival and achievement. Bunions make down-dog unnecessarily painful and many balancing poses, like tree, eagle, and warrior, considerably more challenging. But I could go through my vinyasas with Truman—or even Catherine—keeping up with remarkable ease. And I was unique, older than anyone else in this steam bath studio. This was good, not bad or embarrassing.

And so I said it: for the first time, I faced reality in public, faced the fact that I was an old guy, getting older, but at the same time was pretty damn fortunate to be doing it with some measure of style and grace. The words burst from my mouth, and I could hardly believe I said them. But I did:

"Almost seventy-one."

Forty-Two

THAT INCIDENT AT THE YOGA STUDIO OCCURRED FOUR YEARS ago. I am now, as I finish this book that I started before I turned seventy, seventy-four years old. And by the time you are reading it, I will be seventy-five. Or more. Or . . . okay . . . dead.

But I now recognize that the problem with aging, or my problem with aging—a societal problem for sure, that ism that goes along with sexism and racism—begins with me and people like me. That I believed and accepted the beliefs and prejudices about aging that are unfortunately part of our culture in this country somewhat blindly rather than acknowledging, appreciating, and even reveling in the accomplishment of simply growing old, of making it to three-quarters of a century.

But growing old is quite a confounding paradox, an enigma. No matter what else we do in life, what we aspire to, writing, bowling, music, whatever, the goal in the end is to get old and stay old as long as possible. Even with a walker and a hearing device, even if you shuffle and are engulfed in floaters and annoyed and hampered by bad teeth. Even with all of that and a lot more, some of us, maybe even most of us, can still be in the game. The game might be different. And we may need to play harder, or on the other hand be more accepting of our shortcomings and tone down our expectations, to make it all work. Our life might not depend upon this attitude adjustment, literally, but our sense of self and well-being as we age certainly does. I have pretty much navigated, come to grips with all of this. I think I achieved this transformation—or really began my transformation, finally—with my Catherine and Truman encounter.

The moment I said those words, outed myself with my age, my real age, I could feel relief flow through my body, from my shoulders to my bunioned feet. I understand now, even if I didn't then, that that was just the beginning of a long journey, maybe my final journey, to a different life, gradually realizing and accepting who I was and what I am today: an aging man, but not an old man; a vital man, not a defeated or tired man. A seventy-one-year-old man at that moment, prepared for seventy-two and, as it has played out to today, seventy-five, and for as many more years as I will be fortunate enough to experience and take pleasure from—as well as endure the losses and heartbreaks that will come with them.

I am not the old Lee Gutkind anymore; I am, rather, the new, albeit older, me. A guy with friends, a guy with options, a guy with good health and a good job and continued career aspirations, and a vastly improved attitude toward my past and my future, whatever that brings. Which doesn't necessarily mean I now regard the future with exhilarated glee. No way! I know the truth—the reality of what I am facing as the years pass faster and faster: more people I love get sick and die, or disappoint or mislead me, while my body, my senses, my vital organs may begin, one by one, to fail me.

My mother said it the day she died. She had been in a coma, for a week of ongoing agony. She had tossed and turned and thrashed and moaned, day after day, as Richard, Patricia, and I, along with her caretakers, hovered and hoped that a miracle would occur, that she would suddenly open her eyes and recognize us, at least for a minute—time enough for us all to say how much we loved and treasured her, to say, in our own ways, goodbye.

This hoped-for magical moment did not occur. She never again opened her eyes or recognized us as we huddled around her bed while she was thrashing and moaning. But at one point, quite suddenly, she stopped for maybe thirty seconds. Did she want to tell us something? Maybe. I am not so sure she knew we were there. But regardless, her message was clear as a bell. It rings in my ears today—despite my improved attitude. I recite that message back to myself, again and again. Chant her final words aloud when I am alone and contemplating the realities, the journey of my life. My mother summed it all up for me—ninety-four years of joy and trouble, pain and pleasure—as she regarded the end of her long life with those two unforgettable, undeniable, and indisputable, totally appropriate Yiddish words:

Oy gevalt.

This meant, for those who don't know Yiddish, something like, "Oh fuck. It finally happened. I can't believe it, but there's nothing I can do about it except whine and complain and accept the inevitable. Dying sucks."

Mollie was ready, had climbed aboard her bus, and she was headed out of town.

I am not so ready, however. I am no longer fearing the few years I have to go. If Mollie lived to ninety-four and went out with such a symbolic spark of both resistance and acquiescence, then I need to be motivated to, in this case, not wait and see what happens, because in the end, even though she accepted what was indeed finally happening, she fought and complained and in her own way resisted what was clearly inevitable.

That's the way I intend to go, but I realize now that I have a lifetime yet to live—whatever that means, maybe another eight thousand days, more or less, if I am lucky. Before my own bus pulls up at the curb and beckons me on, I may well pull some Shimmys, or have unexpected setbacks, or even contemplate retirement. Who knows? And I think that's all okay. For just like Frederick Williams, the man who flew off a bridge and landed on the other side still alive and kicking, I have always been and will always be more than a bit *meshuggeneh*.

BOOKS BY LEE GUTKIND

Bike Fever: On Motorcycle Culture

The Best Seat in Baseball, But You Have to Stand!: The Game as Umpires See It

God's Helicopter (novel)

The People of Penn's Woods West

Many Sleepless Nights: The World of Organ Transplantation

One Children's Place: A Profile of Pediatric Medicine

Stuck in Time: The Tragedy of Childhood Mental Illness

Creative Nonfiction: How to Live It and Write It

The Art of Creative Nonfiction: Writing and Selling the Literature of Reality

An Unspoken Art: Profiles of Veterinary Life

Forever Fat: Essays by the Godfather

Almost Human: Making Robots Think

Truckin' with Sam, with Sam Gutkind

An Immense New Power to Heal: The Promise of Personalized Medicine, with Pagan Kennedy

You Can't Make This Stuff Up: The Complete Guide to Writing Creative Nonfiction—from Memoir to Literary Journalism and Everything in Between